ON LOCATION
CANADA'S TELEVISION INDUSTRY IN A GLOBAL MARKET

Film and television production are important components of the Canadian economy. In Vancouver, popular American television series like *The X-Files* and Canadian series like *Da Vinci's Inquest* have boosted the city's profile as a centre for international and domestic productions. Serra Tinic's *On Location* is the first empirical analysis of regional Canadian television producers in the context of developing global media markets.

Tinic observes that global television production in Vancouver has been a contradictory process that has led to the homogenization of culturally specific storylines, while simultaneously facilitating the development of new avenues for international ventures. The author explains how federal and regional network considerations, funding guidelines, and partnerships with international co-producers affect the capacity of Canadian television producers to negotiate culturally specific storylines in the development process. She further investigates the concepts of globalization, culture, and national identity and their relationship to broadcasting from the perspectives of members of the television industry themselves, highlighting the extent to which industry practices in Vancouver epitomize current trends in global television production. *On Location* fills a major gap in contemporary media and cultural studies debates that question the connections between the politics of place, culture, and commerce within the larger context of cultural globalization.

SERRA TINIC is an assistant professor in the Department of Sociology at the University of Alberta.

On Location

Canada's Television Industry in a Global Market

Serra Tinic

UNIVERSITY OF TORONTO PRESS
Toronto Buffalo London

© University of Toronto Press Incorporated 2005
Toronto Buffalo London
Printed in Canada

ISBN 0-8020-8737-X (cloth)
ISBN 0-8020-8548-2 (paper)

Library and Archives Canada Cataloguing in Publication

Tinic, Serra A. (Serra Ayse), 1965–
    On Location : Canada's television industry in a global
    market / Serra Tinic.

    Includes bibliographical references and index.
    ISBN 0-8020-8737-X (bound)   ISBN 0-8020-8548-2 (pbk.)

    1. Television broadcasting – Social aspects – British Columbia –
    Vancouver.   2. Television and culture – British Columbia – Vancouver.
    3. Globalization.   I. Title.

    HE8700.9.C3T55 2005   302.23'45'0971133   C2004-904549-0

Parts of chapters 2 and 3 were previously published as 'Global Vistas and
Local Reflections: Negotiating Place and Identity in Vancouver Television,'
Television & New Media (2005) and an earlier version of chapter 4 was
published as 'Going Global: International Co-productions and the Disap-
pearing Domestic Audience in Canada' in *Planet TV: A Global Television
Studies Reader*, ed. Shanti Kumar and Lisa Parks (New York: New York
University Press, 2002).

University of Toronto Press acknowledges the financial assistance to its
publishing program of the Canada Council for the Arts and the Ontario
Arts Council.

This book has been published with the help of a grant from the Humanities
and Social Sciences Federation of Canada, using funds provided by the
Social Sciences and Humanities Research Council of Canada.

University of Toronto Press acknowledges the financial support for its
publishing activities of the Government of Canada through the Book
Publishing Industry Development Program (BPIDP).

Contents

Preface

[A]ny analysis of the role of the media in the construction of contemporary cultural identities which assumes the existence of a unified and se-
dentary population occupying a unitary public sphere, within the secure
boundaries of a given geographical territory, is unlikely to be adequate in
understanding significant aspects of our contemporary situation.

Morley, *Home Territories*

In our purportedly borderless world of global media and information
flows, the images and symbolic tools incorporated into the construction
of collective identities appear increasingly disconnected from distinct
places of origin. It is one of those interesting ironic moments that while
some herald, and others lament, the possible arrival of Marshall
McLuhan's anticipated global village, the Supreme Court of Canada is
in the process of handing down a ruling that would effectively ban
access to American satellite television services within Canadian borders. The public outcry against the court's decision provides a fascinating glimpse into the ways in which the media connect us to communal
life at a distance. For it is not the loss of access to American news and
popular culture that subscribers bemoan but the disappearance of a
window onto the foreign-language, ethnic, and religious programs that
provide a link to other homelands and that are not available through
Canadian satellite services. These people who exist in multiple communities are the cultural travellers implied by David Morley – people who
use televisual gateways to transcend physical boundaries.

The satellite battle invites us into an ongoing story in the Canadian
cultural landscape: namely, that broadcasting and the nation-state have
been seen as inextricably connected and, as a result, that the airwaves

must be protected as a public good to ensure the maintenance of a sense of national self-consciousness. Such cultural defensiveness sounds rather old-fashioned and idealistic given the current focus on the inevitabilities of the forces of globalization. Some might say it carries the remnants of traditional fears of cultural imperialism – certainly passé given the ascendancy of a transnational media environment. I would argue that the opposite is true and that Canada provides an exemplary case study of the contradictions inherent within contemporary globalizing processes. The origins of nation-building in Canadian broadcasting did develop within the context of fears of imperialism from the American cultural behemoth. Proximity to the world's emerging entertainment superpower also led to policies aimed at protecting and fostering a nascent domestic television and film industry that could provide a countervailing force to the cross-border flow of another nation's stories. This double-edged industry and cultural development model – reflected in the satellite battle – has succeeded to the extent that the Canadian television industry is globally competitive. Indeed, Canada is now the second-largest exporter of television programming worldwide. Cultural development, on the other hand, continues to be a problematic subtext within Canadian media policy and practice. Nation-states do not emanate monolithic, unified identities that are easily translatable into media narratives. Rather, every nation contains competing cultural definitions of collective identity – regional, transnational, ethnic, linguistic – vying for inclusion and representation on the national stage. Canada is no exception to this phenomenon. In fact, as a regionally fragmented nation informed by diverse immigrant experiences and settlement patterns, Canada epitomizes the challenges of connecting cultural identity to the physical space of the nation-state within the symbolic realm of broadcast media production.

In this respect, the Canadian media-identity problematic is at the forefront of the major debates concerning the relationship between places, media representations, and community formations in a global cultural economy. This general thematic, and particularly the disjuncture between culture as a global industry and culture as a communal practice, provides the framework for the chapters that follow. Set within the context of the nation-building mandate of Canadian broadcasting policy, this book provides, through a case study of television production in Vancouver, British Columbia, an analysis of the globalizing forces that compel us to reconsider our perceptions of cultural identity as connected to physical locations. Once a major site of domestic television production for the national network of the Canadian Broadcasting Corporation (CBC), Vancouver as a media *region* – following the restructuring of the national public broadcaster in the late 1970s through the early 1980s – rapidly became marginal to the centralizing processes of national cultural definition. Consequently, the Vancouver production community looked beyond the nation's borders to attract 'runaway' Hollywood production to the province. The effort was facilitated by a federal government initiative already under way in the 1970s that offered tax incentives to foreign filmmakers who relocated their projects to Canada. The proliferation of American 'tax-shelter' film projects, as they came to be known, earned Canada the title of 'Hollywood North.' Soon two major cities – Vancouver and Toronto – were competing with each other for U.S. film business. While both cities were developing highly trained crews to service these projects, Vancouver had a competitive advantage as a locations city because of the diversity of its physical landscape. This, combined with an investment in studio space in the 1980s, allowed the city to attract American television series production in addition to big-budget Hollywood movies. As a result, Vancouver has become the largest production centre for American television series and movies outside of the United States, giving it, some say, first claim to the title 'Hollywood North' (Seguin 2003). The growth of Vancouver as Hollywood North over the last decade and a half coincided with the province's larger globalization strategy to foster economic and cultural links with the countries of the Pacific Rim – two processes that have dramatically changed the cultural landscape of the city of Vancouver.

The industry (or economic) face of Hollywood North indicates a major success, or coming-of-age, story for Canadian television producers. The volume of American television and movie production in Vancouver is such that actors and producers in Los Angeles are calling for U.S. federal government intervention, through tax incentives and trade barriers, to help them compete more effectively with Vancouver for their *own* productions. Interestingly, these are the same groups who only a decade ago were attacking Canadian cultural protection policies as unfair trade practices under the North American Free Trade Agreement (NAFTA). The cultural aspects of Hollywood North, however, paint a different picture for television producers who are interested in developing domestic stories for Canadian and international audiences. These producers, who are often depicted as too 'regional' by the national public broadcaster and funding agencies, are still seen as pitching stories that are too 'Canadian specific' to American production interests (and potential production partners) in this globalizing metropolis. Consequently, Vancouver provides an ideal location from which to examine how the various levels of community – regional, national, global – become contested and reconstructed in the field of television production.

The emphasis throughout this book is on the role that cultural production plays in connecting (or disconnecting) the sociocultural specificities of 'place' (regional and national communities) and media representations of cultural identities. While there is a great deal of rich, theoretical textual and audience analysis within global media and cultural studies, there has been little investigation of the role of cultural producers in the global cultural economy. Indeed, the role of cultural (in this case television) producers is often elided in the scholarship of media globalization, which, by either emphasizing the rapid flow of media content in abstract terms or privileging textual analysis for intrinsic cultural meanings, rarely examines the specific negotiations behind the images displayed on television screens around the world. This book attempts to bridge this gap by exploring concrete examples of how actual media practices influence the global flow of symbolic imagery that shapes transnational identity formations. The central argument of *On Location* is that the 'nation' is an unstable category and that culturally specific programs are negotiated within an arena of competing interests, including the perceived need to gain access to global markets, the political and economic limitations of federal cultural policies and funding practices, and national network programming structures. In the end, regional television production is a constant struggle between attempts to produce programs that reflect a sense of place and community and those that emulate a global generic model.

My central mode of analysis emphasizes the role that cultural producers play in creating televisual stories that seek to construct regional, national, or global frames for their productions. The arguments I present are primarily concerned with the ways in which regional producers reconcile the creative and structural elements of the television industry with the cultural development goals of Canadian broadcasting policy. Although the project incorporates policy and textual analyses, interviews with television producers and production staff provide the central context for my analysis of media representations of community formations. The reason for focusing on these individuals is summed up in Horace Newcomb and Robert Alley's (1983) declaration that 'television is the producer's medium' and, therefore, that any attempt to understand the rationale behind the types of programming we see regularly on television should, at some level, investigate the ways in which producers negotiate the terrain between audience and industry goals and expectations. As the arbiters of both the creative and the financial parameters of any television series or movie, producers fulfil what Newcomb and Alley (drawing on the work of Marshall Sahlins) describe as a 'synaptic function' – they draw upon current sociocultural discourses and reformulate them within the formulas of television narratives in the hope that they will draw the largest and most desired audiences, which then translate into the profit-generating strategies of the networks and advertisers. It is within this role that Newcomb and Alley argue that producers are 'true readers, true analysts of the cultures in which they live and work' (32) and therefore that their voices help us understand how cultural, political, and economic factors influence the ways in which communities are represented in, or erased from, Canadian television programs.

The producer's voice, however, has been largely absent from most Canadian communications research, which tends to treat television as a rather opaque industry by overdetermining either policy factors or the presence of American programs on Canadian television sets. Aside from the exemplary work of Mary Jane Miller (1987, 1996) – whose interviews with the creators of CBC drama programming over the course of ten years provide an important counterpoint to my interviews with regional producers – few scholars have conducted qualitative research into the Canadian television production process. Consequently, the framework for this study is largely derived from the work of researchers who, like Newcomb and Alley, underline the importance of studying the production process through the interpretive lenses of qualitative methods in anthropology and sociology.

As interpretive research in both the United States and England indicates, television producers play an integral role in mediating the ways in which communities are defined within television stories. In an ethnographic study of the production process in the development of a Hollywood television series, Theodore Espinosa (1982) found that producers were simultaneously involved in a variety of levels of cultural practices. At one level, the story-building process was primarily concerned with the conventions of the medium, such as narrative or thematic continuity. However, at a broader level, the producers were concerned that their 'discourse "resonate" with American culture':

> At any moment in time, the story conference is a condensation point for cultural texts circulating widely in American society. This means that the producers tend to present stories, ideas and characters that will have high audience familiarity. The episodic discourse, in reproducing familiar cultural stories, is a manifestation of a cultural mapping of a particular text onto the cognitive system of the audience ... [T]he producers presuppose that connections to the wider cultural knowledge will be made by the audience.
>
> (239–40)

In a similar study, Phillip Elliott (1972) found that British television producers consistently drew upon their own cultural experiences when developing a series. Through his observations and interviews, Elliott concluded that television and cultural context were linked in three primary ways: (1) society as a source of stories; (2) producers as interpreters of cultural stories; and (3) producers' perceptions of the audience's understanding of story form and content.

These studies underline that producers, as part of the larger society in which they operate, bring their own specific cultural interpretations and experiences to the programs they create. Therefore, in order to understand how a place or community is represented within the television story format, we need to examine the cultural perspective brought to the production process by the storytellers themselves. While Espinosa's and Elliott's case studies provide a good starting point for this type of research, they do not adequately address two important aspects of the production process: the economic and political constraints that mediate all cultural productions.

In sociological analyses of the Hollywood production process, Muriel Cantor (1971) and Todd Gitlin (1985) found that economic and organizational factors, such as advertising support and network guidelines and censors, were constant reference points in the production process. These studies, which were also based on in-depth interviews and observation, complement the work of Elliott and Espinosa by emphasizing the organizational culture and structure of television. Together, these research perspectives provide a framework from which to study television production as both an artisanal and an economic activity. This consequent integration of political-economic and cultural models is particularly beneficial to bridging gaps in the Canadian culture and communications debate, both methodologically and theoretically.

My interviews with producers in Vancouver elaborate on these earlier studies by adding the consideration of nation-building communications policies and funding structures into the symbolic and industrial processes of television production in the Canadian context. Following Joli Jensen (1984), the study was based on the premise that an interpretive approach is crucial to understanding how the media produce not just programs but also 'meaningful worlds' and communities for their particular audiences. As such, the production process was viewed as a cultural activity that reproduces the collective social experience shared by producers and their audiences within the boundaries of the everyday constraints imposed by the economic, policy, and aesthetic requirements of the industry.

The discussion generated in this research project was based on formal, in-depth interviews with twenty-two independent producers, public and private broadcasting executives, and locations managers in Vancouver, British Columbia. Informal interviews with approximately thirty other individuals involved in the creative process of television production contributed to the ongoing development of interview protocols and provide much of the background context of study. In accordance with ethics guidelines, confidentiality was ensured for all participants; their voices appear anonymously, linked to occupational title only. Every effort was made to present the participants' perceptions accurately within the appropriate context of the patterns and themes that emerged in relation to the experiences of the larger regional production community. Their experiences are contextualized within the discourses of policy statements and broadcasting production processes that further define the global-local dynamic of collective identities and contemporary television production.

Acknowledgments

All research endeavours are collective acts of labour and this work is no exception. I am indebted to the efforts and resources of many individuals and institutions without which this book would be sorely lacking. I must, however, be solely credited for any errors or shortcomings to be found within the following pages.

There were two phases to, and several border crossings involved in, the project that eventually culminated in this book. I had no idea when I landed stateside that I would eventually decide to write about Canada. Critical distance gave me new perspectives about home and location, and there are many people who allowed me to glimpse them through their eyes. I was incredibly fortunate to have two mentors at formative stages of my work. Richard Barton introduced me to the world of critical-cultural television studies, and his enthusiasm for the possibilities of Canadian culture was contagious. His insight, keen wit, and dedication to his students remain sources of inspiration for me. Michael Curtin continued in this tradition and consistently encouraged me to think outside the box and grapple with the abstract. I am most grateful to have benefited from his collegial guidance and friendship. I began this study at Indiana University, and I owe many thanks to those who first read and commented on the work that would become this book: Christopher Anderson, Carol Greenhouse, and Radhika Parameswaran. It is difficult to imagine a more intellectually generous group of people, and I greatly appreciate the time and energy they invested in my project.

Although they are not mentioned by name, the members of the Vancouver television industry who participated in the study provide the integral voice of this book. I am especially grateful to them for taking the time to share their thoughts and experiences with me. Many thanks also to the individuals at the CBC research department who were so forthcoming with that most institutionally valued category of knowledge: audience research. The extended fieldwork that constitutes the basis of this study would not have been possible without the research fellowship provided by the Academic Relations Office of the Canadian Embassy in Washington, D.C. I thank the officers for their enthusiasm for the project and their continued support for Canadian studies in general. A technical support grant from the School of Journalism at Indiana University was also most helpful in assisting with tape transcription.

Of the many friends who helped along the way, I'd like to thank Gina Carpellotti, Linda Grant, Aaron Harp, Ian Hamilton, Jennifer Kulak, Kevin Newsome, Ryan Patterson, Heather Smith, Steve Stauffer, Nancy Wagers, and Nancy Worthington. You each, in your own way, shared your ideas and supported me through the journey of this work. Chad Tew deserves special mention – our heated discussions and the many diagrams on pub napkins formed the initial map for this project. He and Suzan Ozel went beyond the call of friendship and provided me with a base of operations during my travels between Bloomington and Vancouver. Their warmth and generosity are much appreciated and never forgotten. Shanti Kumar and Hemant Shah invited me to test drive many of my ideas at colloquia and conferences in Madison – thank you; I enjoyed my visits there immensely and appreciated your thoughtful readings and comments.

The manuscript went through its second incarnation at the University of Alberta. Here, a number of friends and colleagues – Aniko Bodroghkozy, Gail Faurschou, Christopher Gittings, Sourayan Mookerjea, and Anne Whitelaw – helped create a supportive intellectual and social space within which I was able to rethink and revise this book. My graduate research assistant, Tosha Tsang, provided excellent archival skills in helping me to update much of the material. Siobhan McMenemy is simply an outstanding editor, and I cannot thank her enough for her guidance, dedication, and commitment to this book. It was an absolute pleasure to work with her and the rest of the team at University of Toronto Press. My thanks also go to Margaret Allen for her judicious copy-editing. In addition, I would like to express my gratitude to two anonymous reviewers for UTP who provided substantial and informed commentary on the manuscript. Their in-depth readings and astute feedback helped me to see through the haze of my own thoughts at crucial conceptual points.

Finally, but definitely not least, I am grateful to my parents for their love and support and for motivating an inquisitive nature. To Atilla Tinic – much love and thanks for providing the ultimate support mechanism: laughter from start to finish. And, most of all, I dedicate this work to Kevin and Declan Haggerty. Kevin held down the fort and picked up my share of the load so that I could bring this to completion. He also made time to read through the manuscript, and his constructive critiques, support, and patience are written throughout the book's pages. Declan endured the last stretch with good grace and great spirits – my hope is that he will always feel a part of the many 'places' to which he is connected.

ON LOCATION
CANADA'S TELEVISION INDUSTRY IN A GLOBAL MARKET

Chapter 1

Local Cultures and Global Quests: Imagining the Nation in Canadian Broadcasting

Over the past decade the terms 'global culture' and 'cultural globalization' have come to the forefront of international communications research. While there is little consensus as to the cultural consequences of the phenomenon of globalization, most scholars will agree that the rapid flow of images and messages in an increasingly transnational electronic media environment has changed the ways we perceive space and time and their relationship to collective identities. As borders are becoming more permeable to the flow of people, ideas, capital, technology, and popular entertainment, cultural and social group identities are evolving at local and global levels that transcend the boundaries of the nation-state (Appadurai 1996). Indeed, it is the questionable future of nation-states and 'national identities,' as we've come to know them, that lies at the heart of most analyses of the global-local cultural dynamic. This book enters into this dialogue by exploring the complex relationship between places, identities, and the globalization of television production within the context of Canada's ongoing project to secure a national cultural community through broadcasting.

The concept of 'place,' which is gaining currency among media globalization scholars, has always been central to the examination of Canada as a political and social community. As literary theorist Northrop Frye has commented, the perpetual Canadian question is not 'Who am I?' but rather 'Where is here?' (quoted in Zemans 1995: 138). With these words, Frye speaks to the larger issue of the relationship between geography and identity that has defined Canada's particular postcolonial experience and struggle to establish a sense of 'self' at the national level. As the expression of a collection of regionally diverse communities that have been loosely united under the colonial political economies of, successively, France, Britain, and the United States, Canadian 'thought has centered on questioning *what it means to belong here*' (Angus 1997: 53, 101).

In many respects, the goals of broadcasting policy, throughout Canadian history, have been specifically to address and define 'what it means to belong here.' From its inception in the 1920s, national public-service broadcasting was seen as a means to unite the various geographic and cultural communities that constituted the provinces into a young nation emerging from the remains of the British Empire. A second, and related, goal was to foster this sense of national unity as a defence against the United States, the new imperial threat from the south. The evolution of the nation-building mandate for public-service broadcasting eventually led to the development of policies that focused on fighting the threat of American media dominance and largely overlooked the divisive elements within Canada, namely, the intense regional loyalties held by the Canadian people.

When regionalism is addressed in Canadian policy discourse, it is usually framed within the context of French Canada versus English Canada, and marginal attention is given to the problematic nature of the state of communication among the English-speaking provinces themselves. Because of the forces of history and geography, these regions developed distinct political and cultural environments based on their disparate resource bases and immigration patterns.[1] This oversight has significantly impeded the formation of culturally resonant broadcasting in Canada, for as R. Kent Weaver (1992) notes, 'Beyond shared grievances with central Canada, there is little in the way of a common culture or collective interest that unites "outer Canada"' (29).

In this respect, national broadcasting policy in Canada developed from the same model as the periphery-centre economic relationship that defined the confederation and the subsequent political structure of the country. In both federal politics and broadcasting, the concentration of decision-making power in central Canada led to the formation of policies that often neglected the incorporation of regional voices in policy formation. This has contributed to the sentiments of regional alienation that characterize Canadian society today. The Canadian Broadcasting Corporation (CBC), as a microcosm of the larger federal-provincial political system, has defined central-Canadian programming as representative of the entire nation at the expense of allowing the regions to communicate the diversity of their own cultures to one another.[2] Even within the private sector, federal funding structures to support independent productions for domestic audiences have largely been limited to the development of vertically integrated television production companies in Ontario.

The examination of English-Canadian identity and regionalism has taken on a renewed vigour since the 1995 Quebec Referendum.[3] With a narrow margin of 1 per cent of the vote deciding Quebec's continued presence in the federal fold (at least until the next referendum), attention has turned to the concept of Canada 'after Quebec.' This latest, and closest, brush with national disintegration has resulted in a long-overdue analysis of the often fragile bonds that tie together a sense of community among the English-Canadian provinces. As new names such as 'Canada-outside-of-Quebec' and 'Rest-of-Canada' (ROC) have entered popular and scholarly discourse, a renewed search to define, or at least to understand, the complex relationships among the English-Canadian provinces has begun. The re-evaluation of the relationship among national cultural institutions, Canadian regionalism, and the global cultural economy has been an integral part of this debate. As Robert Thacker (1995: 176) argues, 'the most pressing issue when defining English Canada will be: Who tells its stories, and how? Who is allowed a voice?'

The following chapters examine the cultural dimensions of regionalism, globalization, and the increasingly problematic construction of 'national' identities through a case study of television series production in Vancouver, British Columbia. Over the past two decades, Vancouver has looked outside of Canada to develop economic, political, and cultural ties with the American Pacific Northwest region and the countries of the Pacific Rim. By positioning itself as a global city, Vancouver has experienced rapid cultural change through Asian immigration and international investment. The city's larger global strategy evolved from both a frustration with the lack of economic and political representation within the federal structure and a desire to diversify a precarious, natural-resource-based economy. An important aspect of this global diversification process has been the provincial government's conscious effort to develop and promote Vancouver as a locations site for the American television and film industry. Today, Vancouver is the third-largest production centre for Hollywood movies and television series after Los Angeles and New York. It is also in the process of becoming an important locations site for the Asian film industry.

In this respect, Vancouver provides a strategic location from which to examine the relationships among regional, national, and global cultural productions. Before the 1980s, Vancouver was the largest production centre for English-Canadian television programs outside of Toronto. However, with the increasing centralization of CBC programming at the network level in Toronto and decreased access to federal broadcast production funds, regional television producers in British Columbia have felt denied a voice in telling English-Canadian stories for almost twenty years. As a result, the Vancouver production community has taken advantage of the Hollywood presence and pursued co-venture agreements with American producers and co-production projects with other international partners to produce programs for global audiences, of which Canadians constitute a small minority. The globalization of the Vancouver television industry can be seen, from one perspective, as the logical outcome of the weaknesses of federal broadcasting policies and institutions that have sought to use nationalism, as defined by central Canada, as a 'conscious strategy of pasting over the cracks' of regional discontent (Melville Watkins, quoted in Laba 1988: 82).

National public-service broadcasting began in Canada in 1932, with the establishment of the Canadian Radio Broadcasting Corporation (CRBC, which became the CBC in 1936) at the recommendation of the Aird Commission – the first of a long line of royal commissions on broadcasting policy. The Aird Report was the first government mandate to institute the concept of national unity as a counterforce to American culture in Canadian communications policy. As Wayne Skene (1993) underlines, the Aird Commission, and subsequent task forces, including the Fowler and Massey Commissions, defined national unity as 'inter-regional communication.' Within this model, programming was to originate in the provinces, and the central network was to serve a dissemination, rather than a production, function. The committee was sensitive to the fact that a centralized programming system might alienate the regionally distinct provinces rather than unite them into a nation. Therefore, the foundation of Canadian broadcasting policy was to encourage local producers to share their communities' cultural narratives with one another, and to avoid a single, centralized definition of 'Canadian' culture.

However, the economic and technological challenges of developing the sizeable Canadian broadcast distribution system eventually led to the exact form of centralization that the Aird Commission had sought to avoid. By 1968, the year of a new Broadcasting Act, the term 'national unity' had been changed to 'national identity,' and television programming (as defined by headquarters in Toronto and Montreal) was seen as the means to simultaneously create a 'Canadian' identity and defend against American cultural domination (Raboy 1990).

As Ien Ang's (1991) work underlines, all national public-service broadcasting institutions face the problem of constructing audiences as publics rather than as markets. This is particularly relevant to the CBC because there is no coherent or essentially Canadian 'public' but rather a collection of diverse provinces, many of which are antagonistic towards central Canada. Therefore, while national identity and cultural sovereignty remain the driving forces behind Canadian communications policy, the meanings of these terms remain enigmatic: How do you protect an identity that cannot be neatly defined and measured?

In fact, as Philip Schlesinger (1991) aptly explains, the concepts of nation-state, national culture, and national identity are usually treated unproblematically and where 'communications are concerned, they are handled as residual categories' (172). According to Schlesinger, communications research should take a few steps back, examine first how 'collective identity' is constituted, and then proceed to locate communications and culture within that larger framework. In brief, we should look at collective identity itself as a problem:

> National cultures are not simple repositories of shared symbols to which the entire population stands in identical relation. Rather they are to be approached as sites of contestation in which competition over definitions takes place ... The national culture is a repository, *inter alia*, of classificatory systems. It allows 'us' to define ourselves against 'them' understood as those beyond the boundaries of the nation. It may also reproduce distinctions between 'us' and 'them' at the intra-national level, in line with the internal structure of social divisions and relations of power and domination.
>
> (ibid. 173–4).

From this perspective we can no longer discuss national identity as a simple concept of unification; instead, we must consider it as a process of both *inclusion* and *exclusion*. In other words, we cannot assume that communities are neatly bounded, or cohesive, cultural entities. Instead, we must examine the competing cultural tensions within regions and nations in order to better understand how communities are formed within a context of ethnic, economic, and political diversity.

The following macro-level analysis of global and local television production in Vancouver complies with Schlesinger's argument and reverses the order of the culture and communications debate. It asks the following fundamental questions: What is the basis of a community? Who defines the boundaries of a community? How are communities formed in a global media environment? How do media producers incorporate local, national, and international cultural influences into the stories they present to their communities?

To address these questions, I have attempted to contextualize the Vancouver television industry within a specific time and place – the 1990s and the confluence of political, economic, and social processes that have been engaged in the larger strategy to construct Vancouver as a 'world class city.' Within this framework, I trace the tensions between broadcasting policies, institutional structures, and the practical realities of the television production process that together have contributed to the current global logic of regional television production in Vancouver. The analysis integrates three components: (1) in-depth interviews with members of the Vancouver television industry, including locations scouts, independent television producers, broadcasting executives, television development personnel, and program managers; (2) archival research on Canadian television programming and policy and analysis of discourse in the industry trade publications and; (3) textual analysis of programming that television producers themselves define as distinctly cross-regional and 'Canadian.'

The central aim of this work is to determine how regional producers reconcile the economic and aesthetic requirements of a global media industry with the nationalist cultural goals of Canadian broadcasting policy. The project emphasizes series, or entertainment, production, as this has been the primary point of contention in the Canadian identity debate. As John Meisel (1991) notes, Canadian news programs consistently outdraw American news by a four-to-one margin, and therefore are not perceived to be as threatened by competition from American television. Similarly, Mark Starowicz (1993) argues that the scarcity of Canadian stories on domestic television, rather than lack of regional and national news content, has resulted in a populace that knows more about American law, society, racial conflicts, and family structures than their Canadian counterparts. Furthermore, it is through entertainment programming, more than news, that regional producers have found entry into the global cultural economy. My conversations with members of the television industry emphasized the following processes in the field of national and global cultural production:

1 The television producers' view of their role in promoting a sense of community and the intersecting levels in which they define community in their program ideas – local, regional, national, or international.

2 The role of audience considerations in the selection and production of television programming.

3 The ways in which regional or national symbols, narratives, and content are defined in the programs and the ways in which producers define these elements in a province that has a large multi-ethnic community and strong ties to the United States.

4 The requisite cultural negotiations that follow entry into the global media arena and, in particular, the means by which regional or national story considerations are transformed in agreements with international production partners and media buyers.

5 The role of national regulations and policies in the day-to-day production process.

As the chapters that follow will indicate, television production at all levels is a constant negotiation between creativity and constraint. The story of Canadian television, as told to me by members of the industry, is one of concomitant frustration, opportunity, ingenuity, and (at times) sheer lunacy, as producers attempt to work their way through the maze of financing, regulation, and broadcaster requirements to finally tell a story that, in the end, may not even make it to the television screen. This dual nature of television production, as both a symbolic and an economic activity, provides the common thread that ties these chapters together and explains the interrelationships among cultures, capital, and places. Proceeding from this perspective, the larger theoretical context for this study incorporates strains of political economy within the framework of critical cultural studies and, in so doing, seeks to redress a current gap in the larger scholarly dialogue about media globalization.

As Graham Murdock (1989) cogently argues, cultural studies has been perhaps the most important intellectual contribution to the understanding of communications through its analysis of the continual negotiation of meaning and expression as they are played out in the practices of everyday life. However, as Murdock also notes, cultural studies has not fully examined the media industries' 'double relation to modernity,' in that the media produce not only commodities but also the 'reper-

toires of meaning' through which societies are constructed or understood: 'It [cultural studies] pays scant attention to the other side of the
duality. It offers an analysis of the cultural industries which has little or
nothing to say about how they actually work as industries and how
these operations impinge on the process of meaning making' (436).

From a Canadian perspective, Rowland Lorimer (1994) similarly argues that, while there is an abundance of literature on symbolic culture,
academics have shied away from examining cultural development:
'the motivation and behaviour of cultural workers and entrepreneurs;
relations between society and creators, their products ... and a full
understanding of the nature of cultural production' (286).

Cultural studies theorists, on the other hand, can justifiably levy a
counter-attack against the tendency within political economy to continually subordinate cultural practices to economic considerations and
the logic of capital. My attempt, within this larger argument, is to
theorize the implications of this dual nature of the television industry in
Vancouver through an analysis of media production as an integrated
social, political, economic, and ideological process in which resistance
exists in both actual and cultural terms between artisanal and industrial
visions of the cultural product (Garnham 1979). As such, this framework 'conceptualizes the relations between these two sides of the communications process – the material and discursive, economic and
cultural – without collapsing one into the other' (Murdock 1989: 436).[4]
The goal is not to establish a simplistic *rapprochement* between the two
schools of thought, but rather to tease out what Lawrence Grossberg
(1997: 13) refers to as a '[return] to questions of economics in important
and interesting ways' in cultural studies whereby we 'consider how
and where people, capital, and commodities move in and out of the
places and spaces of the global economy.'

The premise of this study adheres to the central axiom of cultural
studies that representation is itself problematic. It is a process rife with
political tensions and struggles over the power to define lived experiences in preferred ways. Yet television remains an opaque symbol-
generating industry to the extent that broadcasting policies and funding
practices remain uninterrogated in regard to their ability to naturalize
concepts such as the 'nation' or 'national identity' as cohesive and
undisputed cultural categories. Woven throughout the book are the
words of federal policies that mask the ideological construction of the
'nation' by proceeding from the perception that its definition is a matter

of common sense that can then be merely *reflected* on television screens across the country.

Therefore, in brief, this work attempts to talk with 'what used to be called the [ideological state apparatuses] ISAs' (Bennett 1992) in an effort to understand the ways in which institutional structures, policies, and economic strategies are implicated in cultural practices and their relationship to collective identities.[5] Although this macro-level orientation paints a picture with rather broad strokes of one particular location – Vancouver – the relevant issues and theories are applicable to other sites of analysis in the global-local cultural nexus. In thinking about local, regional, and national communities (and their relationships to electronic media and communications) we need to reconceptualize 'identity,' 'space,' and 'production' within a larger global cultural and political economic context (Mahon 1993). Thus, before turning to an overview of the book's organizational structure and contents, in the following sections I establish the parameters of the debate around the key terms that relate to the Vancouver case study: culture, collective identity, and media globalization.

Culture, Collective Identities, and the Global-Local Nexus

Most scholars tend to discuss globalization as a relatively recent phenomenon by focusing their attention on the changes in the global economy as the Fordist model of production gave way to one of flexible accumulation from the 1970s up to the present. Advances in satellite, computer, and other electronic communications technologies – and the consequent 'placelessness' of international capital – marked the 1980s as the decade of rapid movement into an interdependent global political and economic environment (Robertson 1990). In this era of 'disorganized capitalism' (Lash and Urry 1987), questions of group identity become more problematic as peoples, cultural forms, and symbols cease to be territorially fixed. In communications terms, the electronic media are implicated in contributing to the simultaneous development of supranational and subnational group affiliations that have led some Western nations to confront conflicting conceptualizations of identity – local, regional, and national – for the first time.

To review the growing body of literature on the cultural ramifications of globalization from a Canadian vantage point is to experience an unsettling sense of *déjà vu*. As political economists will argue, the Canadian economy prior to the 1970s is best described as one of 'permeable Fordism' in that its particular characteristic 'since 1945 [was one] permeated by international – or more exactly, continental – effects. Its Fordism was designed domestically but always with an eye to the continental economy' (Jane Jenson, quoted in Angus 1997: 23). The years immediately following the Second World War were a contradictory time in the Canadian national trajectory. It was, in Innisian terms, the brief moment of nationhood between British colonialism and American economic imperialism. By the 1960s, Canadian industry was beginning to be seen as a branch plant of American corporations, and internal fault lines deepened with increasing complaints of colonialism from within – Ottawa against the provinces and Quebec against the country. Aside from brief moments of rallying around the flag, such as Expo 67, national identity has always been an unstable category in the Canadian vocabulary.[6]

Therefore, as theorists debate the dissolution of the nation as final arbiter of a sense of community under the current processes of globalization, they address an issue that echoes the Canadian experience since the passing of the Dominion. Namely, the fact that local, regional, national, and continental/international identities have always coexisted and competed within the political and geographic construct of the nation-state and that such community identifications need not be mutually exclusive. In cultural terms this debate has played itself out over issues of homogeneity versus heterogeneity. In other words, if we can no longer speak of national cultures, do we now speak of a single 'global culture' or of intensified 'local cultures' that operate on a global scale?

For some, the extension and consolidation of a global media system as part of the larger process of economic globalization has led to a singular perception of a cultural system wherein people cannot help but think in global terms (Robertson 1990). But as Anthony Smith (1990) soundly argues, increased cultural contact does not necessarily translate into a sense of collective cultural identity, the latter usually being defined by a shared sense of history, continuity, and common destiny: 'A global culture or cosmopolitan culture fails to relate to any such historic identity. Unlike national cultures, a global culture is essentially memoryless ... There are no world memories that can be used to unite humanity; the most global experiences to date – colonialism and the World Wars – can only serve to remind us of our historic cleavages' (179–80).

Smith does not deny that the globalization of the electronic media has led to a greater awareness that people and political-economic issues are interconnected across national borders, but he underlines that this does not necessarily form a sustained bond of community. Thus there is no global culture, if we define it in terms of the nation-state writ large; there is, instead, a sense of cultural 'relativisation': 'A globalized culture is chaotic rather than orderly – is integrated and connected so that the meanings of its components are "relativized" to one another but it is not unified or centralized ... This relativization may take the form of either a reflexive self-examination in which fundamental principles are reasserted in the face of threatening alternatives or the absorption of some elements of other cultures' (Waters 1995: 125–6).

It is this dialectical relationship between global and local cultural practices that is most evident in the example of the Vancouver television industry and the larger Canadian national identity debate. Among the producers I spoke with, few did not express a desire to operate within three cultural fields at once: the local, the national, and the international. Their intentions, given the opportunity, were to take the particular experiences of their community (which cannot help but be inflected by global themes, given the large, diverse, and active ethnic communities within Vancouver), to set the stories within the larger national context, and to circulate them throughout the international market-place. To some extent, the realities of international television production and the quest for distribution and markets, demand a fusion between the particular and the universal.

The role of cultural producers is rarely discussed in the literature of media globalization, which tends to emphasize the rapid flow of media content in abstract terms but rarely examines the specific negotiations behind the images that end up on television and movie screens around the world. However, this group of transnational professionals can be seen as 'third cultures' who are important conduits of global cultural flows and, while they operate in cosmopolitan circumstances, are just as likely to be 'locals at heart' (Featherstone 1990: 9). It is, in fact, this cosmopolitan-local persona that I heard reflected in my conversations with Vancouver television producers. Whether selling to the national networks or international distributors, the independent producers underlined that stories that were overly particular to place were difficult to pitch. In this respect, the larger the market, the more homogeneous or universal the program needs to be to succeed (at least in market terms). However, a caveat was offered by all the producers in that their choice of stories and the mode in which they told them could not help but be informed by their own cultural and social experiences – the phrase most often used was that inescapably vague 'Canadian sensibility.'[7]

What was most interesting about the definition each provided when pressed as to the nature of this sensibility was the repeated reference to the experience of marginality both within the nation and internationally – the idea that control and decisions were always taken elsewhere. In this aspect, regional location was a strong source of identification for these people, but this was not separable from a sense of being part of a larger collection of regions that were muddling through together, always in the process of trying to define themselves as a group. As these individuals underlined, the idea of the Canadian 'nation' was still an important reference point even when they operated in a global context. But within that context, they retained the sense of regional alienation and lack of participation in the larger definition of the national community.

When discussing a definable 'Canadian' identity, Northrop Frye commented decades ago that 'contemporary Canadian culture, being a culture, is not a national development but a series of regional ones' (quoted in Mandel and Taras 1987: 211). In fact, unlike broadcasting studies, Canadian literary and anthropological analyses have long emphasized the importance of locality or region as a creative force in the articulation of cultural expression. In this respect, the tensions between the forces of regional fragmentation, national centralization, and the American political and cultural presence have been fundamental to the frameworks of literary and ethnographic analyses. Current work in these areas has led to an interesting discussion of the inherent postmodernism of Canadian culture. Here, scholars argue that there is no master narrative of Canada but rather a constant 'questioning of any notion of coherent, stable, autonomous identity be it individual or national' (Robert Fulford, quoted in Karim 1993: 198). From this perspective, the definition of Canada is always one of shifting centres and margins; it can only be articulated in opposition to the 'Other' (Hutcheon 1991). Consequently, the Other defines who an individual is as a Canadian at any given time, and thus identity is in a constant state of flux depending on whether the Other is the United States, Quebec, Ontario, or a different ethnic group or region. Identity stands in relation to perpetually unsettled hierarchies of 'us' and 'them.'[8]

As Rosemary Coombe (1991) argues, postmodern culture as an aspect of the particular 'historical conjunctures in a multinational global economy' forces us to re-examine the foundations of collective identities at all levels (189). The global flow of capital as well as the global reach of popular culture via international media have redefined the notion of local identity. Kenneth Frampton's call for a 'critical regionalism' is an especially useful framework for the study of Canadian culture and communication. According to Frampton, 'local cultures can only be constituted now as locally inflected manifestations of global culture' (quoted in Robins 1989: 161). Therefore, instead of looking for authenticity in local culture, critical regionalism seeks to examine how local identity is constructed through processes of pastiche and bricolage from whatever cultural materials are available or 'at hand' (de Certeau 1984).

David Morley (1992: 282) refers to this simultaneous dynamic of 'globalization and localization' as the 'politics of space and place,' wherein 'places ... are perhaps best seen not as "bounded areas" but as "spaces of interaction" in which local identities are constructed out of resources (both material and symbolic) which may well not be at all local in their origin.' The differentiation of 'place' and 'space' takes on new dimensions in the postmodern dilemma of cultural fragmentation. As David Harvey (1990) explains, 'place' (local culture) becomes crucial to marginalized groups, both intra- and internationally, as they have a better command over cultural definition at this site than they do over 'space,' which is the terrain of national institutions and global capital. Thus, to the extent that fragmentation may lead to an intensified search for collective identity, or 'secure moorings in a shifting world,' it should be explored within the context of place (301–4).

It is in this respect, perhaps, that the arguments of postmodernity are particularly salient to the Canadian case study. As a country that has always had a weak sense of identity, Canada may indeed be the quintessential postmodern nation:

The uncoordinated Canadian cultural reality has always prevailed against projects to define a unified character of 'Canadianism' ... [R]egionalism – the development (economic, political, cultural) and limits of 'local culture' – has been, and continues to be, the fundamental nature of cultural process in Canada. Nationalism, in terms of an integrative and impelling self-concept, has been groundless and, therefore, an elusive objective in the numerous and varied searches for a Canadian sense of nation. Other than occasional officially-directed outbursts of nationalism, the predominance and persistence of regional/local culture have frustrated the pursuit for a Canadian commonality.

(Laba 1988: 82)

It is for this reason that a critical regionalism perspective, which emphasizes the shifting nature of centres and margins in a global media environment, holds promise for advancing the Canadian communications debate.

Culture, Identity, and the Global-Local Nexus

Benedict Anderson's (1991) definition of nationhood as an 'imagined political community' provides a good starting point for the analysis of Canadian national and cultural identities: 'It [the nation] is *imagined* because the members of even the smallest nation will never know most of their fellow-members, meet them, or even hear of them, yet in the minds of each lives the image of their communion' (6). According to Anderson, the development of the print media played an integral role in the establishment of the nation-state as communications allowed populations to link themselves mentally with people and institutions they would otherwise rarely encounter. Of particular significance to this argument is the difference between 'national identity' and 'nationalism' as key terms in the imagined community. As Anderson explains, nationalism is a political strategy that serves to maintain loyalty to the state and the preservation of sovereign boundaries. National identity, conversely, is a social phenomenon that implies a shared 'self-consciousness' of a people in relation to others within the nation.

If we extrapolate from Anderson's work, Canada may provide an example of the ultimate modern imagined community. National public-service broadcasting was intentionally designed to counteract the effects of geographic vastness and provide a sense of national self-consciousness to the diverse regional, linguistic, Native, and immigrant groups within the country's boundaries. The problem inherent in the Canadian communications mandate, however, is reflective of Schlesinger's earlier argument – the perceived need to create a homogeneous definition of national identity, through broadcasting, preceded the analysis and subsequent representation of the various interpretations of national self-consciousness as expressed by the distinct populations within Canada.

The conceptualization of national self-consciousness as an imagined community is also more complicated in an era of global electronic media than the type of imagining that defines Anderson's print-dominant world. International telecommunications networks, and their propensity to conquer time and space, have rendered national borders irrelevant to cultural and information exchanges. Today, electronic communications allow people to imagine themselves as members of both national communities and cultural communities that transcend territorial boundaries. In McKenzie Wark's (1994) words, we have become accustomed to living on two planes: those of 'virtual geography' and of the 'geography of experience.' While the latter is the place we live and work in and experience at first hand, it is permeated by the virtual geography of the global media, which provides an experience that is 'no more or less *real*. It is a different kind of perception, of things not bounded by rules of proximity, of *being there*' (vii). In virtual geography, people form, maintain, and (re)establish cultural affinities, communities, and identities that may or may not coincide with the political and social identity projects of nation building.

These distinctions between national and cultural identities are integral to the study of the global media environment. They underline the problem, in international communications research, of treating national identities or cultures as primordial entities rather than as political and social constructs or narratives (Hall 1992). As Jean-Pierre Désaulniers (1987: 151) notes, 'There is much difference between national identity and cultural identity ... in terms of nationality a person is either Canadian or not, but culturally one may be Canadian in varying degrees.' In fact, the purpose behind the construction of national cultures is often to supersede competing cultural identities or allegiances. It serves as a means to centralize and strengthen authority when '[r]egional privileges and characteristics which have preserved cultural differences [become] obstacles to the national unity which sustains the power of the state ... Cultural integration [makes] it possible to move from the unity of the market to political unity' (Martin-Barbero 1993: 87–8). With regard to the Canadian example, Martin-Barbero's analysis corresponds with the work of Harold Innis and what Martin Laba (1988: 86–7) describes as 'the dialectical struggle in the history of Canadian culture': 'This struggle has been carried out on two fronts: first, in the tension between regional popular cultures and the dominant, acquisitive political and economic practices of the central Canadian power-base (the Ontario bourgeoisie); and second, in the emergence of the Canadian nation as a progeny of British, French and American empires.'

Without digressing completely into Innis's earlier work on the political economy of Canadian culture, suffice it to say that, since the establishment of the national railway, the centralized power structure in Ontario has recognized the importance of constructing and fostering a national identity to maintain access to western markets and to combat the American threat from the south. The federal (core)-provincial (periphery) relationship that evolved from this process also served as the blueprint for future national broadcasting policy.

By reassessing national identity as a constructed narrative rather than a natural attribute of a given collectivity, we can examine the realm of national broadcasting as a contested terrain of competing definitions of a national culture. John Jackson (1991) describes this 'struggle over meaning and representation' in terms of the conflict between 'lived culture' and 'official culture':

> Institutions, by definition, are patterns of beliefs, values, goals, ways of doing and seeing things. The CBC, as a large-scale organization, incorporates a particular institutional mindset and, though the 'Canada' which it has articulated in its formation and broadcasting is restricted, it has been presented as universal. To the extent that the idea of region is incorporated, it is not as a living community, as lived culture, but as a parochialism tied to the centre through bureaucratic hierarchy ... *Lived culture* over and against *official culture* is local rather than cosmopolitan and *tends* to generate and reinforce competing meanings. The function of central institutions is to incorporate, or depress, or eliminate competing meanings.
>
> (196–7)

It is this issue of representation within the national broadcast network that underlines the potential for cultural fragmentation in Canada. If groups feel alienated or unrepresented by the definition of national culture manifested in Canadian broadcasting, they may simply choose not to attend to Canadian programming. In this case, domestic Canadian content regulations appear to hold little promise in building east-west ties between the regions.

This tension between lived and official cultures is not unique to Canadian broadcasting. Rather, it is inherent within the paternalistic nature of most national public-service broadcasting systems. These institutions not only tend to marginalize groups and regions, they also often encourage high-culture programming at the expense of popular culture. As a result, audiences frequently turn to internationally produced (mainly American), commercial alternatives as an act of resistance against official culture (Fiske 1987, Hebdige 1988). In the case of Canada, there is also a strong possibility that many Canadians choose American programming not over Canadian programming but rather over cheap Canadian imitations of American programs, or CBC interpretations of national culture. This idea is reinforced by a 1983 Canadian Department of Communications survey, which found that 70 per cent of Canadians feel that television programming on their stations 'should be more reflective of their own lives,' thereby indicating a preference for 'more and better Canadian alternatives to American program offerings' (Gathercole 1987: 82–3). The idea that broadcasting should be more 'reflective' of Canadians' lived cultures highlights the problematic nature of the national identity mandate of Canadian broadcasting. It underlines the need for greater national representation of the diversity of regional experiences in popular culture and, simultaneously, demands an explanation of what constitute lived cultures in Canada.

As stated above, the crux of the Canadian culture and communication dilemma lies in the mandate of a centralized broadcasting institution to create and perpetuate a single definition of national identity. The construction of a national narrative has been particularly problematic for the CBC, given the lack of strong unifying mythologies, epics, and national from which to generate a universally recognizable portrait of the country. The result has been to treat culture as a product that can be protected through domestic content regulations, rather than a dynamic system of symbolic social and political processes in the anthropological sense of the word. In fact, because of the difficulties of defining a singular and identifiable concept of Canadianism, culture came to be identified from an economic perspective wherein policy makers used a definition of culture that would protect Canadian jobs in a competitive broadcast industry (Ellis 1979). Therefore, to this day, a production qualifies as Canadian if it meets six points on the requirement list (for example, a Canadian director would be worth two points, a Canadian musical composition would be worth one point).[9]

Ironically, it is precisely the lack of strong national myths that led Richard Collins (1990) to claim that Canada exemplifies the modern nation in a global media environment. According to Collins, the Canadian example is one in which culture (myths and symbols) and polity (political and social institutions) have been successfully 'decoupled.' Through a textual analysis of CBC programming, Collins argues that Canadians hold a shared allegiance to the institutions of the social welfare system rather than to any common notion of national culture. Consequently, Collins concludes that the case of Canada indicates that culture and state need not be congruent for a country's continued sovereignty, and as such, the Canadian broadcasting system should be hailed as a model for the European community (33–6).

Collins's work generated an impassioned response from many Canadian communications researchers, who countered that decoupling is the 'problem with Canada, not its promise': 'In other words, it is precisely *because* culture and polity are decoupled, precisely because we have given ourselves unbridled access to American broadcasting, precisely because we have split broadcasting between English and French, that we are unable to generate the common symbols that would hold us together' (Atallah 1992: 224).

The debate between Collins and Canadian scholars is highly instructive for the ideas presented in this book. Whether or not Collins's decoupling hypothesis is an accurate depiction of the Canadian experience, it forces us to ask fundamental questions about social and cultural processes: How do people form collective identities and at what levels (local, regional, national, and international)? And how are these communities reproduced (or erased) by media institutions?

It is this second question, which addresses the politics of cultural identity and its expression within media representations, that forms the basis of the chapters to follow. It follows Stuart Hall's (1990) premise that we should think of identity not as an established state of being but rather as a continually negotiated 'production' that is 'constituted within representations': 'Cultural identity ... is a matter of "becoming" as well as of "being." It belongs to the future as much as to the past ... cinema [is] not a second order mirror held up to reflect what already exists, but ... that form of representation which is able to constitute us as new kinds of subjects, and thereby enable us to discover places from which to speak' (225, 236).

Hall's depiction of identity as a process and a production is particularly appropriate to the discussion of the Canadian identity crisis. The search for Canadian identity has often been regarded as a defining national characteristic in and of itself. It has been seen as analogous to the Arthurian quests – the idea that the Holy Grail of national self-definition will never be found and does not, in the end, matter (Wernick 1993). What is important is the questing and questioning along the way. This particular perception was a recurrent theme in my conversations with regional producers, who saw television as a place to express the diversity of experiences and identities within the national (and international) context but felt limited by the institutional constraints on *which* places were allowed to speak.[10]

Studying the Dilemmas of Canadian Broadcasting

Canadian broadcasting policy has tended to emphasize cultural identity as a product that can eventually be achieved rather than a perpetual process of self- and group definition; and the establishment of some form of national identity has come to be seen as the last line of defence against the Americanization of Canadian television audiences. In fact, by concentrating on cultural imperialism arguments of media analysis, policy makers have been prophesying the imminent erosion of Canadian cultural autonomy for more than seventy years. However, in the words of Roger de la Garde (1993: 29), 'The question is not when will it happen, but why has it not already happened?' The answer, according to de la Garde, and other Québécois scholars, lies in the analysis of resistance and meaning appropriation by active audiences within a 'particular historical, economic, social and political context' (ibid.: 44). Consequently, the explicitly political nature of research in French Canada has focused on the ways in which marginalized Québécois popular culture forms have developed and thrived despite, and often as a reaction against, the dominance of Anglo (both Canadian and American) culture in Canada. Therefore, instead of concentrating on the absorption of American media, these researchers argue that we must consider the ways people incorporate local, national, and international media, intertextually, into the structuring of 'everyday life' within their specific communities (Caron and Belanger 1993).

It is in the consideration of cultural resistance and appropriation that cultural studies approaches to media analysis and audience studies have greatly contributed to our understanding of how people incorporate global media into the context of lived experiences within their local settings. Thompson (1995: 176) refers to this process as 'symbolic distancing,' whereby people engage with foreign media programs, get 'glimpses' of life elsewhere, and subsequently use these images 'to think critically about their own lives and local conditions.' The interpretation of global images through symbolic distancing provides a more sophisticated understanding of social processes than do arguments of cultural imperialism, which tend to depict passive audiences blindly adopting political and cultural mores from foreign television programs.

In fact, as Ted Magder's (1995) personal reflections indicate, symbolic distancing can work to reinforce identity at the local level while it simultaneously incorporates the viewer into an international audience:

> Personally I feel more like a Canadian when I watch violent American television than when I watch *Anne of Green Gables*. I simply cannot identify with the gushing Victorian romanticism of Anne and her Gables; to some extent my reaction is that of an uninvited outsider, someone who, at that place and in that time, would not have fit in and probably would not have been allowed to. When I watch cops and robbers shooting it up in Los Angeles or Miami, I am reminded that the rate of urban violence is much less in Toronto than it is in many American cities ... and this thought is sometimes accompanied by a hint of nationalist smugness.
>
> (176)

Magder's alienation from one of Canada's most acclaimed (and internationally successful) television programs underlines the complex dynamics of the relationship between place, collective identity, and media representations. There are no guarantees that nationally defined programs will bind the people living in a given territory into a national community or that international programs will supplant local cultures and contribute to a homogeneous global community. In fact, a recurring comment in my interviews with members of the television industry was that Canadian policy makers should worry less that people are viewing American programs and be more concerned about the lack of shelf space for Canadian programs that include the stories of everyday life in the regions across the country. From this perspective, it is not American television that poses a threat to the concept of a national community but rather the scarcity of media representations of Canada outside of Toronto.[11]

While English-Canadian media research has yet to completely abandon cultural imperialism theories and experimental and survey methods that attempt to generalize Canadian attitudes as distinct from their American counterparts (e.g., Surlin and Berlin 1991), some scholars have recently begun to examine the internal dynamics of Canadian culture and communication. These researchers argue that central-Canadian control over cultural policy and national programming has been as detrimental to the Canadian national unity project as has American media dominance. At present, however, the discussion of regionalism remains largely theoretical in that it generates further areas of inquiry rather than specific research designs. The few empirical studies that have been carried out have largely concentrated on the national institutional, policy, and programming factors contributing to regional alienation (Vipond 1992).

As McClarty (1988) and Laba (1988) both argue, Canadian popular culture consistently reinforces the dominant view of a singularly de-fined Canada at the expense of local and regional expression. Through analyses of national network programs and broadcasting policies, these scholars found that regional producers have been impeded from com-municating across provincial boundaries as Toronto decides what is 'appropriate' or 'nationally representative' English programming of high enough quality to merit inclusion at the network level:

> In communications terms what happens to the provinces and the regions
> in policy and practice is that they become the spokes of a wheel of which
> Ottawa, Toronto, or Montreal is the hub. Communications among the
> members of the periphery is encouraged *only* if it passes *through* the hub ...
> Ultimately, of course, the struggle to reorganize the communications pat-
> terns of the country becomes a struggle for power. The one-way, central
> Canada-dominated communications pattern is the counterpart to the
> political and economic structure of the country.
>   (Patricia Hindley, et al., quoted in Raboy 1990: 340)

In one of the few empirical studies of CBC television drama production, Mary Jane Miller (1987) found strong support for Raboy's analyses. Through interviews with producers, and a historical study of cultural policy, Miller was unable to find any consistent broadcasting policy either at the government level or within the corporation concerning the role of regional drama in either the regional or the national program mix (327). Rather, decisions appeared to be based on the subjective opinions of quality and the financial bottom line. Miller found the following commentary to be common among CBC staff: 'There's no way they can make stuff for the network out there.' According to Miller, 'out there' was used to describe 'all points east, west, or north of Toronto' (328).

While all of these scholars have recommended greater interregional communication, there has been no substantial investigation of how cultural products are developed within the regions. In brief, there have been no empirical media studies of the English-Canadian regions as culturally diverse lived communities. And, more importantly, given the renewed interest in regionalism and community, there has been no research into the processes of television production at the regional level itself. Jackson's (1991) research on regional radio drama production, however, is instructive for the case of local television production. Jackson's historical overview of provincial public-radio broadcasting from 1945 to 1986 illustrates how producers of a local medium were able to engage in a form of regional 'storytelling' that provided a sense of history, continuity, and place or community for listeners. While Jackson argues that this 'last' venue of regional expression was lost with the CBC takeover of provincial public-radio broadcasting, he overlooks the fact that, to some extent, regional television serves this function in modern, urban societies. It was with this idea in mind that I set out to analyse the ways in which regional producers draw upon the popular discourse of their communities during the story development process and the institutional, policy, and market constraints that contribute to the structure of the final cut.

At first glance, it would seem reasonable to equate different spheres of community – local, regional, national, and international – with concomitant levels of television production – community television, the Vancouver CBC, and the major private television broadcasters in British Columbia. However, as the following chapters indicate, this notion appears facile in light of the interconnectedness of the seemingly distinct broadcasting institutions. Television production is a particularly mobile industry, and to narrow it into convenient packages/sites or case studies is to set artificial boundaries around the interaction of the production community. Most producers work independently and pitch their stories to whichever broadcaster they think will give the project at least a second glance. While community television, as a first impression, appeared to be the most fixed and local production community, many of the people I spoke with were simultaneously working their way into the field of independent production. At the same time, independent producers who could not pin down a private broadcaster would sometimes turn to the community television station if their idea was sufficiently 'local' or 'regional.' The CBC, in turn, was in the midst of strengthening ties with independent producers as the latest cutbacks from Toronto had decimated the in-house production teams. Despite the emergent Vennlike diagram of overlapping production-broadcaster teams, each sphere of production remains governed by its own particular mandate – regional programming (with an eye to the national network) that could be defined as 'Canadian' for the CBC; local or regional programming for the province's largest community television station in Vancouver; and anything that would draw the largest audiences domestically and internationally for the private broadcasting sector. The disjunctures and connections between these disparate mandates and spheres of production, and the types of narrative content that emanate from them, form the substance of the larger arguments presented in this book.

In 1996, at the beginning of this study, the Vancouver production community was in an interesting state of flux. The Canadian Radio-television and Telecommunications Commission (CRTC) had just announced that it was accepting applications for twenty-three new specialty channels (eighteen English language) and that it would grant a licence for the first new private television station in Vancouver in more than twenty years. As all these enterprises would be contingent on a commitment to regional and national programs, Vancouver producers were gearing up for the opportunity to pitch ideas to several new broadcasters. At the same time, CBC staff were poised to announce a strike in protest of the loss of in-house production teams that had resulted from the regional cutbacks over the past decade. Throughout this industry shake-up, the British Columbia Film Commission was predicting that 1996 would be a record volume year for American television and movie productions in the province.

Chapter 2 depicts this point of entry into the study. It sets Vancouver within the context of the larger issue of globalization and the province's goal to establish Vancouver as a 'world class' city or city-region. The focal points here are the turn to Pacific Rim trade and immigration and the promotion of Vancouver as a service locations industry for American producers. Lorimer's (1994) description of these processes in British Columbia reasserts the arguments of the vanishing nation that characterize many theories of globalization: 'Such developments would seem to encourage enhanced loyalty to the local, and an orientation to the international. What disappears? Perhaps the regional, certainly the national – if only because there will be fewer economic, political, and cultural transactions' (277).[12] This chapter places Lorimer's commentary in a critical light and examines the rationale behind Vancouver's global strategy and the possible cultural ramifications of the internationalization of the local television industry. It suggests that the outward-directed gaze of the Vancouver television industry has as much to do with marginalization within the national sphere as it does with a desire to reach international markets. Herein, the incorporation

into the Hollywood production structure provides an avenue for producers who are unable to gain access to the national network.

Chapter 3 elaborates on the issues of regional marginalization through
a consideration of the policies and funding structures that have favoured
the development of television production in central Canada. The consequences of these actions are illustrated through a discussion of the
current realities facing the two most culturally mandated television
broadcasters: community television and the Vancouver CBC. When I
began this project there were no prime-time series in production for
either the regional or national level at the Vancouver CBC production
centre. However, towards the end of my fieldwork a new regime of
'Canadianization' had been announced, and the CBC declared the revival of regional production in Vancouver beginning with the production of two new prime-time series for the network's fall schedule. As
this chapter illustrates, the region was revived under the watchful eye
of the Toronto network, with the end result that the least regionally
representative story ideas were approved for pre-production.

The case of community television provides an interesting counterpoint to the CBC context. Community television in the summer of 1996
appeared to exemplify the goals of the Canadian cultural identity
mandate and the emphasis on representing the diversity of the local
community to its audiences. The structure of community television
corresponded with the importance of neighbourhood affiliation and
identity to the cultural geography of Vancouver by establishing small
production centres throughout the city and scheduling half-hour to
one-hour time slots for current affairs and entertainment programs
from each sector. Community television also epitomizes the shifting
boundaries between level of production and community definition, as
this most local of broadcast media was also the most effective at televis-
ing depictions of the globalization of Vancouver. Herein, grass-roots
volunteers, many of whom were members of diverse ethnic diasporic
communities, produced programs that represented the province's changing cultural and political landscape as British Columbia turned its focus
to Pacific Rim interests in a manner that highlights the inextricable
connection between the local and the global. By the spring of 1997,
however, community television became a victim of its own success. At
that time, the station's parent company, Rogers Cable, conducted its
first ratings study and discovered, much to its surprise, that community
television stations were drawing in close to 1 million viewers nationally.
Envisioning the potential for national sponsorship, Rogers collapsed

Vancouver's neighbourhood stations into one central production centre and introduced generic program formulas for all large urban community television stations under its control across the country. While it is too early to reach conclusions about the consequences of the Rogers restructuring of community programming, the loss of another site of local production presents striking parallels to the current structure of the CBC network.

The discourse around audience ratings and international markets is further explored in chapter 4. The tensions between national cultural development and market forces have always been a central problematic in the private-public broadcasting structure in Canada. Our small population of approximately 30 million people makes it difficult to recoup production costs on indigenous programs within the domestic market. Consequently, international sales have always been important to both independent producers and the CBC. While the relationship between the symbolic and the economic aspects of television production is the common theme connecting all the chapters, chapter 4 emphasizes the roles played by gatekeepers (broadcasters, policy makers, and funding agencies) and international co-production partners in the development of story ideas. Specific attention is given to the way in which Canadian producers must negotiate culturally specific ideas – or universalize the particular – in order to produce and sell programs to a wider market, usually the United States.

Chapter 5 brings the project full circle and questions whether it is possible, in a global media environment, to produce domestic programs that are distinctive and popular across the Canadian regions. When I posed this question to television producers, they unanimously agreed that Canadian comedies exemplified the possibilities for a successful domestic television industry. *This Hour Has 22 Minutes* was one of the most frequently mentioned programs, and therefore is the focus of analysis in chapter 5. The program illustrates the way in which marginalized groups use irony to subvert the dominant discourses of official or hegemonic cultures. Its satirical attack on both central Canada and the United States reflects the dual core-periphery relationships at work within the Canadian context.

Chapter 6 concludes on a cautiously optimistic note and suggests that globalization is a contradictory process and provides both limits to and new opportunities for Canadian television. With the introduction of the new specialty channels, and the possibility of a relevant and newly 'Canadianized' CBC, all that is necessary is the attendant political will to relinquish some degree of control to the regions and return to the initial goals of national broadcasting – national *unity* not national *identity*. In this respect, this project does not anticipate the death of national institutions or nation-states within the context of globalization. Rather, it points back to the original intent of broadcasting in Canada: to convey a sense of unity within diversity in a country that has always been defined by regional, national, continental, and international forces. This chapter also argues for a reconceptualization of the discourses that underpin our notions of the local, national, and global as they pertain to cultural production. Working within a Foucauldian framework, I argue that these terms are discursive constructions, or regimes of knowledge, that serve the disciplining and governance goals of policy makers and broadcasting executives but mask the fluid cultural processes that define the relationship between communities and their depiction in the field of televisual production in the global cultural economy.

The issues raised in these chapters are not limited to the Vancouver case study. As older nation-states such as France, England, and Germany move towards continental integration and begin to address the relationship between geography and community, they do so in terms that reflect Canadian dilemmas since Confederation. The European Union's attempt to establish a policy of 'television without frontiers,' which simultaneously unites diverse regional (once national) cultural communities and defends against global (read 'American') media intrusion, echoes the goals of Canadian communications policies since the development of radio in the 1920s. Ironically, the European Union's path to averting what EU members refer to as 'Canadianization' (the perception that a smaller nation's culture can be overwhelmed or destroyed by the inundation of American programming) is to follow the same problematic route of the example they are attempting to avoid – namely, the attempt to define a common *European* identity that can be translated into content and policy regulations (Morley and Robins 1995). Where Canada could not succeed in uniting two linguistic and cultural communities, Europe will try to unite several. To reword Melville Watkins's earlier phrase, the European Union is attempting to use continentalism as a conscious strategy of pasting over the cracks of nationalism. By re-examining the relationships between culture, communication, and the diverse interpretations of collective identity at the ground level of Canadian media production, we can see implications that contribute to both Canadian communications policies and the larger theoretical debate about the nature of communities and identities in a global cultural arena.

Chapter 2

Constructing the Global City:
Contextualizing 'Hollywood North'

In the 1980's the B.C. Ministry of Small Business, Tourism and Culture developed the 'Super Natural British Columbia' campaign, which promoted travel to the province by extolling the beauty and variety of British Columbia's natural landscape in a series of advertisements directed at both the American and out-of-province Canadian markets. While 'Super Natural British Columbia,' remains the province's official tourism motto to this day, by the mid-1990s the slogan became more closely associated with the fact that Vancouver was the production home of nine of the top American 'supernatural' television series, including *The X-Files, Highlander, The Outer Limits, Poltergeist: The Legacy, Sliders, Strange Luck, Millennium, Stargate,* and *The Sentinel*.[1] The connection here is not meant to appear facetious. The rationale for producing these series in Vancouver is, in fact, largely the diversity of locations available in a coastal province that also contains a glacier mountain range and a dry, rugged interior region. The Lower Mainland's grey, rainy, and foggy winters also provide the natural light and settings that writer-producers and directors of photography (DOPs) relish in their efforts to establish the necessary atmosphere for such programs. And it is no coincidence that the B.C. Film Commission, the organization largely responsible for recruiting 'runaway' American television and film production, works under the auspices of the Ministry of Small Business, Tourism and Culture.

The connection to small business, however, is misleading. In British Columbia, film and television production and tourism are multimillion-dollar industries that are integral components of the province's larger economic globalization strategy and goal to establish Vancouver as a world class, or global, city. In 1997 the television and motion picture industry spent directly an estimated $700 million in Vancouver, an increase of $100 million from 1996. During that year, the B.C. Film Commission provided service to $2.7 billion worth of productions (one-third of the potential market) and confirmed Vancouver's status as the third-largest production centre for American movies and television series (B.C. Film Commission 1997). In fact, of the approximately 200 television programs and movies shot in the province between 1996 and 1997, only an estimated 20 per cent were indigenous Canadian productions (Rice-Barker 1997a: 3). By 2000, spending by the film and television industry had surpassed the $1.18 billion mark.

This integration of the Vancouver locations industry into the larger Hollywood production structure has led some people (e.g., Gasher 1995) to argue that foreign production has not only displaced indigenous production in British Columbia but that it is has also erased any sense of 'place' by commodifying it or selling producers 'an industrial setting (physical sites and services) rather than a cultural and historical site (a source of stories and characters)' (233): 'The B.C. example illustrates how the locations industry denies British Columbia its sociocultural specificity. It empties this place of its sociality, its status as community, and frames it simply as geographical space' (ibid.: 239).

Gasher's indictment of American and other international productions in British Columbia is partially accurate. Foreign producers do not choose to bring their projects to Vancouver to tell Canadian stories or portray Canadian settings. In fact, much of their pre-production work consists of finding sites that can stand in for other places, usually someplace in the United States, and then 'dressing' it accordingly (which means removing any physical objects that could identify the location as Canadian in any way).[2]

However, Gasher's argument, which is based primarily on archival analysis of industry promotional documents and production figures, misses the point in two very important respects. First, unlike other forms of international capital and resource/production flows, the 'globally mobile' film and television industry does not merely 'create and use up places for the purposes of production or consumption' (N. Thrift, quoted in Morley and Robins 1995: 31). In other words, merely by filming projects in Vancouver, international producers do not first exhaust the labour, resources, or sites needed for indigenous production and then move on to the next locations city, leaving Vancouver a depleted resource town. In fact, before British Columbia was able to attract runaway American production, local producers were dependent on the transitory whims of central-Canadian broadcasters and policy makers to support and maintain any level of domestic television and film production in the province. The fact that there were far fewer domestic productions prior to Hollywood's arrival in British Columbia further contradicts Gasher's implication that the foreign television and film industry somehow supplants the domestic.[3]

The second, and related, problematic assumption in Gasher's argument is that increased indigenous production automatically guarantees the portrayal of British Columbia's 'sociocultural specificity' as a place rather than as empty 'geographical space.' However, as chapters 3 and 4 indicate, domestic producers also often disguise the culturally specific aspects of their stories and settings in order to sell them to international audiences and even, sometimes, to national broadcasters. Also missing from Gasher's analysis are any description of what constitutes the sociocultural specificity of British Columbia that has supposedly been erased by the development of the Vancouver locations industry and any discussion of what types of depiction of community and place experiences might potentially be developed by the domestic production industry.

This chapter begins to address some of the critiques of international, especially American, film and television production in Vancouver through a consideration of the development of British Columbia's locations industry within the context of the province's larger strategy of economic and cultural globalization. The first section examines the goals and rationale behind the provincial government's efforts to attract runaway American television and film production as a component of a larger plan to attract global capital. The second section follows that theme with an analysis of the evolving sociocultural dimensions of Vancouver that have resulted from the province's economic and cultural movement away from the national and towards the global, beginning with the 1986 World Exposition (Expo 86) and culminating in the establishment of Vancouver as Canada's gateway to the Pacific as evidenced in the province's special relationship with Southeast Asia. The final section explores the ways in which the specificities of culture and community in the global-local dynamic of Vancouver have been erased, or neglected altogether, in both foreign and domestic media production. Here consideration is given to the contradictions in the Vancouver-Hollywood production relationship; namely, that runaway American production does erase Vancouver as a *lived community* but simultaneously provides the necessary opportunities and infrastructure for domestic producers to develop independent local stories – facilities and opportunities denied them by the central-Canadian broadcasting powers (a topic examined further in chapter 3).

'The British Columbia shooting gallery: We can give it to you for a song'

The above title, from the B.C. Film Commission's centrepiece promotional brochure, is perhaps the best illustration of Gasher's argument that the locations industry commodifies Vancouver as geographical space to be sold to international television and film producers. *The Shooting Gallery* is a glossy, thirty-page magazine that underscores the reasons why foreign producers have flocked to Vancouver over the past decade: the diversity of British Columbia's geography, the cheap Canadian dollar (which fluctuated in a range between 79 and 89 cents U.S. throughout the 1990s and declined below 65 cents in 2002), well-trained film crews, and, importantly, the proximity to Los Angeles, the centre of the American industry. The discourse of commerce provides the subtext of the publication and uses a play on words and song titles to frame snapshots of Vancouver communities frozen into stage-set vignettes with generic locations identifications: 'The Big City,' 'Urban Ethnic,' 'Deep Woods,' 'Industrial,' 'Residential,' 'The Mountains,' 'The Period Look,' 'The Railroads,' 'The Countryside,' 'The Farm,' 'The Wild West,' 'Small Towns,' 'High Tech,' 'Coastlines,' 'Ranch Country,' and 'Wilderness.' Beginning with the subtitle 'We can give it to you for a song,' the brochure tells foreign producers that 'This land is your land' and that, for a fraction of the costs elsewhere, Vancouver can be made to look like anywhere in the world, with the closing invitation to 'Come and get it ...'[4]

Attracting and facilitating international production in Vancouver is, in fact, the central objective of the B.C. Film Commission. The commission was created in 1978 by a provincial government that sought to diversify its resource-based economy by creating an industry that would not be subject to the exigencies of commodities markets. To this extent, the B.C. government's economic strategy exemplifies Jenson's (1993) depiction of the patterns of post-Fordism in Canada from the mid-1970s through the 1980s. At the time, the provinces found themselves increasingly in conflict and competition in their efforts to restructure politically and economically in ways 'which often implied abandoning efforts to protect the borders of the domestic economy' and favoured 'accommodating new regimes of accumulation' (159). An important aspect of this process was the attempt by provincial governments, using the neoliberal discourse of globalization, to encourage 'unions to participate in new kinds of tripartite bodies to design programs for restructuring industry and re-locating Canadian production in the new global economy' (ibid.: 158). The B.C. Film Commission's mandate exemplifies this strategy. The first step towards developing the Vancouver locations and service industry was to negotiate a cooperative agreement with the B.C. film and television unions and thereby establish an attractive economic environment for American producers. The next step was to send a team to Los Angeles to convince the studios and producers that Vancouver would be the ideal city for their production needs. One member of the commission summarized the province's initial strategy:

> L.A. has always been based around the top five or six major studios. Each of those studios has a major executive in charge of production for features, for television, et cetera, so you go and you sit in their offices with pictures, a portfolio book, with the union hand in hand – government and the union walking into the office and saying whatever it takes to get them up here and they would come. Sometimes a feature is going to come here anyway because it's locations driven. For instance, when Fred Schepisi's going to do *Iceman* where are you going to get glaciers that are within twenty or thirty minutes' flying time from downtown? Vancouver has that option – anything that's wilderness based, which is exciting for viewers – you can stay at the Sutton Place [a luxury, downtown hotel], go to the Seymour Demonstration Forest, and look like you're actually lost in the woods – work for twelve hours and drive back to the Sutton Place. It's great and they like it.
>
> (interview with the author, 13 August 1997)

It is precisely these amenities – and the Seymour Demonstration Forest, in particular – that made Vancouver home to *The X-Files* for the show's first five seasons. The show's creator, Chris Carter, needed a forest for a UFO landing scene in the first episode and, as forests are somewhat scarce in Los Angeles, he found what he needed in Vancouver. Carter is one of the city's biggest boosters: when asked why he stayed in Vancouver, he replied,

> First of all because I have a great crew ... *second of all because it's the biggest backlot in North America*. It really has so many different looks and it

doubles for anywhere in the U.S. ... People say, 'Oh you save money,' and I always tell people that I don't save any money being in Vancouver: I actually get to put more onscreen by being in Vancouver. That's the difference. I actually get to produce a better product for the money that they would have given me to make the product anyway.

(quoted in Leiren-Young 1995b: S12, emphasis added)[5]

Vancouver's capacity to serve as the 'biggest backlot in North America' was actually noticed long before *The X-Files* and the creation of the B.C. Film Commission. In the 1930s, when Canada was still a British dominion, Hollywood producers took advantage of the fact that shooting movies on location in British Columbia would allow them access to the highly protected film market in the United Kingdom. These 'quota quickies,' as they were called, constituted the first stage of the B.C. locations industry until 1938, when Britain revised its quota system to exclude productions from the dominions as domestic content (MacIntyre 1996: 132). The second stage of the B.C. locations industry did not begin until the early 1970s, when directors such as Mike Nichols and Robert Altman moved their productions on location in search of greater 'realism' (ibid.: 133). The development of the B.C. Film Commission, and its ability to capitalize on the positive experiences of the early American directors and producers who had worked in Vancouver, can thus be seen as the third, and most enduring, stage of the city's evolution into a Hollywood service centre.

The B.C. Film Commission has played a fundamental role in Vancouver's emergence as 'Hollywood North.' Run by a staff of eight, the commission focuses many of its activities on making the city a production-friendly site. This involves everything from breaking down scripts for locations scouting and maintaining a locations photo library to acting as a community mediator between city residents and business owners when productions take over the city's streets. The commission's primary role, however, is to continually market Vancouver internationally and sustain strong ties to the key market: Los Angeles (B.C. Film Commission 1997). In this respect, the commission has seen itself as a key player in maintaining the annual 21 per cent growth rate of the Vancouver locations and service industry. To reinforce this relationship, the commission holds an annual 'Friends of B.C.' reception in Los Angeles as an official thank-you to the American filmmakers who bring their productions up north (Come Again 1996: 12). Attendees include representatives from the major American studios, television networks, and cable channels who gather to hear updates about new tax incentives, the labour situation, and the overall benefits of working in Vancouver.

Perhaps the greatest barometer of the commission's efficacy, aside from the hundreds of movies and television programs filmed in Vancouver between 1996 and 1997, has been the recognition it has received from its counterparts across North America. As one U.S. film commissioner has said, 'This place [B.C.] gets everything.' His words were echoed by Jack Valenti, president of the Motion Picture Association of America, and a vehement critic of Canadian content regulations and cultural protection policies, who told a delegate of film commissioners, 'If B.C. gets one more production, this province will sink into the sea' (quoted in Caddell 1997: 8). In fact, the volume of runaway American production that has relocated to British Columbia has led to a new inter-city competition between Vancouver and Los Angeles. In 1996, Los Angeles mayor Richard Riordan, in partnership with actor Charlton Heston, announced that the opening of the Los Angeles Film Office was part of a strategy to 'bring the movies back home' (Haysom 1996: A6).[6] Prior to the development of the L.A. Film Office, American producers had to deal with ninety-one different permit-granting jurisdictions for locations shooting in Los Angeles County, as opposed to the one-stop shopping process available through the B.C. Film Commission. According to Cody Cluff, the president of the L.A. Film Office, the B.C. Film Commission will provide the model for the development of his new office because 'You guys in Canada have been doing it right. We've been doing it all wrong. You made it easy for moviemakers. We made it impossible' (quoted in Haysom 1996: A6).

However, it is not the B.C. Film Commission alone that has guaranteed the longevity of the Vancouver locations industry. The provincial government, as mentioned earlier, is committed to maintaining the necessary infrastructure for what has become one of British Columbia's primary economic resources after tourism and forestry. Not only has the government taken an active role in cultivating a favourable labour climate in British Columbia, it has also invested millions of dollars in building studio space in order to avoid losing any potential productions because of a lack of production facilities.[7] Prior to the boom of the locations industry, the only available studio space in Vancouver was in the city's CBC production centre. Given the severe regional production cutbacks that began in the early 1980s, the underused CBC studios were available for rent to American productions passing through Vancouver.

The space, however, was not capable of meeting the demands of the growing locations industry and lacked the capacity (both physically and politically) to serve as a permanent production home for American television series in Vancouver. To keep the industry growing, the provincial government spent $4.4 million to build The Bridge Studios in 1987. A one-time steel fabricating factory, The Bridge Studios (The Bridge) opened with four sound stages and the largest special effects stage in North America, facilities that have enabled Vancouver to attract high-budget Hollywood features such as *Jumanji*, *Alive*, and the $100-million Disney movie *The Thirteenth Warrior* (Leiren-Young 1995a: S7). The Bridge has an added competitive advantage in that government ownership qualifies the studio complex as a Crown corporation, which exempts it from paying provincial income tax. The savings allow for a 'low-margin, high-volume business' that keeps the studios at full capacity year round and generates more than $1 million in annual revenue for the province (Edwards 1996b: 22).[8]

The government's commitment to maintaining a secure environment for runaway American production has led to spin-off effects in attracting international capital investment in other studios and sound stages. Two years after The Bridge was built, Stephen J. Cannell decided to make Vancouver the production home for his episodics *21 Jump Street*, *Booker*, and *Wiseguy* and built North Shore Studios to accommodate his production needs. At the time, North Shore Studios was the largest sound stage in Canada, and Cannell's confidence in Vancouver as a production environment provided the impetus for other L.A. producers to go beyond using the city as a temporary locations site and actually move their television series production there. While Cannell continues to use one-third of the North Shore Studios for his productions, the rest of the sound stages have been semi-permanently booked by Chris Carter, first for *The X-Files*, until the show's relocation to Los Angeles in 1998, later for the short-lived series *Millennium*, and the recently cancelled *The X-Files* spin-off *The Lone Gunmen*.

The provincial government, meanwhile, continues to accommodate the interests of international capital investment in Vancouver and in 1996 agreed to a partnership with MGM Worldwide Television to build a fifth sound stage at The Bridge. The agreement allowed MGM a five-year lease on the sound stage for the television series *Stargate*, which began production in 1997. The partnership was heralded by then B.C. premier Glen Clark as a profit-generating vehicle that would result in 400 new jobs, $75 million in direct investment, and $4.5 million annually in rental and tax revenues (MGM/B.C. Government 1996: 28). However, the MGM-government agreement met with a mixed response from local Vancouver producers, who were concerned not so much with the amount of American production in the city but with the government's reluctance to transfer some of the revenue into a fund that would support indigenous film and television production. MGM's senior vice-president of television, Mel Swopes, responded to these concerns by stating, 'When you look back at earth from space you see no borders and no boundaries. Let's celebrate our differences and build our global filmmaking community' (quoted in Wilson 1996: C13).

It is statements like this that fuel the arguments of those who see the locations and service industry as displacing domestic production and denying the sociocultural specificities of place as Vancouver becomes assimilated into the Hollywood production structure. It is, after all, difficult to 'celebrate our differences' when the concentration of effort appears to be directed at helping to produce another nation's stories. The difficulty here is in reconciling the sometimes conflicting interests between 'spaces' and 'places.' As Beynon and Hudson (1993) explain, the domain of 'space' is one 'where we find capital largely involved in a one-dimensional assessment of localities, understood in terms of their capacity to yield profits.' 'Places,' conversely, are not reducible to the interest of global capital (although they cannot be unaffected by it) but rather are sites of community where

> [people] have networks of friends, relatives and acquaintances, where they have learned about life and acquired a cultural frame of reference through which to interpret the social world around them; their place is where they are socialized as human beings rather than just reproduced as bearers of commodity labor power. As a result, people have often become profoundly attached to particular places, which have come to have socially endowed and shared meanings that touch on all aspects of their lives, helping shape *who* they are by virtue of *where* they are.
>
> (Beynon and Hudson 1993: 182–3)

In this respect, American producers are primarily interested in Vancouver as a space in which to invest capital in order to garner greater profit rather than a place about which to tell stories. To this end, they largely ignore the 'place' of Vancouver as long as it does not interfere with capital accumulation. But the question then remains: What defines Vancouver as a place and what types of stories does it offer to domestic producers who are interested in telling them? The following section explores the sociocultural specificities of the place of Vancouver before turning to the second, related question: Does the growth of the *space* of Hollywood North somehow preclude the possibility of telling stories about the *place* of Vancouver?

Vancouver: Exploring the Global-Local Nexus

> It's not Terminal City. It's not the little village on the edge of the rain forest. What it is is a new kind of city, one that is inventing new ways to be, uh, globally important.[9]

Incorporated as a city in 1886, Vancouver is a mere infant compared to global cities like Tokyo, London, New York, and Paris. Nevertheless, the focus of the provincial government's economic plans for more than twenty years has been to transform Vancouver into a world class or global city that could function as a semi-autonomous city-region within the confines of the Canadian nation-state. While the development of the television and film industry provided an early foray into the process of attracting foreign capital, it was not until 1986, the city's centennial year, that Vancouver arrived at the pivotal point in its globalization strategy.

In 1986, Vancouver hosted the World Exposition (Expo) and in welcoming the world also hoped to welcome and attract international business interests that would remain long after the fairgrounds were dismantled. Fortuitously for Vancouver's business community and Expo planners, the World Exposition took place during the same year that then Prime Minister Brian Mulroney introduced the Immigrant Investor Program in Canada. The new investor program was developed as an extension of Mulroney's economic policy whereby business immigrants would be targeted over more marginalized groups seeking resident or citizenship status in Canada. Under the regulations of the program, people applying for landed immigrant status would be required to have 'a net worth of $500,000 (CDN) or greater, and commit to a five-year investment of between $250,000 [and] $500,000 (CDN) in a business, private investment syndicate, or government-managed joint venture fund' (Abu-Laban 1997: 79). As Canadian immigration falls under both federal and provincial jurisdictions, British Columbia has consistently fought for greater provincial control over immigration decisions since the introduction of the Investor Immigrant Program; and Expo 86 provided the ideal environment to sell Vancouver to a preferred business community: Hong Kong corporations and entrepreneurs looking for a safe financial haven before the 1997 handover to China. British Columbia's attempts to wrest greater control from Ottawa over provincial immigration patterns is indicative of the historical tensions between the region and the federal government. In order to more clearly understand the province's turn to the global, and the changing geocultural landscapes of pre- and post-Expo Vancouver, it is important first to consider the province's particular place within Canada.

British Columbia did not become a province of Canada until 1871, four years after Confederation, and then did so with the caveat that the deal would be null and void if the Canadian government failed to live up to the terms of union, of which extending the Canadian Pacific Railway to Vancouver would be the key proviso. As Black (1996) maintains, British Columbia, from 1871 until the present day, has 'held firmly to a contract theory of the association' (40). While the federal government fulfilled its promise of the railway and established Vancouver as 'Terminal City,' since that time British Columbia has echoed the demands it made during the negotiation of the terms of union by repeatedly seeking greater control over natural resources while expecting greater federal responsibility for social programs and structural development. In fact, the province's 'constant complaints upon joining the young nation' led to its nickname as the 'spoilt child of Confederation.' The term resurfaced during the constitutional debates of the 1980s and 1990s when British Columbia opposed Quebec's claims to status as a distinct society while simultaneously seeking constitutional recognition for itself as a 'distinctive fifth "region" of the country' (ibid.: 32–3).

In many respects, British Columbia epitomizes Soja's (1989) depiction of the subnational regionalisms inherent within all nation-states wherein the resultant spacialization arises from 'competitive struggles and particular conjunctures, filled with tensions, politics, ideology and power' (163). In the case of British Columbia, the province has attempted to declare autonomy as a fifth region, thereby limiting Ottawa's desired control over the Pacific port and the province's natural resources, while concurrently bemoaning the federal government's political and economic neglect of the province. The resulting sentiment is encapsulated nicely in a popular B.C. saying that, 'British Columbia may be three thousand miles from Ottawa, but Ottawa is three million miles from British Columbia.' This is reinforced geographically through the physical separation of British Columbia from the rest of the nation by the Rocky Mountains and through the psychological alienation that accompanies the core-periphery relationship between Ottawa and the regions. The resultant spacialization, following Soja's terms, is one in which British Columbia has long-seeded and 'hardened attitudes to central government' and has evolved as a 'self-conscious community with more oceanic ties to the rest of the world than to Canada' (Keith Ralston quoted in Barman 1991: 346).

The province's 'oceanic ties' date back centuries to the imperial conflicts among Spain, Russia, and Britain, all of which sought to claim the territory in the interests of geographic expansion and access to natural resources. British Columbia's ties to the countries of the Pacific Rim developed early in the province's union with Canada, when hundreds of Chinese and Japanese men came to the province seeking the riches of Gold Mountain and found themselves with few opportunities other than working as cheap labour for the building of the transnational railway. This early wave of immigrants, amid intense racial hostility, managed to establish large Asian communities throughout the province that would, four generations later, enhance Vancouver's Expo 86 claims to be Canada's gateway to the Pacific in the hopes of attracting a new, and wealthier, generation of Asians to immigrate to British Columbia.

While it is often implied that Expo 86 marked a somewhat smooth transition point at which Vancouver moved away from the national arena and into the global, the idea of a costly, international event was not an easy sell to city residents, despite the promises of an economic boom proffered by the business community. The provincial government began to develop its bid for the World Exposition during one of the most severe economic recessions the province had faced; the same economic downturn that had expedited the initiative, begun in the late 1970s, to bring American television and film production to Vancouver. Taxpayer resistance was further aggravated by the Exposition Committee's proposal to develop the Downtown Eastside or 'skid row,' the city's poorest neighbourhood, as the site of the World's Fair. Vancouver is a city with a long history of social and political activism, and the Downtown Eastside Residents' Association (DERA) had, since its inception in 1973, lobbied government to build affordable public housing in a neighbourhood that consisted primarily of run-down hotels for transients and welfare recipients.[10] DERA immediately recognized the threats to potential social housing development, and the consequent displacement of hundreds of downtown residents, if the city won the bid for Expo.

The government and Expo chairman Jim Pattison, a billionaire Vancouver entrepreneur, attempted to sell Expo as a loss leader that would pay for itself in the resultant increases in foreign investment and tourism. Moreover, Pattison stated that Expo would not run a deficit to be paid by taxpayers and that any losses would be covered by revenue from the province's portion of the national lottery (Lotto 6/49). To finalize the process and counter growing opposition from city residents, the government promised that the Expo lands would be developed with future community development and social housing in mind. An estimated $1.5 billion was spent on construction for Expo 86, with $706 million paid by the government and the rest contributed by sponsors and participants. Expo attracted 22 million visitors and generated $369 million in revenue, leaving a deficit of $337 million. While the lottery covered approximately $277 million of the debt, $60 million remained to be covered by the end of the fair (Hatten 1987). Expo chairman Pattison later admitted that the committee had known they would run a deficit of at least $311 million for a year and a half before Expo (Tafler 1985).

DERA saw its fears confirmed both prior to and during Expo 86. Owners of downtown hotels for transients evicted between 500 and 800 long-term residents in order to raise their rates and offer tourists rooms within walking distance of the Expo grounds. Seemingly overnight, room rates went from $200–$250 a month to $45–$65 a night (Ley 1994: 716). The government, however, dealt the worst blow to community activists after Expo when it broke its promise to develop social housing and instead privatized the land and sold it to Hong Kong developer and billionaire Li Ka-shing. In turn, his son, Victor Li, built luxury condominiums on the site, which comprises one-sixth of downtown Vancouver, and transformed it into one of the city's most expensive residential areas (Mitchell 1993: 263). It is notable that Li Ka-shing is also a global media mogul in his own right. He and his son Victor developed the first pan-Asian satellite television service, Star TV, in 1991 and sold it to Rupert Murdoch in 1993.

In retrospect, commentators and scholars agree that such was the intent behind Expo 86 all along, and in this respect, Expo 'exemplified the central themes of the 1980s – privatization, polarization, and internationalization': internationalization was the explicit intent of the fair, with marketing slogans such as 'Invitation to the world' and 'What your world is coming to in 1986' (Ley, Hiebert, and Pratt 1992: 239). It is not coincidental, either, that the theme of the fair was 'Transportation and Communication.' In all facets, the government's goal in hosting the fair was to attract foreign capital and effectively globalize the province's economy for the long term. It is in the execution of Expo that we see the process of globalization unfold at the ground level, in Gramscian terms, as an 'economic accumulation strategy and a hegemonic political project' (Bob Jessop, quoted in Todd 1995: 194): 'The pursuit of globalization certainly qualifies as such a strategy. A hegemonic political project seeks to resolve the more abstract problems of conflicts between particular and general interests by mobilizing political support and appealing to common-sense understandings of the economy' (Todd 1995: 194).

This is precisely the method that was employed in selling Expo to the residents of Vancouver. Not only was globalization touted as the only means to revive a depressed economy, but the fair itself was framed in easily understood terms of economic mobilization. The Expo committee and the government promised $970 million of incremental economic activity, 15,000 person years of employment, $187 million in tax revenue, and a 'catalyst for the re-development of an old downtown industrial area with many permanent facilities that will remain for community use' (Public Affairs 1986: 2). Whether or not Expo's promises were fulfilled was of little relevance to a government that had managed to mobilize support, or at least marginalize dissent, for an event that played a major role in transforming the British Columbia economy and rapidly altered the sociocultural 'place' of Vancouver.

It is important not to underestimate Li Ka-shing's role in solidifying the relationship between Vancouver and the Pacific Rim. Between 1989 and 1996, approximately 80,000 residents moved to Vancouver from Hong Kong as a result of uncertainty over China's plans for the British colony. According to Bramham (1997: C1), two factors made Vancouver more attractive than other North American cities with Pacific Rim interests, such as Seattle and San Francisco: (1) the 1986 Immigrant Investor Program, and (2) Li Ka-shing's decision to pay $145 million for the Expo lands. Vancouver banker Richard Wong called the land deal a 'turning point' and said that 'If Li had not bought the Expo site, Vancouver would not have developed anything like it has today. As 1997 approached, the people in Hong Kong looked to him as an indication of where to put their capital as a safe haven' (quoted in Bramham 1997: C1–C2). The infusion of Hong Kong capital into Vancouver had a rapid impact on the development of the city.[11] Not only was British Columbia the first province to emerge from the recession of the 1980s, it boomed economically and sustained the strongest provincial economy in Canada for more than a decade. According to the Canadian census, Vancouver's population grew to 1,831,665 by 1996, an increase of 14.3 per cent from 1991 compared to the national average of 5.7 per cent. Immigration also increased as Hong Kong's hand-over date drew closer, with 40,000 immigrants arriving between 1994 and 1996.

Although Vancouver residents reaped many benefits from the province's economic strategy, the accumulation of Hong Kong capital and integration into the global economies of the Pacific Rim countries was not without its disorienting effects on the social and cultural land-scape of the city. The arrival of a new and wealthy immigrant class eventually played itself out in a struggle over spatial and civic politics or *le droit à la ville*, '"the rights to the city" in Lefebvre's terms, the power of citizens to control the social production of space' (Soja 1989: 153). The fight over 'the rights to the city' brought issues of place definition to the forefront of Vancouver politics, and the ensuing struggle to define what a community is, or should be, is perhaps the most enlightening illustra-tion of the sociocultural specificities of Vancouver.

In her work on global cities, Saskia Sassen (1994) paints a picture where immigrants tend to be disadvantaged populations in sites of internationalization where ethnic diversity is seen at the 'low end' of the economy, or in the non-professional, labouring class. Vancouver provides an antithesis to Sassen's argument in that the largest immi-grant group is one of the wealthiest and, therefore, in a position to significantly alter the social meanings of place as well as to subordinate the interests of members of the domestic professional classes. In this respect, racial and class conflicts in Vancouver have primarily occurred between Anglo-Canadian and Hong Kong elites over the city's real-estate market. As Smart and Smart (1996) explain, the Hong Kong view of real estate as a source of profit to be continually 'flipped' rather than as a source of sentiment, as it is within Anglo-Canadian culture, has inflated the market value of the city's real estate to a point where most middle- and upper-middle-class residents can no longer afford to buy a house in the metropolitan area. By 1991, houses on Vancouver's west side had risen in assessed value by 300 per cent as a result of flipping. At the same time West Vancouver was named the wealthiest municipal-ity in Canada (Ley, Hiebert, and Pratt 1992). The conflict, however, has been greatest in the city's established elite neighbourhoods where wealthy Hong Kong immigrants have torn down existing homes and gardens and replaced them with extravagant mansions with little or no yard space. These 'monster homes,' as they came to be termed in public and media discourses, averaged approximately 5,000 square feet and became the foci of a cultural struggle to maintain control over the definition of Vancouver's landscape. It has been referred to as a battle of ideological labels between 'ostentatious/*feng-shui* principles' and the 'picturesque/English garden' in defining what is to be considered 'natural' in two conflicting cultural spheres (Ley, Hiebert, and Pratt 1992). The result has been the development of a new citizens' movement to lobby City Hall for stricter zoning and building by-laws. But what the issue really speaks to is the larger concern over the displacement that ensues from the processes of globalization:

> One main theme in the discussion of Hong Kong property investment is simply that of money and its connection with the emerging Pacific Rim economy. Hong Kong is important for funneling a share of that money to Canada and for creating a much tighter linkage between local property markets and emergent global property markets. Hong Kong is thus seen as the leading edge of globalization, dramatic change, and the erosion of local and national sovereignty. In Canadian cities, this loss of control becomes represented by 'monster homes.'
>
> (Smart and Smart 1996: 43)

The debate over 'monster homes' became a prominent feature of news coverage throughout the 1990s and, in its path, sowed the seeds of a wider racial, ethnic, and class conflict over the boundaries of capital restructuring in Vancouver.

Long considered one of the more liberal and progressive cities in Canada, Vancouver became a contested site of multicultural political struggle as community groups clashed with business interests over the ramifications of economic displacement in ways that became increasingly articulated in racial and ethnic terms. In this respect, tenant action groups and the political left, seeking government action to address growing income and property disparities, found themselves in the ironic position of being labelled racists by globalization and free-enterprise proponents (Mitchell 1993). By framing the debate in the discourse of race, the economic right was able both to effectively neutralize its opponents and, simultaneously, to obscure the economic basis of inequality resulting from the unfettered accumulation of global capital. Consequently, community groups such as DERA found themselves increasingly marginalized in their quest for equitable housing solutions at both the municipal and global levels as they saw their political arena 'shift from local slumlords to national and international public and private corporations' (Ley 1994: 714).

In the end, however, the most detrimental effect of the confluence of economic and racial discourses was the backlash against multiculturalism felt by the Chinese-Canadian community and new immigrants who were not members of the elite 9 per cent of high-profile Asian investor immigrants. Regardless of class, citizenship, or ethnic background 'those of Chinese origin were systematically equated with immigrants, and immigrants conflated with wealthy entrepreneurs from Hong Kong' (Creese and Peterson 1996: 131):

> The Chinese-Canadian population, however, is far from homogeneous: a significant number are second, third, or fourth generation Canadians who have been joined more recently by refugees from Southeast Asia and China, and by independent immigrants and wealthy business entrepreneurs from Hong Kong and Taiwan. Though the class positions of Chinese-Canadians are as varied as among the rest of the population, popular attention has focused on the small but influential class of wealthy entrepreneurs, whose investments, particularly in real estate, have reshaped the city.
>
> (ibid.: 121)

This is not to imply that Vancouver's experiences of globalization have only been characterized by racism and class polarization. In an effort to promote cross-cultural understanding, most public schools in Vancouver have now included Asian cultures and languages in the curriculum. There has also been a general 'rise in interest for "things Asian,"' as Vancouverites now participate in numerous Asian cultural activities from film festivals to the annual Dragon Boat Races on False Creek (Barnes et al. 1992). Vancouver's cultural markers have also become reflections of global hybridity as classical Chinese gardens blend with English-style landscapes and Asian-style malls contrast with the Anglo-parliamentary architecture of many downtown buildings.

There are, in fact, many parallels between the histories of Vancouver and Hong Kong, arising from their particular experiences as ports, colonies, and frontiers, that in many ways establish a congruent relationship between the two globalizing cities. The national chairman of the Hong Kong Bank of Canada illustrated this point when she said that Vancouver was preferred by the Hong Kong business community for its more familiar, 'freewheeling' business environment, compared to Toronto's 'stuffier corporate climate': 'Vancouver is more like a frontier, you have more manoeuvrability' (Lucy Roschat, quoted in Wood 1996: 13). The frontier mentality has long been a characteristic of the Vancouver imagination. As the port city at the edge of the nation, Vancouver has a dual focus: inward, to the Canadian centre as a periphery-resource base, and outward, to Pacific trade. In many respects, the city's emergent cultural geography is reminiscent of Abbas's (1997: 74) illustration of the salience of the nature of the port in the experience of colonial Hong Kong:

> The nature of the port may have changed, but Hong Kong has not changed as a port. In contrast to international cities like New York, London, or Tokyo, which are in relation to their respective regions, central sites for the production of goods and culture, Hong Kong is primarily a space of facilitation. It is less a site than a *para-site*, in that its dominance in the region is due largely to its geographic proximity to China, together with its accessibility to the rest of the world ... The *para-site* therefore connotes a position that in some strange ways is both autonomous and dependent at the same time, a position in which autonomy is paradoxically a function of dependence.

Vancouver also resembles a 'para-site' to the extent that it is primarily a space of facilitation, whether it is for American film and television production or Asian capital investment, rather than a site of production or manufacturing. Moreover, its situation as a Pacific port grants it nominal autonomy from central Canada, as it is able to look outward and operate internationally. And its autonomy, too, is a function of dependence on the maintenance of business relationships with partners in Los Angeles and the countries of the Pacific Rim. Ian Waddell, a B.C. MLA (Member of the Legislative Assembly) aptly summarized the province's relationship to the latter: 'You can't understand Vancouver without understanding Hong Kong. Our ties are so close now that what happens in Hong Kong will influence Vancouver immensely' (quoted in Ward and Goldhar 1997: A11). Indeed, in its role as a 'para-site,' Vancouver has achieved its goal and badge of status in becoming a global city. While world-city researcher John Friedmann excluded Vancouver from his 1986 (an interesting and telling date) list of world cities, he included it in his 1995 list after the city had entrenched its link to the Pacific Rim (Friedmann 1995: 38. See the Appendix of this book).

As the preceding discussion indicates, the sociocultural specificity of Vancouver is one in which the local is suffused by global cultural and economic forces. Consequently, to speak of the possibility of fostering an indigenous, television and film industry that acknowledges the local specificity of the 'place' of Vancouver presents some interesting challenges. Part of this problem lies in defining, and often differentiating, the local from the global in terms of cultural identity and representation. As Michael Smith (1995) argues, any emphasis on a global-local duality 'rests on a false opposition that equates the *local* with a cultural space of stasis, ontological meaning, and personal identity (i.e. the "place") and the *global* as the source of dynamic change' (257). Vancouver epitomizes this perspective as a site where everyday life in the immediate community is, in one way or another, imbued with the influences of global capital and political power. The relationship, moreover, is not oneway but rather a dialectical process, as the flow of people and finances into the place must also adapt to the particularities of the community. In the end, 'the world city becomes a place where the symbolic economy of new cultural meanings and representations takes place ... At one level, the juxtaposition of cultures, the contestations, become the very material from which new cultural conflict arises, yet simultaneously, these also provide the new cultural content for the movies, videos, theatre, or literature' (King 1995: 228).

If this is the type of sociocultural specificity that Gasher alluded to, then he would be correct in his assessment that the lived aspects of the 'place' of Vancouver are erased, or largely ignored, by the television and film locations industry. But then, defining and representing the cultural community of Vancouver was never the intent behind the development of the locations and service industry, which exists, primarily, to facilitate foreign productions. The questions that remain are, Who *should* define the sociocultural specificity of British Columbia? Is there any interest, among local producers, in telling stories that depict life in the region? and, What are the real constraints against domestic production?

In my conversations with B.C. producers, I found the patterns of response to be as follows: Yes, there is an interest in developing stories about the region and the global-local nexus that is Vancouver. The major constraint against these types of productions was not the development of the Hollywood service industry but the lack of access to the central-Canadian policy makers and the necessary government funding structures. In fact, one locations scout and part-time producer expressed a strong desire to eventually develop a project that depicted the globalization of Vancouver:

> In a way, I can't believe no one's done a show about it yet. I've lived here most of my life, and my experiences are informed by this city. This place really changed after Expo and so did my perspectives on many things. There are probably hundreds of great story lines about intercultural contact, interracial relationships, and just the way the economy changed everything for people of my generation [thirty-year-olds]. I think there'd be a market for that type of story, not just here but with people going back [to Southeast Asia] there's a market there as they become familiar with experiences in Vancouver. They'd really recognize it, too. A quote I really like is, 'Being a Vancouverite is always following and always moulding to other people's agendas.' Being raised in Vancouver, for me, has always meant being caught in other people's worlds. Always.
>
> (interview with the author, 27 June 1997)

When asked why he had not pursued that type of project, he replied: 'Where would the money come from?' While this area will be pursued in greater detail in the next chapter, a representative from the B.C. Film Commission described the problem quite succinctly:

> Canada has always been a highly centralized country. They had to build a railroad out here before they recognized it as Canada. And communications-wise and media-wise, a lot of indigenous industry is based on government funding ... We're contending with a distribution system that's almost solely controlled by five square miles in L.A. – that's a worldwide problem -- and unless you have some support to get a project up and running and to get distribution then obviously you're dead in the water, no matter how good your project is ... Indigenous producers have been quite reliant on funding – a lot of that has been federal funding – obviously, if you are close to the source, physically and politically, and your lobbying efforts are good, whether it's from Montreal, which picks up half the Telefilm money, or in Toronto, which picks up most of the rest, then you're going to be more successful in getting your production done ... One point that's quite contentious is that we have 'superfunds'; the government draws $200 million from the cable companies, who we as cable users pay a fee for and that's a tax that goes back to the government. British Columbia contributes something like 16 per cent of the $200 million that goes into that fund and, since it's been established, there's not been one

year in the last three years that we've pulled back more than 4 per cent because the board that runs that fund is out east. There's no membership from the West Coast on it, and even though $100 million of that goes directly to the CBC, the CBC doesn't have a big production mandate out here. It's discouraging ... Again, it's a distance thing.

(interview with the author, 13 August 1997)[12]

This was, indeed, the common grievance of most of the producers I spoke with. Neglect from central Canada and unequal access to financing were seen to be far greater barriers to developing indigenous productions than was the presence of the Hollywood production machine. Ironically, many of the producers found that spin-off benefits from working within the American system, at home, somewhat filled the void left by lack of federal support. In this respect, the training and income derived from working on American projects were seen to be invaluable to their eventual plans to develop their own stories. Therefore, before this discussion turns to the discord within the Canadian broadcasting environment, brief consideration is given to the relationship between domestic producers and the service industry that is Hollywood North.

Life in the Grid: Erasing and (Re)Presenting Vancouver

According to Stephen Miller (1994), there is the City of Vancouver, where people live, work, and play and then there is the Grid: 'the area within which the various artists' and craftspersons' unions that govern productions allow their members to work at the basic rate of pay. If your production travels outside the Grid you have to pay more in wages and penalties. Sometimes lots more' (287). The estimated 1,500 square kilometres that constitute the Grid are the parameters of what Chris Carter referred to as Hollywood's biggest backlot – the location sites that are dressed to look like American or other international cities by the removal of any markers that could identify the sites as specifically Vancouver or generically 'Canadian.' While the most obvious references such as flags, mailboxes, and newspaper boxes are the first signs or markers that must be altered to represent the place of the story, it is the more subtle aspects of locations selection and dressing that illustrate the cultural signifiers distinguishing American from Canadian cities and their representations on television and in movies. At a seemingly basic level, one of the first things that American directors, like tourists, notice about Canadian versus American urban environments is the cleanliness of Canada's larger metropolises. However, what delights tourists creates work for American production crews attempting to project the gritty, urban look of parts of New York or Los Angeles. As one Vancouver locations manager related,

> To de-Canadianize it you've got to dirty it up. You've got to throw some garbage around, you've got to do some spray painting. There's an old story that's become a myth in our industry; it happened in Vancouver five or six years ago. An American film crew went into a lane somewhere down near Gastown and blocked the whole place off and painted the walls, painted the dumpsters, and put prop garbage all over the place. It was a real good-looking dressed lane for backstreets New York. They propped it up and were going to shoot the next day. And, of course, the city works crew came by that night and they went back the next day and the whole lane was cleaned out – pristine. Oops.
>
> (interview with the author, 8 July 1997)

However, it is at a deeper level that the more subtle nuances that differentiate the socio-economic, cultural geographies of Canadian and American communities, or at least their media representations, are reconstructed to signify the disparate connotations of class, ethnicity, and everyday life in the place. One Vancouver locations scout, who has worked on various projects with Toronto, American, and local Vancouver producers, aptly summarized the divergent perspectives that are brought to the use of Vancouver as a backdrop:

> The locals, when they show Vancouver as Vancouver, they'll show it as not always the prettiest place. The houses they've requested are houses in South Burnaby – box houses, working-class houses – which the Americans would not request. Their [Americans'] idea of a working-class house usually has B.C. Sugar behind it [non-residential, industrial area]; that means working-class to them. In Vancouver, working-class to us means South Burnaby or maybe box-style specials in Richmond where houses [were] built in 1960, there's no character to them and they're all that weird grey colour. The locals are willing to show the Fraser Canyon and stuff like that. The houses are down and the poor look poor.
>
> From Toronto, what they want from B.C. is B.C. as a kind of tourist ad. They want beautiful woods, beaches out by Furry Creek, or they want a

beautiful forest with mountains or an old-growth forest with lots of moss. They want what the tourist ad says B.C. is.

The Americans are trying to always get from B.C. what it isn't. They try to get somewhere else. For the most part they use a lot of forest to make something the 'Northwest,' and the middle-class American neighbourhood would be a place like Dunbar with nice, small houses all in a row. You either have that or a mansion, which is always the same four or five houses that exist in Vancouver for that purpose ... The Americans, of course, never show Vancouver as Vancouver. They rarely show the water. For example, X-Files is rarely ocean-bound; it's always interior, foggy U.S.A.

(interview with the author, 27 June 1997)

Of course, the representation of place will always vary according to the nature of the story being told, but in general terms the above locations description was not uncommon among local producers. Toronto producers use Vancouver as a setting for what the industry refers to as 'beauty shots' in both advertising and television projects. And, as already mentioned at length, American producers seek to portray it as 'somewhere' in the United States. However, while the aforementioned neighbourhood of Dunbar might signify a middle-class enclave to American audiences, Vancouverites would probably be less inclined to imagine middle-income families and individuals residing in houses that fall into the $250,000 to $300,000 range. Consequently, when playing Vancouver as Vancouver, local producers must ground their representations of the city more within the lived experiences of members of the community.

One of the less frequently mentioned aspects of the Vancouver locations industry, however, is the fact that non-American, foreign producers are increasingly moving their productions to Vancouver and developing projects that *appear* to take place in the United States. In a manner similar to that in which Hong Kong capital followed Li Ka-shing's venture into Vancouver, many Asian filmmakers now consider the city to be a filmmaking hotbed after Jackie Chan made his phenomenally successful movie *Rumble in the Bronx* there in 1994. As a result, one Hong Kong film producer and recent business immigrant, Danny Hui, has established his company, United Film and Video, in Vancouver and plans to develop and produce three television series in the city. While Hui acknowledges the advantages of being able to draw on the city's Southeast Asian community and Chinatown for casting and atmosphere, his interest is not in telling stories about the immigrant experience in Vancouver but rather in developing Asian storylines that move between the United States and abroad. Indeed, his words echo those of *The X-Files* creator, Chris Carter: 'Vancouver is unique. It can give you a different look of North America all in one city, most within 30 minutes travel time. This gives us lots of flexibility' (quoted in Chow 1997: D12). As illustrated by his projects' titles, *New York Tempest*, *Escape from America*, and *Passage to America*, Hui is primarily interested in the large and lucrative Asian audience markets and, more tangentially, the Chinese communities in North America.[13]

As I explore further in the discussion of international co-productions in chapter 4, the true extent of American hegemony in the global media environment goes beyond the absolute quantity of movies and television programs disseminated by Hollywood and into the processes whereby other countries attempt to place their stories in American settings – which have become familiar to international audiences – and then to circulate them worldwide. It is in this respect that Vancouver has become a revolving door, in a manner of speaking, for producers seeking to develop inexpensive, American-looking programs for the global entertainment market. The question as to whether or not this actually displaces the production of culturally specific Canadian projects remains uncertain. However, the implication is that the integration of the Vancouver production community into the larger Hollywood structure is a contradictory process that at times limits the labour and resources invested in indigenous production but also provides the requisite capital and experience otherwise unavailable for domestic productions.

The sheer number of American productions in Vancouver would appear to reinforce the perception that Hollywood has supplanted indigenous production. Of the more than 100 movies and television programs produced in Vancouver in 1997, only thirty-eight were Canadian productions. Of those thirty-eight, most were 'industry shows' – the term applied to domestic productions that fulfil CanCon's industrially defined cultural requirements but are actually intended for the American market. Industry productions included *Poltergeist*, *The Outer Limits*, and *Highlander*, all co-ventures between international, American, and Canadian producers that contain no implicit or explicit references to Vancouver or Canada. The fallacy of the cultural goals of CanCon requirements is underlined in a statement by the American co-producer of *The Outer Limits* and *Poltergeist*, Richard Lewis, in a magazine interview: 'I'm applying for Canadian citizenship. So by the time your story comes out our shows will be 100 percent Canadian produced' (quoted in Edwards 1996c: 7). It is this industrial aspect of cultural production in Vancouver that has extended the long-standing American branch-plant perception of the Canadian manufacturing sector into the television and film industry. In fact, when speaking of the Vancouver television and film service industry, one individual at the B.C. Film Commission used the analogy of automobile production in Canada:

> It's like the car manufacturing industry. Detroit research and development – Detroit puts up the money for the development of a product and the production of it. That's their money, it comes from the Big Three. And they actually distribute the product and make a profit on it. But that doesn't negate the fact that 25,000 people work in the car industry, unionized positions, in southern Ontario, which is one of the big drivers of the economy. That doesn't include all the ancillary stuff that people are building: the dashboards, the chairs, the ashtrays, and all that stuff. You can see we're identical to their industry in many ways. California distributes the product. We're a service town – a branch plant, and unfortunately, a lot of people in Ontario will talk about their indigenous television industry, but they're also delivering directly to CBS, NBC, ABC, and saying, 'Oh, it's Canadian.'
>
> (interview with the author, 13 August 1997)

The Vancouver locations and service industry parallels the automobile industry in other respects: almost 35,000 people are employed in the television and film sector, and with an estimated three dollars in indirect spending and ancillary services per one dollar of production spending, the province sees an economic net impact of $3.3 billion annually, making the industry also a 'big driver' of the provincial economy. However, there remains an important difference between the two 'branch plant' industries. While it would appear inconceivable for labourers at General Motors' southern Ontario plant to leave and build their own automobile production facilities, it is not uncommon for Vancouver's local 'service' producers to work within the Hollywood North structure only until they have amassed the capital and connections they need to stabilize their own production companies for domestic television and film development. This is the central contradiction of the American production presence in Vancouver: It simultaneously absorbs labour and resources while also creating opportunities for local producers to independently fund and distribute their own programs.

The federal government recognized years ago that large, vertically integrated production companies were integral to the maintenance of a viable Canadian television and movie industry. For that reason, the government subsidized the creation of Ontario-based companies, such as Atlantis Communications and Alliance Communications (the two companies merged in 1998 to form a global media presence as Alliance Atlantis Communications Inc.), that would be capable of project development, production, and distribution. The government, however, never invested in the development of similar large, independent production companies in British Columbia.[14] Therefore, until the Los Angeles production community arrived in Vancouver, local producers were reconciled to building piecemeal funding packages to produce and distribute each project on an individual basis. Service work on American productions not only provided these producers with the capital to build their own companies but also opened doors that were previously closed to them in terms of providing distribution networks for the final productions. As one local independent producer explained, these companies are now positioned to advance the indigenous television and film industry differently from those that concentrate on 'one-at-a-time' productions that rely on government funding structures:

I have one friend who was a first AD [assistant director] on an American production. That's how he makes his core living. Every now and then he does a big project and lives high off the hog for six months. I'm exaggerating, but there are various ways in which people do it. There is the distinction between people who are doing one-off kind of productions, which I'm one of. But there is the other very important way, which is more significant in terms of helping the television and film industry overall, and that is the people who work in the service industry and build companies on the basis of the service industry. This has helped everyone a lot. The kind of business I do is not going to help the industry ... It doesn't employ a lot of people, it doesn't generate a lot of dollars that flow through the system. A lot of people and bigger companies – well, PMP [Pacific Motion Pictures, co-producer of *Poltergeist* and *The Outer Limits*] is a good example of a company that started out in service production in order to create the cash flow to do what they wanted to do, which is independent, local production. And they have done very well and they employ a lot of people. That kind of activity certainly grows the industry much more so than what I do.

(interview with the author, 19 August 1997)[15]

Similar to PMP, other local independent production companies have found that, through working in the American locations and service sector, they have been able to develop the necessary critical mass to finally branch off into domestic production. Crescent Entertainment, the Vancouver company that co-produced the American *Titanic* television miniseries, announced in 1996 that the program would be its final service project as it moved into '100 percent indigenous production.' According to Crescent's president, Harold Tichenor, 'We went into service production in order to finance our own productions ... It's served its purpose. We need to move on to other things ... We've invested between $300,000 and $400,000 in development of independent projects over the life of the company' (quoted in Edwards 1996a: 6). Crescent announced that its first 'homegrown' production would be a feature film, written by a local playwright, about the Canadian experience during the First World War.

Runaway American television and film production, and the subsequent development of the Vancouver locations and service industry, can thus be seen to have a variety of incongruent implications for domestic producers and the representation of the 'place' of Vancouver. On the one hand, through their incorporation as service labour, Canadian crews and production teams assist American producers in the erasure of cultural markers that invoke a sense of place. On the other hand, participation on runaway American productions provides economic and experiential spin-offs that enable producers to step out of Hollywood's shadow and develop their own locally or regionally inflected projects. It is in this respect that indictments of the Hollywood North structure of the Vancouver production environment fail to account for either the sociocultural specificity of British Columbia or the void left by government funding cutbacks to the regions outside of Ontario. However, before we optimistically predict the birth of a new era of indigenous, regional production in British Columbia, it is important to note that Vancouver's involvement within the global media environment does, to some extent, imply a 'disappearance of the national,' as Lorimer indicated in the previous chapter.

This is not to imply that the sociocultural dimensions of national life lose their impact on quotidian practices within the local sphere of

Vancouver. To return for a moment to the distinction between 'place' and 'space,' I would extend Lorimer's argument and propose that the move towards the global cultural economy and the concomitant emphasis on the local dimensions of capital accumulation have to a noticeable extent resulted in a turning away from the 'space' of the nation (defined as the institutional and structural arrangements that impose constraints on local manoeuvrability). As chapter 3 elucidates, the Vancouver television community has long felt alienated from and marginalized by the centralized network programming and funding structures that have culturally defined the nation from their preferred vantage points. Consequently, many local producers have strategically positioned themselves to attract opportunities through partnerships within the Hollywood North structure or through alternative international co-production arrangements, as is further explored in chapter 4. It is in this regard, where the nation is seen as a space of political, economic, and cultural constraint, that we see a diminishing emphasis on the national through a reduction in the number of cultural transactions at that level, as Lorimer so aptly anticipated.

This 'disappearance of the national,' however, was not, as nationalists might argue, expressed as a desire on the part of local producers to assimilate into the American production structure and abandon Canadian storytelling. In fact, several producers see it as an opportunity to move away from the high-culture aspirations of central-Canadian definitions of 'national' programs that merit financial support. In yet another allusion to the automobile industry, one independent producer and locations manager described the development of Hollywood North as an opportunity to develop regional projects at the popular level:

A lot of people give the Americans a lot of crap for their stuff, but American filmmaking at this point in time is Detroit in the 1950s: It is the world. It has it, if you want to learn how to do it you go there, and the only people who were able to swallow their pride and go to Detroit and figure out how they were doing it were the Japanese ... We have an amazing opportunity here. Filmmaking is very complicated. It's not invisible. It's very intellectual, oddly enough, and it takes a lot of skilled people. We've almost been given a golden opportunity to make something of it. In my opinion, Canadians and Americans put out, on par and time after time, the best productions in the world. Yeah, the British do good productions and yeah, the Germans do good productions, but on par, hour upon hour upon hour, we're building Honda Civics and we don't even know it. I think that what's weird is that *we* don't know it, not until you're in Singapore watching *The Littlest Hobo* followed by *The Beachcombers*. Not everything we make has to be like *Exotica*. We should be proud to make *The Littlest Hobo*. We should be proud to make something like *Rumble in the Bronx*. *We* should be doing that ... We shouldn't think that every one we put out there has to be a Ferrari. Part of it is that Canadian thing – we rip apart what we think we're above. We're too good for a lot of things, we're *too good* to act like Americans ... We're Canadian and the definition of being Canadian is being too good. We're so good that we don't get anything done.

(interview with the author, 27 June 1997)[16]

Moving away from the national, or more accurately *official*, definitions of Canadian cultural representations and toward more *popular* depictions of local and regional community also implies a greater international inflection in the case of Vancouver productions. As the city and the province become more globally oriented, both culturally and economically, the stories that producers develop for television will inevitably blend the particularities of the local with universal themes that strike a chord internationally. While this process is attributable to the increasingly international composition of Vancouver's population, and hence the story material provided by everyday life in the province, it is also substantially a result of the production community's exposure to new development, funding, and distribution opportunities in the global cultural economy of media production.

In this respect, federal cutbacks to indigenous production in British Columbia have had contradictory effects on the types of stories and regional representations depicted in television production in the province. In one sense, the opportunity to develop dramatic programming that focuses on narrowly defined constructions of the region, and that therefore lacks broad appeal outside of the national context, has been severely curtailed. On the other hand, Vancouver producers have contributed to the development of a production infrastructure that has decreased their reliance on national funding structures that dictate a centrally formulated, and often nostalgic, definition of the 'local' worthy of financial support. As a consequence, a greater latitude in storytelling emerges in the midst of diminished support for indigenous production. As Stephen Miller (1994) explains, the opportunities provided by working within Hollywood North have enabled local producers to develop stories that probe the region's identity as an evolving process within the local-global nexus rather than as a fixed or frozen image of a static locality:

> For those of us who live and work inside the imaginary Grid, we no longer have doubts about our potential. Vancouver filmmakers no longer have any limits. We can do an awful lot right here in town ... A lot of local artists feel freed by all this scrutiny, whether intentional or inadvertent. They can turn outward to international or abstract themes. There is no obligation to define the city ... Sooner than we think, we will have our own long-sought-after identity. As we sit, a bowl of cornchips in our laps, the blue light of the television illuminating our upturned faces, a flash of recognition will pass through our consciousness – Yes! That's Vancouver, isn't it? *Yes. It is.*
>
> (294, emphasis in original)

This sense of liberation from national mandates requiring a contribution to identity formation in Canadian television and the turn to 'international or abstract themes' is not, however, completely unproblematic. There remain many local producers who seek to develop indigenous programs that may not resonate globally and who, for this reason, have consistently sought greater access to the national television networks while attempting to maintain some degree of creative control or autonomy over the depiction of regional stories. Since the early days of television in Canada, the CBC national network was intended to provide this arena for the regions to communicate stories representing their lived experiences to one another. However, over the past two decades the national public broadcaster has faced drastic financial cutbacks that have been borne, primarily, by the regional production centres. As creative control for English programming has become increasingly concentrated in Toronto, Vancouver producers who wish to develop locally specific programming have found their most important access to the national stage limited, if not closed all together. The next chapter examines the creative constraints on these producers in the light of the peripheralization of the Vancouver CBC production centre. Ironically, towards the completion of my fieldwork in Vancouver, the CBC national network announced a complete 'Canadianization' of programming on the public broadcasting system; a move intended to finally differentiate (and justify the continued existence of) the CBC from private broadcasters in Canada. The Canadianization plan called for a revitalization of the regional production centres and a significant increase in the level of regional drama in the network schedule. As is illustrated, this revitalization process did not include a concomitant extension of creative control or decision-making powers to the provincial CBC management. Rather, Toronto maintained power over which proposed programs would represent the lived realities of Vancouver to Canadian audiences.

Within this framework, a brief comparison is made between the mandate of the regional CBC centre and local community television in Vancouver. In several aspects, Vancouver's community television provided the only venue for local producers to define the sociocultural definitions of 'place' in the city after the provincial CBC cutbacks. As will be seen, this most local of all broadcasters was uniquely positioned to address the discourses of culture and community within the global-local dynamic of Vancouver by drawing upon the grass-roots resources and efforts of volunteer producers – many of whom are members of the city's diverse ethnic diasporic communities. Yet in 1997, the community station's parent corporation, Rogers Cable, announced a centralization program remarkably similar in tone to that of the CBC, whereby local variations of nationally formulated programs would come to dominate the community channel's schedule. Together, the processes of national centralization in community television and CBC production illustrate how the dilution or dislocation of local expression often leaves producers with few alternatives but to turn away from the nation and look outward to the global cultural production environment.

Chapter 3

The Politics of 'Space' and 'Place': Mandating 'National' Identity in Canadian Media Policy

Hating Toronto. Moving to Toronto. Wishing you could move to Vancouver. Staying in Toronto. Hating Vancouver.

Ferguson, *Why I Hate Canadians*

Broadcast One: One place on earth like no other place on earth but connected to every place on earth.

Vancouver CBC station identification

Television to call our own.

CBC national network station identification

When I first entered the Vancouver CBC offices in 1996, there was not a single television series in development or production at the largest of the public broadcaster's English production centres outside of Toronto. The latest project shot in the centre's vast studio facilities had been a series of American-produced television advertisements for Ford cars and trucks, featuring the former star of *The Bionic Woman*, Lindsay Wagner. It was difficult to miss the irony of the situation, given that the CBC's *raison d'être* has, since its inception, been to serve as a bulwark against American cultural dominance in Canada. These types of revenue projects are intended to generate financing for regional CBC production through the rental fees charged to the production companies. And, in this respect, it would appear that even the Vancouver CBC centre now relies on runaway American television and film production to fill the void left by government cutbacks to domestic regional production. This impression was further reinforced at the time by the fact that CBC employees, from studio crews to directors and producers, were on the brink of a strike to protest the latest round of cutbacks from Ottawa that had resulted in the loss of all regional in-house producers of drama and variety programming.

The situation in 1996 marked a noticeable break from the early days of the CBC when the Vancouver studio was not only a vibrant arena for the production of local and regional television but was also a primary contributor to the national English network schedule. This chapter examines the marginalization of the regional voice in the CBC and explores the ramifications for local producers who are left with few channels in which to produce programs that tell the stories of their community. It begins with a brief background of Canadian broadcasting policy and the structuring of the CBC national network and then provides an overview of the resulting content and cultural definitions that regional producers must negotiate in an increasingly centralized funding and broadcasting domain. A brief comparison with similar restructuring processes in community television illustrates how the discourses of power, commerce, and the perceived threat of new competition in the broadcasting environment work to limit local expression at the periphery and, in a sense, compel regional producers to develop stories for international rather than national audiences.

National Broadcasting Policy and the CBC

The founding principles of national communications policy in Canada were established in the 1929 Aird Commission report on radio broadcasting. The report proposed the establishment of a national broadcasting service, the Canadian Radio Broadcasting Company (CRBC), to serve the nation-building needs of a federal system defined by an overwhelming geographical land mass. The rationale behind the CRBC was twofold: (1) to compensate for the scarcity of airwaves, and (2) to provide a countervailing force against American broadcast signals that freely spilled over the border. With the following declaration, nationally funded public-service broadcasting was established in Canada:

> We believe that broadcasting should be considered of such importance in promoting the unity of the nation that a subsidy by the Dominion Government should be regarded as an essential aid to the general advantage of Canada.
>
> (Royal Commission on Radio Broadcasting, 1929; quoted in Bird 1988: 50)

Thus, with the formation of the CRBC, the broadcasting mandate of national unity was cemented into Canadian communications policy and would continue as the cornerstone of the CRBC's successor, the CBC, which was created by the 1936 Canadian Broadcasting Act.

It is important to discuss briefly the report's definition of 'unity of the nation' because the vagueness of the concept has allowed for numerous, and often conflicting, interpretations when broadcasting policy is translated into practice. As mentioned in chapter 1, the Aird Commission was attuned to the fact that the geographic expanse of Canada was leading to the development of regionally distinct cultures; it therefore defined national unity as 'inter-regional communication.' Consequently, in the first ten to fifteen years of national broadcasting, the CRBC was to be based on a model that borrowed from the British Broadcasting Corporation's (BBC) 'Regional Scheme' and the 'Lander System' of German broadcasting. Within this framework, programming was to originate in the provinces, as it was assumed that local producers knew their communities better than national producers and would, therefore, be the most capable of developing stories that portrayed the diversity of life in the young nation. The national broadcasting office in Ottawa was intended to serve only as a disseminator of programming to allow the provinces to share their stories with one another, relatively unimpeded by a central control mechanism. However, the Aird Commission's haste to develop a distribution system that would reach all Canadians as quickly as possible would precipitate the failure of its interregional broadcasting goals. As a result of the rapid development of the technological infrastructure necessary for national broadcasting, Canada quickly developed one of the finest and most extensive broadcasting distribution networks in the world. Unfortunately, there were scant funds left over to develop regional production centres or the programming that would unify the nation. Consequently, until production centres could be built in the regions, Ottawa took over responsibility for overseeing the initial organization and programming of the CBC, thereby beginning the centralization process that the Aird Commission had tried to prevent.

While national unity and fears of American cultural imperialism remained the dominant discourses in Canadian broadcasting policy from the days of radio to the entrenchment of television, regionalism did reappear as a cultural issue in the 1960s. The issue of regionalism had been a consideration in the CBC's own internal deliberations throughout the decade, but the 1968 Broadcasting Act was the first federal communications and culture mandate explicitly to mention regionalism in relation to the need for a decentralized national public broadcaster. However, the act framed regionalism as a division between English and French Canadians and decentralization as the move from the central headquarters in Ottawa to one in Toronto (English CBC) and one in Montreal (French CBC). Regional antagonism among Anglo-Canadians was not recognized in the act, which now spoke of the development and protection of a non-problematic 'Canadian identity' in addition to 'national unity.' The act also created the Canadian Radio Television Commission (CRTC), which would become the Canadian Radio-television and Telecommunications Commission in 1976, to oversee the regulation of Canadian content and programming in the new public-private system that began to develop in the early 1960s.

The 1960s was a paradoxical decade in Canadian broadcasting to the extent that it was simultaneously considered the 'golden age' of Canadian television drama and the decade that introduced the initial policies that would eventually undermine the efficacy of the CBC as a national public broadcaster (Raboy 1990). During this period, the CBC was the nation's primary program producer and broadcaster and, in the absence of competition for audiences, Canadian programming was marked by experimentation and drew on the realism and techniques of the Canadian documentary tradition. Not only were the programs distinct from their American counterparts, they were also very popular with Canadian audiences.[1] While the CBC headquarters in Toronto had consolidated all decision-making power over scheduling, programming, and production decisions at both the regional and network levels, the necessary volume of prime-time content exceeded Toronto's production capacity, and regional programs and series were relatively well represented on the national network schedule.

Of all the regional CBC production centres, Vancouver was the most active contributor to the network, with several anthology pieces and dramas such as *Caribou Country*, *The Manipulators*, and *Studio Pacific* airing nationally at the time. All the programs were in-house productions and conveyed themes and representations of life in British Columbia. Consequently, at the height of production in the 1960s, Vancouver's CBC studios reflected the spirit of the Aird Commission's mandate translated into practice:

Television drama from Vancouver has been a distinctive voice from a distinctive region of the country, suspicious of Toronto centralism and the hated and envied East, which often seems to begin at the Manitoba-Ontario border and end at the frontier of Quebec ... Too often, around the English network corridors, people say without much thought, certainly without knowledge of what has gone on over the years, that the regions cannot make good drama – at all, ever. This is of course nonsense ... this city, with its mountains, sea, lush growth ... harbours and windswept beaches in the city itself, with its casual dress and prosperous, middle-class populations of Japanese, Chinese, and native peoples ... this city so different from the rest of Canada ... becomes a special visual presence in drama as a counterbalance to Toronto.

(M.J. Miller 1987: 334)

As Miller (ibid.: 332) further notes, part of the success of the programs generated in Vancouver at the time was attributable to the fact that regional producers were often 'out of sight and out of mind' of Toronto headquarters and therefore somewhat free to develop and produce regionally relevant programming for the network as long as the budget allowed. Indeed, it was this 'relative freedom' that led to the production of the longest-running and most successful television series in Canadian broadcasting history, *The Beachcombers*.

In 1971 the CBC, seeking a family-adventure series and wanting to ensure that British Columbia was represented in prime time, asked the Vancouver drama production team to develop a television series that would meet the network's requirements (M.J. Miller 1987). The result was *The Beachcombers*, a series about a group of quirky characters and their life in Gibsons Landing on the Sunshine Coast. The series, which ran on Sunday nights for nineteen years, was regionally distinctive and tied to the issues of the West Coast. Episodes would regularly intertwine plots concerning the environment, ethnicity, island life, and Native culture, politics, and social issues. Stylistically, it was similar in tone to many Canadian series in that it was a drama with comedic elements and ambiguous storylines and characters, where there were no steadfast heroes or consistent villains. The series was a sustained hit with Canadian audiences and maintained an average of more than 1 million viewers per week until its cancellation in 1990.[2] *The Beachcombers* further defied the idea that 'the regions cannot make good drama' through successful international sales to forty countries.

For the Vancouver production community the cancellation of *The Beachcombers* has become a symbol of the continuing marginalization, some would say annihilation, of the regional mandate of the CBC that began in the late 1970s and continues today. The show had maintained a steady audience, both nationally and internationally, when the Toronto offices began to exert greater control over its production during its last few years and eventually cancelled it in 1990 to make room for new programs on the Sunday night schedule. The result was an increased level of distrust towards the network. In the words of one local independent producer,

> *Beachcombers* was one of the huge Canadian success stories. It was all over the world. It was in twenty-six different languages. There was a lot of politics behind that one. It was shut down by the East, by Toronto. There was no reason, but it was some bureaucrat or some top producer pulling funding on it in Toronto, basically shutting it down ... [nineteen] years of success, you know, and they wouldn't even talk to the people who were selling it. They wouldn't even talk to the distribution arm who were saying, 'Wow, we've sold this thing to [forty] countries.' And it also increased tourism. It brought in dollars, not just through advertising but in other ways. If you have this [success] and you can't prove it to people [in Toronto] to let you produce something, then how do you get Vancouver producing anything for the national level?
>
> (interview with the author, 8 July 1997)[3]

The year that *The Beachcombers* was cancelled was a critical turning point for the CBC. In 1990, the national public broadcaster faced the most severe cutbacks in the network's history, and regional drama production, which had borne the greatest weight of every budget reduction since the 1970s, was completely curtailed.

As mentioned earlier, the 1960s was a contradictory decade for national television in Canada. In 1958, the Conservative government initiated hearings concerning the possibility of private ownership of television stations and the establishment of a private national network. The process was approved, and in 1961 the Canadian Television Network (CTV) became the CBC's first domestic rival. Competition with a private network might not have proven entirely problematic for the CBC had the government maintained a secure financial structure for the national public broadcaster. Until 1953, the CBC had been funded through a combination of user licensing fees and parliamentary appropriations. Licensing fees were abolished that year, and the CBC has depended on advertising to generate 30 per cent of its production and operations budget since that time. The situation was further aggravated by the fact that no sitting government has ever accepted the repeated recommendations of various task forces to provide the CBC with five-year budget appropriations. Rather, the CBC is granted an annual budget by the federal government and therefore must plan production goals on a year-by-year basis. This public-private structure has been the core of the CBC's problems since the federal government began regular and drastic reductions to the broadcaster from the late 1970s onward. Not only was the CBC placed in direct competition with private stations for advertising dollars, but it was still mandated to produce large numbers of domestic programs while the private stations could fill their prime-time schedules with more cheaply purchased American programming. By the 1970s, the golden age of CBC television had ended, and the broadcaster began to carry American network programs whenever the schedule allowed; it also began to produce inexpensive imitations of American programs in order to attract advertisers who would otherwise finance private television stations. A discussion with a CBC regional manager (RM) in Vancouver underlines the dilemma that the network has faced for the past two decades:

ST: Does the rather schizophrenic public-private nature of the institution impact the ability to carry through the objectives of the mandate?

RM: Oh, listen you've hit it. On the one hand, we are pushed into a commercial mode and we have to produce commercially viable programming in order to generate about one-third of our budget out of commercials. It would be much easier for us to become a true public broadcaster if we didn't have to do that. But those are the fiscal realities. We have come to live with this. Our programming would look a lot different if that was not the case. The dollar drives a lot of our decisions, unfortunately ... And the privates shamelessly exist for one reason alone. We exist for making programs, but the private broadcasters exist for making money. That's it. The money which we now generate goes back into programming while the private broadcasters present programming that is big money for their shareholders. Sometimes our decisions as to what hits the schedule are shamelessly made for commercial reasons. Years ago, we had *Dallas* running, I think at 9:00 on Friday nights. An ultra-American program for CBC prime time. The equation was very simple. We bought an episode for $80,000, which generated about a quarter of a million dollars in revenue per episode. So we have about $170 million, which you can make programs with – Canadian programs.

(interview with the author, 14 May 1996)[4]

The revenue raised from airing such programs, however, remains in the central CBC headquarters in Toronto where the decisions are made as to what constitutes appropriate or nationally representative programming of high enough quality to merit inclusion at the national network level. Regional programs that do not meet these criteria are relegated to local audiences or are not produced at all. It is in this respect that centralized control over production decisions has impeded the Canadian regions from communicating across provincial boundaries. The process is particularly challenging for regional producers, as standard criteria for programming objectives and decisions are not clearly defined by network CBC production officials.

The role of drama production in the larger network schedule, and particularly regional drama, has long been a matter of debate within the CBC. The network recognizes that television drama, which according to the broadcaster includes any form of fiction including comedy, dramatic series, miniseries, and made-for-television movies, is essential to the fulfilment of the 1991 Broadcasting Act mandate to 'reflect Canada to all Canadians.' However, the story sources, genres, and their placement on the schedule remain a matter of uncertainty. Therefore, in the spirit of all Canadian national broadcasting decisions, there have been numerous committees established to address the drama 'question.' The 1987 Subcommittee on Drama came closer to addressing the problem than most of its predecessors in stating that there was a need for serials and series that provided a 'stronger sense of daily life, the workplace, the streets ... Too rarely do we recognize ourselves, our neighbours, our neighbourhoods on the screens. Too rarely do we recognize our own fears or our own concerns' (quoted in M.J. Miller 1996: 329). Although it was recommended that the programs should be topical, contemporary, and 'have an edge, and be close to the edge,' there were few guidelines as to suggested storylines or whether new dramas should be developed in Toronto or in the regions. Thus, while the subcommittee raised the importance of airing images of 'daily life,' it declined to specify *whose* daily life should be recognized. Instead, the final report evaded the issue of regional representation by presenting the issue as an ongoing debate among opposing voices rather than as a coherent strategy for interregional communication, as the following excerpts indicate:

> This sub-committee believes that most locations should not produce network drama. We fear a situation where ... increasingly deflecting scarce regional resources we, as a system, cannot afford to have so dispersed.
>
> (ibid.: 443)

> Maryke McEwen feels strongly that the crisis is overriding: The issue is to produce hours upon hours of new and good Canadian drama, and to cloud the issue with considerations of where to produce it is irresponsible.
>
> (ibid.: 443)

> Bernie Zuckerman ... stresses how complicated the production process is, how advocates of regionalization fail to understand the extraordinary support network required, and the scarcity of craft skills ... [He] also fears indiscriminate and naive regionalization.
>
> (ibid.: 443)

> John Hirsch fought decentralization passionately ... and [says] there are no regional points in Canada where drama can be produced without massive infusion of outside help.
>
> (ibid.: 443)

In the end, the report stated, 'No one is opposed to regional drama production for the network per se ... None of this is an ideological issue of the regions versus the centre' (ibid.: 444), and the subcommittee accompanied their conclusions with the telling qualification that 'We cannot even agree among ourselves in this network on what a "regional" production is' (ibid.: 458).

Ultimately, the report of the Subcommittee on Drama exemplifies the circular reasoning that has dominated the discourse surrounding regional drama production within the CBC for twenty years. It begins with a question of regional capability to produce quality television and concludes with an emphasis on the allocation of scarce resources. The process becomes a self-fulfilling prophecy as the network decreases the requisite funding that would enable the provincial studios to produce quality television drama. This is aptly illustrated by the fact that regional programming carried the burden of all federal budget cuts between 1984 and 1989. By 1989, 75 per cent of the CBC program budget was allocated to national programming, while regional programming received 25 per cent, and little of that was invested in the production of regional drama (Hoskins and McFadyen 1992: 279–81). What little remained of regional drama production was lost in 1990 when the CBC was forced to address a corporate financial shortfall of $108 million and did so by closing or downsizing several regional stations and cancelling hundreds of hours of programming, primarily in regional television. In the end, regional production suffered a loss of $46 million, while only $12 million was cut from the national network in Toronto. Former CBC president Gérard Veilleux delivered the news to CBC staff across the country in a closed-circuit broadcast in which he announced that 1,100 positions would be terminated, that regional production at all remaining stations would be reduced to daily news and information programming, and that 'all other local and regional programs [would] be cancelled' (CBC 1990).

The emphasis on financial arguments in the process of streamlining or restructuring the role of regional television serves to mask more subtle issues of power within the CBC production structure. Aside from the problems of reallocating diminishing resources there is also a utilitarian strategy of bureaucratic self-preservation at work within CBC programming circles. Florian Sauvageau, co-author of the 1986 Caplan-Sauvageau Report on Broadcasting Policy, described the task force process as a bargaining situation with groups who are unwilling to forsake jurisdictional authority (interview with the author, 26 October 1993). The Caplan-Sauvageau Report put forth one of the most innovative and radical recommendations for Canadian communications since the Aird Report of 1929 – the complete decentralization of broadcasting through the creation of 'multiple points of entry' or autonomous production centres in five or more regional locations. Not surprisingly, Sauvageau's recommendations were conspicuously absent from the government's new Broadcasting Act in 1991. According to Sauvageau, the significance of territoriality within the civil-service structure of the CBC had provided a strong oppositional force to any possibility of radical decentralization.[5] However, this should not diminish the importance of the debate generated by the report's findings. As Marc Raboy (1989: 73) explains,

The most interesting thing about the Task Force Report was its implicit undermining of the myth that Canadian culture could only be promoted by strong central agencies under exclusive control of Ottawa. This did not attract as much attention as its call for 'Canadianization,' but the idea that the sociocultural objectives of Canadian broadcasting could be met by multiplying the points of entry to the system was the most significant ... aspect of the report. The Caplan-Sauvageau Report legitimated the various hitherto marginal forms of broadcasting – community, provincial, native – as tools of social development, and argued for their recognition in law.

In this respect, the Caplan-Sauvageau Report presented the strongest argument, among the recommendations of a long line of policy research committees, against a centralized production system as the best structure to realize the nation-building goals of broadcasting in Canada. As a document, it was the result of almost ten years of policy recommendations and commission reviews by groups and individuals from various sectors including business, the arts, and broadcasting. A brief examination of this process provides insight not only into the final version of the 1991 Broadcasting Act but also into the philosophy of the CBC administration.

The Canadian broadcasting debate took on a new economic tone in the mid-1980s, introduced by the Liberals and continued by the Progressive Conservative Mulroney government. As a result of advances in communications technology such as direct broadcast satellites (DBS) and pay-per-view television, policy makers began to speak less about 'culture' and more about 'cultural industries' and competition for audiences. The contradictions inherent within a public-service broadcasting system that also relied on advertising revenue also became intensified as the terms 'profit' and 'viability' were introduced into policy discourse. This internal tension became explicit in the report of the Federal Cultural Policy Review Committee (FCPRC) in 1982 (hereafter referred to as the Applebaum-Hébert Report).

The Applebaum-Hébert Report, a forerunner of the Caplan-Sauvageau Report, presented an interesting overview of the problems facing Canadian communications in an era of technological determinism. While it introduced the concept of culture as an industry, it also juxtaposed the threats of new technologies with the cultural realities of Canada. It is perhaps the first report to emphasize the issue of Canadian regionalism:

As a country with two official languages, each a link to several different cultural traditions, and with many other traditions that are all part of the fabric of *a complex society composed of regions*, Canada offers a unique

setting for the creative process. Taking the fullest advantage of this resource requires that we allow our various cultural traditions to reach out
freely to each other ... *The fact of regional diversity should inform cultural
policy from beginning to end.*

(Applebaum and Hébert 1982: 9–10, emphases added)

The rhetorical nature of this pronouncement comes to the fore when we
consider how the intent of the Applebaum-Hébert Report was incorporated by the federal government after its presentation to then Minister
of Communications Francis Fox.

In his report *Building for the Future* (1983), Fox concentrated on the
'cultural industries' aspect of the Applebaum-Hébert Report and gave
secondary consideration to the issues of cultural processes. In fact, in
describing the new communications environment, Fox wrote, 'There is
now less need for the CBC to provide such comprehensive programming service, given that there has been a startling increase in the number and reach of private Canadian broadcasters' (7). He also stressed
that the policies set out in his report would recommend ways to create a
'more efficient and accountable CBC' (ibid.: 19). It is at this point that
the private-enterprise component of the CBC structure takes the leading role. In terms of regionalism, Fox agreed with Applebaum-Hébert
that the 'CBC must have a strong regional presence.' This definitive
statement was immediately followed by a call for a 'reduction in over-
head costs at regional centres' (ibid.: 14). Statements such as these,
combined with a proposal to increase the use of independent or 'out-of-
house' producers in the development of CBC programs, led many to
predict the imminent dismantling of the CBC (Sauvageau, interview
with the author, 26 October 1993). While the CBC remains (somewhat)
intact today, the fiscal crisis of December 1990 and the restructuring of
the CBC were foreshadowed in Fox's report.

In the final analysis, after ten years of task force research, the 1991
Broadcasting Act refused to formalize a strong commitment to the role
of regional production recommended in both the Applebaum-Hébert
and the Caplan-Sauvageau Reports. Rather, a vaguely worded clause
stating the need for 'regional representation' left the implementation of
a regional strategy to the interpretation of the administrators in Toronto,
who continued to reposition the corporation in the manner outlined by
Francis Fox. And, as a regional manager at CBC Vancouver explains,
the network's strategy thus far has been to maintain as much production volume within Toronto as possible:

[A] sort of corporate jealousy comes into play to some extent. [They'll say about a Vancouver proposal], 'Why don't we do this program in Toronto?' The corporate culture at CBC has downplayed the role of the regions. We used to have a vice-president of regional programming. That's gone, and we now just have a director of programming, which is probably okay. We have far too many vice-presidents anyway, to begin with. But there should be some attention paid to regionally produced programming. And regional programming should have more access to the network airwaves. I think Toronto is very much like any major corporation around the world. It behaves according to an industrial model where large corporations and large entities have the centre protecting itself. Whenever they get into trouble, they will let the periphery fall by the wayside. And actually the periphery really only exists to protect the centre. You find this at IBM and you find it in the CBC. So as soon as the structure gets threatened, the centre will protect itself. The CBC is no different. Although the Juneau Report and other reports have put a lot of emphasis on regional programming, and the fact that they should play a very strong role in making up the network's schedule, we haven't seen much of that. This is, I think, the year we have had less program orders from the network than any other year since I've been here.

(interview with the author, 14 May 1996)

The above-mentioned Juneau Report was the most recent government task force to examine the role of broadcasting and Canadian cultural policy. Unlike its predecessors, however, this Mandate Review Committee was not established to recommend revisions to a new Broadcasting Act but instead was asked to determine whether or not institutions such as the CBC, Telefilm Canada, and the National Film Board (NFB) remained relevant in a time of financial challenges and new technological delivery systems. The Juneau Report, which was tabled in 1996, not only concluded that all three institutions remained crucial to sustaining Canadian cultural goals but also emphasized that the CBC could not 'be truly national if it is not rooted in the regions':

We think it is of the utmost importance that this aspect of the CBC mandate be maintained. Some commentators argue that in order to reduce costs, the CBC should become strictly a national network ... and that its regional stations should be closed or sold. We disagree strongly. In our consultations throughout the country, the positive view of CBC's regional role was expressed forcefully by everyone, including provincial and federal politicians. *In Toronto, Ottawa and Montreal, we occasionally heard a different opinion on this subject.* Our view is that the CBC will not be able to 'contribute to shared national consciousness and identity' if people from various parts of the country do not hear or see themselves on CBC.

(Mandate Review Committee 1996: 45, emphasis added)

The Juneau Report went farther than all other task forces in recommending that, in addition to giving local managers greater control of production decisions and producing network programming across the country, the CBC should resolve the contradictions of its public-private structure by instituting a new user licence fee or tax that would replace reliance on advertising revenue.

Although the CBC was not given the power to implement user fees, the corporation echoed the regional wording of the Juneau Report in its 1996 mission statement, *A Vision for the CBC*:

The very nature of Canada is expressed through its regional reality, which is a source of cultural richness to all Canadians. The national public broadcaster must be a part of Canada's regions if we are truly to reflect the diversity of a people living in one of the world's largest national geographic entities. Canada's regionalism adds immeasurably to our opportunities, but it can also sometimes be an obstacle to mutual understanding and tolerance. For both reasons, CBC must tell the regional story to the nation, a job that can't be done from afar. To achieve this goal means that we must not only make programs in the regions but our programming must also be a genuine reflection of life in them. Even with diminished resources and difficult choices, the principle of regional reflection is central to our mission. As a national broadcaster, rooted in the regions, we are uniquely positioned to explain both the richness of our diversity and the transcendent values we hold in common.

(CBC 1996: 5)

While the CBC's 1996 mission statement implies something of a regional revival within the network programming structure, it is important to consider one of the missing elements that the Juneau Report had considered integral to the regional mandate – the allocation of greater power to local managers over regional production and programming decisions.

During the golden age of CBC television the regional centres had in-house drama production teams who developed stories that, to a great extent, 'genuinely reflected life' in that region. When regional managers were called upon to produce a network series, it was largely left to them to determine the project's course of development. Following the cut-backs of the 1980s, the CBC complied with Minister of Communications Francis Fox's recommendations and moved to build links with independent or out-of-house producers whereby regional managers would serve primarily an intermediary role between the out-of-house team and the network in Toronto. This remains the model for the regional mandate outlined above, and it is one of the major points of contention that led to the threat of a CBC strike in 1996. The argument is not that out-of-house regional producers are somehow less qualified to develop quality programs but rather that many enter the agreement with mixed interests – their goals are often to universalize a series so that it can be sold internationally. Therefore, the concern is that the unique elements of the story that represent everyday life in the community may be diluted to avoid narrowing audience potential. The problem is further compounded by the fact that regional managers have no control over these forms of production agreements – all final decisions remain in Toronto's hands. It is with this in mind that former Vancouver CBC producer Wayne Skene (1993) remarks that,

> On the west coast *Beachcombers* ... was the last vestige of a truly regional CBC production, and even that series was controlled and massaged out of existence by Toronto network executives in its last few years ... *Beachcombers* was an excellent example of the application and need of pure, as opposed to adulterated, regional production in a national public broadcasting system. *Beachcombers* was conceived, nurtured and survived for nineteen years through the energy and creativity of CBC personnel, not in Toronto, but in Vancouver. *Beachcombers* was originally produced by local CBC producer Phil Keatley, who had been instrumental in pushing the concept to reality, often against the preferences of the network. If left solely to a Toronto network decision-maker, the folksy little program idea about a bunch of happy beachcombers who spent most of their time either arguing in a leaky boat or sitting in a coffee shop, would never have made it to the small screen ... As a television program, *Beachcombers* was delightfully entertaining, reflecting life on the west coast – people, lifestyles, issues – injected into the Canadian social and cultural mainstream. It helped define a region to the rest of the country. And, by and large, it did that *authentically*. The people who made the shows lived on, and knew, the west coast, with all its particular quirks, personality and idiosyncrasies.

As a consequence, Canadians received a pretty real and entertaining slice of Canada. Unfortunately, there will never be another series like *Beachcombers* on the CBC.

(156–7, emphasis in original)[6]

It is this argument over the nature of 'authentic' portrayals of regional life through television drama that lies at the heart of the Canadian national broadcasting debate. The politics of location are nowhere more apparent than in the often unwieldy process of cultural negotiation and the conflicting goals among independent producers, regional managers, and Toronto network executives as they attempt to develop drama that represents life in the region to national audiences.

Producing in the Periphery

It's funny, when you talk about UBC you probably mean University of British Columbia but when we say UBC, we mean the University of *The Beachcombers*. It really has been one of the training grounds for Canadian producers and directors. Most producers and directors who have been successful have at one time done some *Beachcombers* episodes.

(CBC Vancouver regional manager, interview with the author,
14 May 1996)

The relationship between the Vancouver CBC production centre and the English network in Toronto epitomizes Jackson's earlier depiction of the struggle between 'lived culture' and 'official culture' over the power to define the many facets or representations of Canadian culture through national public-service broadcasting. The enduring sentiment for *The Beachcombers* among Vancouver's CBC staff, as reflected in the quotation above, is a manifestation of a tactical victory for the region in the battle with the network for access to the national schedule. The longevity and popularity of the series challenge the network's central tenet that the regions are unable to produce quality drama and that Canadian audiences are uninterested in folksy contemporary stories that are not set in dynamic, urban settings. Therefore, the ability to keep the memory of *The Beachcombers* alive serves as a constant reminder of regional production capability and a negation of the network's centralization strategy or rationale that only the centre can define the nation.

The struggle between the network and the regions to define the parameters of identity and community illustrates, somewhat, a Foucauldian example of the ways in which power relations are established within the production of discourses. At issue here are the contentions surrounding the question of what constitutes the 'true discourse' of culture, both regionally and nationally. *The Beachcombers* marked a momentary shift of power in the discursive struggle by illustrating how a specific portrait of regional life could resonate nationally and sell well internationally; thereby underlining that the local is not a bounded area but, rather, is always nationally and globally inflected. While this may accord with the goals of the earliest broadcasting policies, it does not serve the interests of power within the central network, which, to reiterate Jackson, seeks to exclude or eliminate meanings that compete with the orthodoxy of 'official culture.'

The English CBC network maintains power over cultural definition in various ways but most notably through the discourse of economic rationalization of scarce resources and by maintaining a monopoly on the knowledge of the story proposal and development process at all times. The latter is, in fact, one of the greatest sources of frustration for regional producers, who see the CBC as the only venue for domestic broadcasting and then encounter a time-consuming, labyrinthine process that often ends in rejection because the network already has a similar project in development in Toronto. The process is aggravated by the fact that regional managers currently serve only a screening or clearing-house role between independent producers and the network; they are not informed as to what the network is considering at any given time:

RM: We always try to have three or four different projects on somebody's desk at the network ... regional relevance is important to us but ... a proposal has to have first of all a clearly defined target audience and obviously we look for projects that are not represented in the schedule ... They should be somewhat Canadian. That is important ... For example, we've had four or five [projects] and some of them were real attractive properties ... There were interesting production techniques, some of the producers had funding, and so we think the network would just grab hold of something like that. But the offer was simply this, 'We like it but we already have three or four other things in development.' Which we [in Vancouver] don't know about until they hit the screen. Those kinds of deals are popping up all over the place.

ST: So, once they get to Toronto you don't know what you're competing against?

RM: No, we don't know. Sometimes we hear. Sometimes a producer
might shift a thing to Toronto – an idea – without even telling us.
Some people don't use us at all. They just go straight to the network.
But most of them come through here, especially when there are
resource considerations involved where we would become the
production centre rather than Toronto just buying the idea and
producing it as a story out of Toronto.

ST: Given this scenario, is it possible to have a vision of what the role
of Vancouver is within the larger structure?

RM: We struggle with that constantly and we have maybe one perception of Vancouver and the network might have another. For years
we saw ourselves, our role, primarily as a production centre for the
network, but that depends on who runs the ship ... [Programming
from here] all should be regionally relevant – a very strong B.C.
imprint on it ... At the moment we had hoped that the Juneau Report would put some clarity into the role of the regions because
some regions hardly produce any material other than maybe sports
events for the networks anymore ... [Now] there is really no obvious
mandate for the region.

(interview with the author, 14 May 1996)

The process is highlighted through the experiences of one independent producer (IP) who bought the rights to a true-crime story that had
taken place in Vancouver and eventually sold it to CBS after dealing
with the frustrations of the Canadian funding and broadcasting systems. As a condition of the U.S. sale, all of the story details and, specifically, the location, were Americanized. The details of this case will be
discussed further in the next chapter, but the initial attempt at domestic
production is revealing:

ST: Would it have been different [i.e., the story would have remained
intact] if you had sold it to a Canadian broadcaster or the CBC?

IP: If the CBC had been involved it would never have been made because they have the slowest headless monster in terms of a development department over there. I don't even know how to respond to the way they operate versus the way the American networks do business. [At NBC or CBS] I get answers when I pick up the phone, as opposed to receiving letters back from projects that were submitted, oh, some months ago. [CBC] takes months to even get a response, and then it's ambivalent. I don't even know what the letter says ... They've got to staff these departments properly, and they've got to create a decision-making structure that can respond to the business community because that does not exist. And, complicating this further is the fact that they're all this little club back in Toronto with their little offshoot in Montreal for French language. And we just don't exist. We get the occasional give-the-dog-a-bone, but we don't exist ... Maybe I'd feel different if I moved to Toronto and was on the lunch circuit. But I'm not, and I'm more apt to jump on a plane and go to L.A. than Toronto – it costs less and it's in the same time zone. And, frankly, a sale in the States is worth way more to me.

(interview with the author, 7 August 1997)

The process is equally frustrating for regional development managers at the Vancouver centre who see good story ideas come through their offices and have little input beyond their role as intermediaries:

RM: We don't make decisions on drama. It's either pass on it or pass it on [to Toronto] ... We get a lot of scripts and proposals here – most of them we don't bother sending on to the network. We'll help. We might say, 'This isn't really for the CBC, we suggest you go here or back to the drawing board,' or we'll partner up with somebody ... In a couple of instances, we saw something that looked like a good show and we flagged it right away and said, 'This is wonderful,' and sent it off. And, bang it's off to another network and they've snapped it up right away. That kind of thing can happen. It would've taken a long time for it to get through the network process. It can sit on someone's desk for quite a while before they read it and get through their proposals. So we can flag it, but essentially it is network's approval and it is a Toronto decision. And that will often cause a lot of consternation in the independent production community and even here [in our office]. You know, 'They're [Toronto] not paying any

attention to us.' But this is a network and you either buy into it or you don't ... It can be a source of frustration but that's how it works.
(interview with the author, 30 July 1997)

As the preceding comments indicate, proximity and geography are paramount in the CBC drama development process. And producers and executives in Toronto acknowledge that fact:

Ivan Fecan (former CBC director of programming and vice-president of arts and entertainment):
Every department had producers who seemed to get preference because they were there, as opposed to producers who were working on their own or in Vancouver, Calgary, Halifax, or Winnipeg.
(quoted in M.J. Miller 1996: 475)

Alice Sinclair (CBC story editor):
[U]nless you work on the fifth floor [drama development] it's difficult to know what we want from day to day.
(quoted in M.J. Miller 1996: 112)

These methods by which the central network maintains control over the development of television drama, and thus over cultural definition, are best understood through Foucault's (1977) depiction of the ways that knowledge functions as a form of power in which 'There is an administration of knowledge, a politics of knowledge, relations of power which pass via knowledge and which, if one tries to transcribe them, lead one to consider forms of domination designated by such notions as field, region and territory' (69). Following Foucault, we see that the CBC maintains a geography of power whereby access to, and information about, the development process is concentrated at the centre and is withheld from the periphery. In this respect, 'knowledge functions as a form of power and disseminates the effects of power' in the final determination of what constitutes regional and national expression within the official culture of the network schedule.

Ultimately, the struggle over the power of cultural definition is embodied in the differing conceptualizations of regional expression. While the report of the 1987 Subcommittee on Drama conceded a lack of agreement as to what even defined a regional production within the larger network structure, regional managers at the Vancouver CBC consciously engage in an ongoing debate about the nature of 'lived culture' and its translation into television drama. At this site, the mandate to produce regionally relevant programs that 'represent a region to itself and the nation' as set forth in the 1991 Broadcasting Act is a primary concern. And as one regional manager explains, the challenge lies in identifying a story idea that both captures the character of 'place' and simultaneously anticipates the network's expectation of quality national programming:

> I think the difficulty here in terms of developing for the network is that it's hard to pinpoint what the indigenous culture is here. What is it that we can pack into it that will be of interest to the network? People out East call us Lotus Land – everyone's laid-back, you know. Well, sort of but not really. The Maritimes is so easy to identify, there's an accent and a real look to the place, which they play up greatly both in their comedy programs and in their drama programs. It's very distinctive, very easy to recognize. It has a certain romanticism about it. The West Coast doesn't have that. It tends to have a type of L.A. feel to it, which isn't very romantic – without that high energy feel to it [that L.A. has]. Also, it's very young, whereas the Maritimes have this very ancient tradition. This is a young place. So we don't have the wealth of heritage in the same way. The trick is to play into what is really distinctive about the West ... One way is to show it [the physical landscape]. But what's more difficult to show is the sensibility, the attitude. What are you actually reflecting? I mean, did *The Beachcombers* reflect the West Coast? I'm not sure. It certainly reflected what the West Coast – the actual coast – looked like. Did it necessarily reflect what Vancouver was about? I don't think so. It was very rural. It was very maritime and that's one way of doing it.
>
> (interview with the author, 30 July 1997)[7]

Notable here are the impressions of how the province, or even just the city of Vancouver, must somehow be essentialized culturally (and preferably in an urban context) to gain the attention of the network management in Toronto. Consequently, British Columbia must conform to an easily identifiable metaphor of how the East perceives or constructs the West Coast.

The debate over what constitutes an 'authentic' domestic culture is an interesting one. Culture is a multi-discursive term, and to attempt to freeze-frame it in some form of quintessential portrait within a television series would be a futile endeavour. However, to capture prevailing sensibilities or attitudes, described above as a difficult feat, is the central objective of most of the independent producers I spoke with. Indeed, the term 'sensibility' was a recurrent description of the ways in which regional and national culture was translated into content for these individuals. In other words, regardless of topic, they felt their stories could not help but be informed by their experiences of place. As one independent producer explains,

> I love certain stories that take place here. I'm from here. I'm third-genera-
> tion Vancouver. British Columbia is my home. There are certain stories
> that are soul stories for me, and I will find the way to get them out there ...
> I have stories that take place on this coast. I've got logging stories that take
> place in boats going up the coast, things like that is what attracts me as a
> local. Hard sell! ... I have a great story about Clara Brett Martin, the first
> woman lawyer in Canada. Try and sell that. Great script. Well written.
> Characters, dialogue, fabulous story. Where do you sell it? Even the
> Canadians are starting to shy away from their own stories ... The material
> that I choose, while it may not be Mounties and Indians and all that kind
> of stuff, still does have a Canadian sensibility to it. And this has been a
> conflict that I have had ... philosophically ... for a long time, because if I
> come up with a story that happens in a 'galaxy far, far away,' it doesn't
> make it any less Canadian to me because I'm Canadian – I think that
> way.
>
> (interview with author, 7 August 1997)

It was, in fact, this combination of regionally specific stories and sensibilities that led to the continued success of *The Beachcombers*. Although the program may not have addressed the urban realities of Vancouver, as the aforementioned CBC manager underlined, it did provide an impression of everyday life in a coastal town on the Sunshine Coast as translated within the conventions of television drama. In a textual analysis of the long-running series, M.J. Miller (1987) argues that *The Beachcombers* successfully portrayed 'a strong sense of community' through the incorporation of 'West-Coast values and lifestyles' in dealing with locally relevant themes, including Native values and land-claims disputes, environmentalism, and even historical processes such as reparations to Japanese Canadians interned during the Second World War (103, 108–9). As a result, it exemplified the ways in which regional producers drew upon the experiences of their audience and community to reproduce the collective social experience in fictional form.

Conversely, regional production as defined by the CBC network since the late 1980s has had little relationship to the stories and sensibilities connected to the 'place' of Vancouver or British Columbia. From that time onward, the mere fact of shooting a television series in the Vancouver studios qualified as contributing to the regional mandate of broadcasting policy, regardless of its source of origin or whether or not it resonated with life in the province. Examples include the series *Northwood* (a high-school drama that could be described as a middle-class *Beverly Hills 90210*) and *Mom P.I.* (a comedy about a suburban mother negotiating child-rearing and her activities as a private investigator), which were initially proposed by producers in Winnipeg and Toronto and finally given to Vancouver for production because 'politically, it was right to keep Vancouver busy' (M.J. Miller 1996: 72). Given the generic nature of the storylines in these types of series, 'they could have been shot anywhere in Canada' (regional manager, interview with the author, 14 May 1996).

The most vivid example of the network's conceptualization of regional expression came in the development and production of *Pilot 1*, an afternoon entertainment series for teenagers. According to Skene (1993), the intention was to produce a regionally based, conceptually challenging program for the youth market. The program ended up in the full control of the Toronto network, from creative development to direction and production, with regional managers and producers playing a supporting role. It also greatly upset the sensibilities of its audience:

> When *Pilot 1* went to air January 13, 1989, letters of protest started pouring in immediately. The show was aimed at the young and hip and hit the rest of the audience right between the ethical and moral eyes ... the general in-your-face-tone of the show was perceived as pure Toronto ... The series seemed to be drawing more angry mail than viewers. The average audience for the show was 105,000 viewers – 50,000 less than for the inexpensive music video program *Good Rockin' Tonite* [hosted by a popular Vancouver music pundit] it temporarily replaced ... to do it that way – to control the design of a program concept in Toronto and send the idea to Vancouver, along with the Toronto staff, to produce the program and call that a regional production on our national broadcasting service – reflected little more than Toronto's biases about the country and how it is constituted. Toronto ... would end up being our cultural filter.
>
> (Skene 1993: 151, 154)

Regional producers, within the current structure of the television industry, are thus doubly marginalized in any effort to develop domestic stories. They are either subject to the whims of the CBC network decision makers or forced to pursue co-production agreements with private broadcasters or international partners and, in the process, to negotiate creative elements to suit the needs of market expectations or foreign audiences.

In light of the alternatives, many regional producers persist in their efforts to produce for the CBC network because there remains a perceived commitment to the goals of a national public broadcaster. Thus, despite the public-private tensions of the corporation and the continuing funding cutbacks, the CBC is still seen to respect the audience as composed of citizens – rather than consumers – who actively seek out domestic television programming. One independent producer who primarily co-produces with the Vancouver CBC explains the underlying rationale:

> When I pitch stories to the CBC, I pitch my best ideas because only the CBC would buy them. Any other place I would take my ideas, I'd have to think of an angle, some way of selling it or some way I could sell it to get money. Whereas when I'm pitching ideas to the CBC, I'm thinking of stories for the good of whichever viewing audience I think would want to see it. It's a really different thing than doing it for the privates. I think the CBC is one of the few places where you can work toward an ideal that has nothing to do with commercialism – that has something to do with good programming. I don't think we could make the kind of shows we make for the outside because they're driven by people who put money in. At our show we are as separated from the sponsors as you can be … to their [CBC management's] credit they keep me totally separated from the sponsors, they want to be protected from that influence. Through that buffering process, we are left being able to do a show that has a high set of standards, unencumbered by outside forces. I don't know how the CBC manages to do that but they do.
>
> (interview with the author, 7 May 1996)

To a great extent this is attributable to the fact that the CBC is expected to be not a profit generator but a program producer, so that advertising revenue is invested in television production, with even the dwindling government funding providing the 70 per cent buffer between producers and advertisers. The private broadcasters, as described earlier by a

CBC regional manager, exist to produce profits, not programs, for their shareholders. As the CEO of one of Canada's largest private broadcasters succinctly stated, 'Our primary reason for existing, quite simply, is to sell eyeballs to advertisers' (interview with the author, 27 July 1997).

While this is not a startling revelation, given that private broadcasters in most countries are driven by the commodity form of television, Canadian private broadcasting may be somewhat different in that the privates are rarely interested in airing, let alone financing the production of, domestic television. Rather, the goal of most private stations is to garner advertising revenue for cheaper, imported American programs that Canadian audiences would otherwise watch on cable television or through border spillover. The practice of simulcast, or signal substitution, where Canadian private broadcasters run popular American programs at the same time that they air on the U.S. network stations, generates an estimated annual profit of $100 million in advertising revenue, of which a scant portion is invested in local production beyond daily news programs (Winsor 1997: A7).[8] These news programs, combined with sports coverage, allow the privates to comply with CRTC regulations that demand 50 per cent Canadian content during prime time as a condition for holding a private broadcasting licence. The practice, referred to as the 'book-ends approach,' of beginning and ending the 6 p.m. to midnight prime-time designation with an hour of news while showing American programs in between, has allowed the private broadcasters to circumvent the spirit of Canadian content regulations while complying with the letter of the law in their contract with the CRTC (ibid.).

When, in 1997, Heritage Minister Sheila Copps contemplated removing sports and news programming from the CanCon qualifications criteria, the president of the Canadian Association of Broadcasters (CAB) – the industry organization for private broadcasting – rallied with the comment 'We should take another look at the point system to see if we can do things that look less Canadian' (Rice-Barker 1997b: 24). CAB has spent the last several decades, practically since the introduction of private broadcasting in Canada, lobbying the government and the CRTC to release its members from Canadian content obligations. The privates' lack of commitment to domestic production is based on their estimation that quality one-hour domestic programs would require $1 million in production expenditures while only generating $200,000 in advertising revenue (ibid.). Therefore, the implicit threat above is that if private broadcasters were forced to develop domestic drama, it would be with a global audience in mind. Indeed, the few indigenous series that do appear on private television are largely the result of promises to the CRTC to win among competing licensing bids for new stations across the country.[9] Consequently, with yet another viable avenue for domestic production closed, many independent producers see few alternatives to seeking production deals with the American networks and cable stations or other international partners.

Some producers, however, attempt to work in both domestic and international arenas simultaneously in order to benefit from Canadian funding opportunities while maximizing audience potential for their productions. As a result, CBC regional managers have seen a noticeable increase in story proposals that are only tangentially or superficially Canadian in either tone or content:

RM 1: We see these type of 'watered down' or generic, 'Europudding' proposals come through here all the time. And the producer's going, 'But, but, that's what really works and this could really sell.' So, then market it to the States because what works there won't work here. Or take it to the privates. We're here to do Canadian programming in every sense of the word: Canadian talent, Canadian producers and directors, Canadian stories set in Canada, not San Francisco. We hear them [independent producers] say, 'How dare you. Don't you want to make money? Here's a wonderful show and you don't want it.'

(interview with the author, 30 July 1997)

RM 2: We're looking for Canadian content – amazing how many people don't realize that – Canadian stories ... It really is about the Canadian aesthetic in all of these subjects – a lot of these programs wouldn't work in another market because they're so Canadian in attitude.

(interview with the author, 30 July 1997)

However, with limited access to the larger, eastern-based production companies and faced with uninterested regional private broadcasters, it is likely that independent producers, regardless of Canadian content, will continue to pitch their ideas to the CBC. A broadcast agreement with any Canadian network, public or private, is the key to triggering access to government funding for television production, and as a substantial portion of these funds are earmarked for the CBC, the public broadcaster is an attractive co-production partner for independent producers. However, given the paucity of CBC regional production and the lack of regional representation on sitting funding committees, the current funding-broadcast structure has more often served as a source of frustration rather than a source of support for the Vancouver production community. This has been particularly true for those producers who hope to develop domestic programs that are not amenable to alternative financial structures such as international co-production arrangements.

'Superfunds': The Canada Television and Cable Production Fund

The Canada Television and Cable Production Fund (CTCPF), mentioned briefly in the preceding chapter, is an amalgamation of two previously separate production development funds: the Cable Production Fund (CPF) and the Telefilm Canadian Broadcast Fund. The collapsing of the CPF (which is financed through contributions by cable companies of 5 per cent of their annual profits) and the Telefilm fund (which is financed through government appropriations of approximately $100 million a year) created the CTCPF 'superfund,' which provides up to $200 million annually for independent television production across Canada. It has since been renamed the Canadian Television Fund (CTF). The intent behind the development of the CTF was to create an efficient, sizeable, and stable source of funding to assist in the development of a higher quality and greater quantity of Canadian television programming. A second fundamental objective was to encourage and increase regional contributions to network television by fostering production 'in all regions of Canada' (Telefilm Canada 1998: 4).

The establishment of the CTF was lauded by regional producers in British Columbia who had long felt excluded from both the CPF and the Telefilm broadcast funds in their earlier incarnations. To reiterate the earlier comments of the representative of the B.C. Film Commission, cable subscribers in British Columbia contributed 16 per cent of the CPF throughout the fund's existence, while only 4 per cent of the financing was allocated to regional producers. At the same time, Telefilm divided its existing funding almost exclusively between producers in Toronto and Montreal. For example, in 1995 the federal government's total expenditures for film and broadcasting in British Columbia amounted to approximately $60,000, while $800,000 was invested in Ontario (Statistics Canada 1996). During the same period, Telefilm contributed to the development and production of 114 hours of television drama in the city of Toronto and 29 hours of drama programming in the entire province of British Columbia (Telefilm Canada 1996). It has long been the contention among regional producers that these disparities in funding distribution were the direct result of the eastern control of both the CPF board and Telefilm Canada, neither of which included western representatives in their decision-making structures.

The inception of the CTF and the renewed commitment to a Telefilm development department in Vancouver appeared to signal a positive change for the B.C. independent production community. Not only did the executive director of the CTF say that consideration would be given to B.C. representation on the independent board that administered the fund, but Telefilm announced that it would increase its commitment to indigenous production by requiring eight instead of the usual six CanCon credits to qualify for funding, with added incentives for regional productions outside a 150-kilometre radius from Toronto and Montreal. CTF investment decisions, on the part of Telefilm, were to be based on four criteria: cultural content, national audience appeal, exportability, and recoupment potential (Telefilm Canada 1997). While the contradictions between cultural factors and profitability are readily apparent here, the more acute problems for regional producers came in the form of eligibility requirements to gain access to the funds – namely, the need to have a broadcaster's commitment to the project at the time of application for financial support.

In the end, the development and execution of the CTF became a catch-22 situation for regional producers. According to the rules of the superfund, a producer would be required to have both a distribution deal and a licensing fee from a broadcaster in place at the time of the request. The licence agreement required the broadcaster to provide a cash contribution of 20 per cent (15 per cent if the project meets regional qualifications) of the production costs and a contract to air the project within two years of its completion. Within this scenario, producers who required CTF money to begin production on a project would be expected to have a deal in hand with a broadcaster, who would not normally consider investing in a project until it had seen the final product. Therefore, the immediate competitive advantage for gaining access to CTF funds fell to independent producers with established out-of-house production relationships with the Toronto CBC network and to the large independent production companies in Toronto, such as Alliance and Atlantis.

Even prior to their merger in 1998, Alliance and Atlantis were both vertically integrated companies with their own distribution arms and sufficient seed money for story development. They were therefore well positioned to apply for CTF funding at the earliest stages of a television project. Moreover, they were doubly advantaged in that they had also completed several co-productions with the CBC network and were viewed as reliable partners, which gave them greater access to that part of the fund that was set aside for the national public broadcaster.[10] Approximately $100 million of the CTF originates from the cutbacks of direct parliamentary appropriations to the CBC. This money is now recirculated to independent producers who supply programming to the corporation and cannot be used for in-house CBC projects. Moreover, as illustrated earlier, few regional productions have been able to reach the network level. The final link in the centralized funding-broadcasting circle that Vancouver producers regard as that 'little club' in Toronto came with the election of a new board for the CTF in 1997. In its final constitution, the independent board remained an eastern-controlled body without a B.C. representative. The CTF's broken promise led to outrage in the Vancouver production community. As one local producer, Alan Morinis, fumed, '[The situation] is intolerable. It's getting to the point where it's not accidental. It has reached a point of crisis. In 13 years, I've never seen the level of frustration of Western producers as high as it is now. People like me are cutting back' (interviewed in Edwards 1997b: 12).

Ironically, just as morale flagged among Vancouver producers after the CTF board decision, the CBC announced that it was proceeding with its long-delayed project to Canadianize the CBC network schedule. The corporation, anticipating the need for a number of new dramatic series that would exceed the production capacity of the Toronto studio, concomitantly announced a process of regional revitalization and named Vancouver and Halifax as the two primary regional production centres for the network. While it remained uncertain what form regional revitalization would assume – whether it would be Toronto stories shot in provincial studios, as was the case with *Pilot 1*, or true domestic regional stories developed by producers based in the community – story submissions literally poured into the newly established television development office at the Vancouver CBC. In the final analysis, regional revitalization was a combination of the competing centre-periphery perspectives of the regional role within the network. The dramatic series chosen for development was set in Vancouver and produced by a local independent producer. However, the entire process, from selection to story development and initial production, was overseen by Toronto's drama executives with scant input from the Vancouver development office.

'Canadianizing' the National Broadcaster

The term 'Canadianization' has been bandied about in CBC circles since the 1980s. In the midst of cutbacks and debates about the relevance of national public broadcasting in an age of new technologies and global delivery systems, the CBC decided that it would have to eliminate American programming from the network schedule in order to remain a viable institution in the new millennium. After twenty years of direct competition with an ever-increasing number of private television stations and specialty channels, the corporation realized that it would have to gamble on a return to its roots, if for no other reason than to establish a niche for itself in the multihundred-channel environment. Consequently, it was announced in 1996 that the CBC prime-time schedule would be completely Canadian in content by the fall of 1997 and the entire schedule would be Canadianized within another two years. Moreover, this ambitious resurrection would be accomplished during another round of parliamentary cutbacks that would total $414 million upon completion in April 1998 (Vale 1997).

Despite the impending, and supposedly final, budget reductions, Vancouver producers remained optimistically focused on the key words 'regional revitalization' that were said to be essential to the success of the CBC's new direction. And they did not have long to wait; almost immediately after the Canadianization proclamation, the network announced that it would begin considering script proposals for one, and perhaps two, new dramatic series to be developed in the Vancouver production centre for the following fall season. All that remained to be clarified was exactly how the network planned to define the regional role in the new vision for the corporation.

In the end, regional revitalization turned out to mean different things to different people. Managers at Vancouver CBC had hoped that it would indicate a return to in-house production or, failing that, at least an out-of-house co-production agreement where the new Vancouver development office would act autonomously as the central production liaison with an independent producer. However, in a manner that was described by one Vancouver CBC manager as paying 'lip service' to regional revitalization (interview with the author, 30 May 1997), Toronto controlled the entire process from optioning scripts to the final selection of the program, with the Vancouver development office once again serving as an initial intermediary between the producers and the network. As one regional manager described the process, their role was primarily to vouch for the producers whose projects had made it to the final round of consideration:

ST: Did you have any involvement in the decision process?

RM: There was to an extent. But basically, at the end of the day, it's up to the network. What they do is use us as a sounding board for things: 'What do we know about these people [producers]?,' et cetera. By and large, they know who the producers are, we just keep them apprised of what's going on. For instance, if someone's being sued ... that sort of thing. We read the scripts, but the process was pretty much under way.

(interview with the author, 30 July 1997)

Interestingly, in that process the regional development office and the network had different opinions as to which proposal should be chosen:

ST: Was it Toronto's decision alone which show would get the go-ahead?

RM: Yes. They narrowed it down to five, then four, then three. It's hard to speak for them. I know it was a difficult decision for them. There were two that they really liked. At the end of the day it's a judgment, right? I mean, we're happy that we got a drama series. We had our favourite, which wasn't the same.

(ibid.)

As Jensen (1984) explains, in order to interpret the production process as a cultural and symbolic activity, we have to consider 'what is being negotiated ... what eventually becomes public from what is suggested and how that is determined by people's beliefs about business, materials, audiences, the times' (114). Although Vancouver regional managers were quite diplomatic in refraining from stating to me which series idea they preferred, the implication was that the two offices were looking for different concepts. A brief description of the final short list and the winning project provides some insight into the differing perspectives on regional stories as they apply to the national network:

1 *These Arms of Mine*: a series about friends struggling to navigate contemporary Vancouver.[11]
2 *Tofino*: a series about a Vancouver Island town struggling with the end of the fishery and the war in the woods [between environmentalists and loggers].
3 *Crosstown*: a series about life on the gritty Eastside of Vancouver.
4 *Watchdog*: a series about Vancouver parole officers.
5 *Da Vinci's Inquest*: a series about a Vancouver coroner.

(The Gatekeepers 1997: 33)

What is notable here is the extent to which the first three series proposals address the specificity of the 'place' of Vancouver or Vancouver Island in establishing the context for their storylines. In this regard, they all hold the potential to speak to the sociocultural ramifications of economic restructuring under the province's globalization strategy – inner-city class struggle, the instability of a resource-based economy, current challenges and change facing young people in the new intercultural arena of the 'world city.' As such, they epitomize King's conclusions, in the preceding chapter, that the new cultural meanings, representations, and contestations within the evolution of the global city provide the symbolic framework for television and movie content. The latter two proposals, in contrast, fall more within the generic, urban-crime category of television drama and have, in fact, been described in trade publications as 'multi-genre series à la *Law and Order*' (Edwards 1997a: 22). The network's final decision to proceed with *Da Vinci's Inquest*, a 1990s version of *Quincy* merged with Britain's *Cracker*, reinforced the enduring sentiment that Toronto's definition of regional production was primarily concerned with setting rather than sociocultural specificity in prime time.

From the initial announcement of regional revitalization at the CBC, the network assumed full control of the development process for Vancouver. Indeed, the entire operation was overseen by the network's creative head of drama series, Susan Morgan, who described the type of series they were looking for as 'something that was urban West Coast' (quoted in The Gatekeepers 1997: 33). The selection of *Da Vinci's Inquest* not only fulfilled these criteria but also illustrated, using Jensen's words, the corporation's view of 'the business, the materials and the times' –

namely, that the urban-crime drama held high audience possibilities both domestically and internationally. This point is reinforced by executives who predicted that the show could become a 'tent-pole series for the CBC with enormous potential for foreign markets' (Ontario Scene 1997: 14). Given the above criteria, it is not surprising that the corporation selected a series proposed by a producer with perhaps the most Hollywood experience among the local contenders. The show's creator, Chris Haddock, had formerly worked on the American series *MacGyver* and cited NBC's *Homicide: Life on the Street* as his source of inspiration for *Da Vinci's Inquest* (Brioux 1998: 5). Although regional managers at CBC Vancouver did not disclose the exact details of the differences in opinion between the region and the network during the selection process, it is probably not inaccurate to surmise that Toronto was basing its decision about what would constitute a regional success story on economic as well as cultural factors. The implication is that any series that concentrated too specifically on the local realities of the region would fail to generate the audience numbers necessary for a profitable fulfilment of the corporation's mandate, despite past domestic and international success stories such as *The Beachcombers*. As a result, the network's final decision, and its control of the process, underlined Toronto's continued lack of confidence in the regional capacity to develop and produce quality drama programs that simultaneously presented issues and stories of salience to the locality.[12]

This is not to say that *Da Vinci's Inquest* erases the 'place' of Vancouver in a manner similar to industry projects designed for the global market. In fact, the series self-consciously and explicitly refers to the site and context of the city but in a manner that emphasizes the generic markers of any crime or murder-mystery program. In this light, the series should definitely not be seen as a failure in including a form of regional representation on the network schedule. Rather, the fact that it became the network's sole choice signals another lost opportunity to fulfil the spirit, as well as the letter, of the Broadcasting Act by allowing local producers to develop and generate stories that draw on everyday life throughout their community. As another door closes for local producers who seek to develop indigenous stories that may not meet the genre requirements of the centralized funding and broadcasting structures, there appear few alternatives to diluting domestic content and participating within the global cultural economy instead of the regional or national arena. However, for many producers who do not yet want to abandon the effort, the turn to the less prestigious (but decidedly local) venue of community television has, until recently, been the alternative of last resort.

A 'Real' Sense of Place? The Case of Community Television

In 1994 the *Canadian Journal of Communication* devoted a special issue to the consideration of questions of media and cultural development within the context of global free trade zones and satellite communications, or what the editors referred to as the 'open economy' for cultural production. The majority of articles argued for greater support of media that upheld national cultural goals as a counterweight to the consumer model of media production that dominates the global cultural economy. Nevertheless, there was at least a tacit acknowledgment among all contributors that the lack of government commitment, internationally, to national public-service broadcasting has perhaps permanently undermined the capability of such institutions to fulfil cultural development mandates. What was most notable, however, was that, rather than arguing for an abandonment of the effort to sustain a sense of cultural community through broadcasting, some researchers advocated expanding public support to include traditionally overlooked media forms within the cultural development model. Of particular interest to these contributors was the relatively low investment and highly localized community broadcasting media:

> In the present context, it is equally urgent to support the mainstream public service broadcasting institutions and to draw smaller public service media out of their condition of marginality. The development of community media, closer to the communities they serve and more sensitive to their needs, is thus fully coherent with our definition of cultural development. Not only do community media facilitate participation in public life, but also they provide an alternative basis for linking communities in addition to what is possible through traditional public service institutions.
>
> (Raboy et al. 1994: 307)

What Raboy and colleagues are giving voice to is something that community television programmers in Vancouver have long realized – namely, that they have been fulfilling the spirit of the CBC's regional mandate for local and regional community expression for decades at a fraction of the cost and with even less policy attention or support than that given to the national public broadcaster. This is not to say that community television should become a replacement for the CBC, as it lacks the resources to execute the second component of the corporation's regional mandate, which is to represent the local to the national community. What community television does illustrate, nonetheless, is the capacity to convey the sociocultural specificity of place through broadcasting to an audience that has, until recently, escaped the notice of market researchers.

Community television was never intended to fill a void left by the CBC; instead, it was developed to provide an alternative forum for local groups and issues that were underrepresented in both the commercial and the national public broadcasting sectors. It became an integral component of Canadian broadcasting in 1975 when the CRTC required all cable companies to include a community channel within their service area as a public contribution in return for the benefit they would enjoy as a monopoly operation. As a part of their licence, and depending on the number of subscribers, cable operators would be required to invest up to 5 per cent of their profits annually in equipment and expenses for community television facilities.

What differentiates community television from both the private and the public networks is that it is expected to be user-defined television that provides a forum for local community participation in both informational and entertainment programming. As Kim Goldberg (1990) emphasizes, it is important not to confuse community television with the numerous citizen-access stations that exist throughout North America. While people living in the community are welcome to walk into their local station and suggest an idea or ask to participate in the production process, the community channel has become a semi-professional broadcasting endeavour with a highly developed training program administered by the parent cable company. Consequently, community television is best described as a 'collectivist, pluralist, egalitarian concept embedded in a hierarchical, privately controlled, corporate structure' (Goldberg 1990: 38). Despite the apparent contradictions within this framework, community television in Vancouver, until 1997, provided an example of innovative local programming freed from the profit demands of commercial broadcasting. Indeed, Vancouver community programming thrived for two primary reasons – first, it was largely ignored by its parent company, Rogers Cable; and second, it drew on the resources of a large group of committed volunteer producers and crews within the community.

Aside from a small cadre of full-time program coordinators, community television is largely the domain of production volunteers with varied reasons for their participation. For some it is a part-time hobby, for others an opportunity to train for professional broadcasting careers. Still others see it as a means to serve particular community needs and interests. When I began my conversations with community television producers in 1996, the station was in an interesting state of transition. With advances in portable and lower-cost broadcasting technologies, the community station had reached broadcast quality and was beginning to 'bicycle' (a term for the non-profit exchange of programs between broadcasting organizations, with complementary mandates, outside of the community jurisdiction) its programs to larger educational and cultural channels such as Knowledge Network and Vision Television, as well as some specialty channels, including the Life Network. The increasingly professional look of the programming combined with the availability of a well-trained volunteer production crew thus made community television an attractive alternative for local independent producers who faced limited opportunities and avenues for domestic production. According to one program coordinator, in the mid-1990s they began to see

> more and more people approaching us because they were frustrated by the broadcast and film process. They just couldn't get a foot in the door. Everyone wants the product finished before they buy it and they [independent producers] were looking for someplace to do it. We did a couple of one-off specials with those kind of producers who were really looking for a way to take the next step up the ladder. Some of us were hoping and optimistic that we could be the intermediary in the Canadian Production Fund. What if people could access the fund and then come here and do it with these facilities? It would be really beneficial to our senior volunteers ... and it would draw more people into the system who were trying ideas that were new and interesting.
>
> (interview with the author, 27 April 1997)

There are, however, limits to the extent to which community television can serve as a viable alternative for Vancouver's independent production community. According to the community television mandate, programming must be unlike that being done anywhere else in commercial or public broadcasting, and there must be a local and regionally relevant focus to all program proposals. Given these factors, and the struggle to control the CTF by existing power interests, it is highly unlikely that such a marginalized medium could ever become a major player in the administration of the current broadcasting superfunds.

Yet for those producers who seek to develop ideas that draw upon the experiences of life in the 'place' of Vancouver, community television does offer a structure and level of access that is particularly suited to the representation of the sociocultural specificity of the city. Until the CRTC deregulated the community mandates of cable providers in 1997, Rogers community television was organized according to the particular cultural-geographic needs of the Lower Mainland. Within this structure, fourteen community television offices covered the region, and four neighbourhood stations were given the specific task of programming for metropolitan Vancouver (Kitsilano-Westside, Vancouver main office, Vancouver West End, Vancouver Eastside). Vancouver is very much a neighbourhood-oriented city, and in many ways the neighbourhoods are like towns in that they differ culturally, economically, and socially from one another. The capacity to produce programs from each neighbourhood and then air the variety of stories on a single channel allows Vancouver community television to operate as an idealized and local microcosm of the original vision for the regional-national mandate of the CBC. In this respect, the emphasis given to the importance of Vancouver's cultural geography contributes to an exploration of place that is distinct from that of traditional broadcast networks in that members of the community identify and generate the programs that portray the everyday lived realities of life in Vancouver. Thus, community television has often been at the vanguard in examining the new cultural formations and struggles that have evolved through the localization of global processes. The issues of immigration, economic disparity, and environmental crisis, as described in the previous chapter, have been translated into regular television series on the community channel while appearing only as episodic news events on mainstream television.

The priority given to the processes of sociopolitical and sociocultural contestations within the 'place' of Vancouver is a key distinguishing feature of community television. As one program coordinator underlined, the community channel emphasizes 'groundswell issues' – longstanding issues within their historical and social contexts – as opposed to the 'topic/event of the moment' that characterizes most mainstream television programming:

> We always want to see the *next* issue and we've been pretty good at that. We have the next hot topic before anybody else. For example, our environmen-

tal show *Silent Winter* about Clayoquot Sound [the battle between loggers and environmentalists] began two years before the story broke. We were up there filming. We could see it coming. Same with *Fish Story*, it won an award, the scientists and environmentalists came to us with that story and said, 'We're going to lose this industry.' The broadcasters want hot news or flashpoints. CBC Newsworld literally said, 'Unless they're shooting bullets at each other in Georgia Strait, we don't want the story.' So, it wasn't until last year, when they were practically shooting at each other over the herring, that they said, 'Okay, now we'll go cover it.' We had already done it documentary style and all the media came to us later and wanted our footage.

(interview with the author, 27 April 1997)

While documentary-style programs like *Silent Winter* and *Fish Story* cover regional concerns and run approximately six episodes per year, neighbourhood productions such as *Eastside Story* and *Chinatown Today* are weekly series that explore the sociocultural struggles that provide a symbolic televisual map of the city in the manner suggested by King's analysis of life in the global city. *Eastside Story*, an award-winning community television production, provides viewers throughout the city with a critical portrayal of the politics and culture of everyday life in this neighbourhood community and relates the impact of the area's marginalization to the growing class struggles within metropolitan Vancouver. From a similar perspective, members of the Chinese-Canadian community produce the only regular television series in British Columbia that addresses the quotidian experiences of life for the province's largest ethnic community: *Chinatown Today*.

Chinatown Today deserves consideration within this discussion, as it exemplifies the underlying goals of the cultural development aspects of the Canadian broadcasting 'mission' – in particular, the stated need to examine the cultural negotiations within regional communities and circulate these experiences back to the larger society. The idea for the program was brought to the community channel by a group of Chinese Canadians who wanted to address the lack of mainstream television attention given to their community – a rather important matter of exclusion given the rapid changes occurring both within and between Anglo and Chinese-Canadian communities during a decade of record levels of immigration from Southeast Asia. As one community programming coordinator explained, *Chinatown Today* began as an attempt to address the internal politics of the community and eventually found itself playing a mediating role in the new ethnic conflict arising from globalization processes:

What we have in B.C. is not only multiple cultures but some cultures that have been here for one or two hundred years. Not just the Anglo cultures but also the Asian – Chinese and Japanese – and then all of a sudden you have the next waves. Some are here to establish new homes and a new life in Canada, and others have set up a satellite life here in case everything blows up in Hong Kong after 1997 ... That's one of the issues we deal with on *Chinatown Today*. There's a lot of friction now between the generations that have been here for two, three, four generations and the new incoming Cantonese from Hong Kong. The older Chinese and Hong Kong communities are saying, 'These newcomers, all they want is just a good time and they're going to take the money and run. They're not going to give my people work, they're just passing through. They're not interested in us as a community, why should we pay attention to them? We've been here two or three generations, our families work here. We've built our lives and our businesses here.'

(interview with the author, 27 April 1997)

Today, the program has evolved into a multidimensional weekly series that speaks to the intercommunity conflict described above by providing informational programming to assist new immigrants to adjust to life in Vancouver, and that also serves as a direct forum in which both Chinese Canadians and new immigrants from Southeast Asia can develop and produce programs that represent their own interests as members of the larger community. In regard to the first purpose of *Chinatown Today*, many of the weekly episodes deal with issues that immigrant service providers have identified as the major issues confronting newcomers to Vancouver: housing, access to health and counselling services, English-language training, coping with new forms of intergenerational conflict, and employment issues (Abu-Laban: 83). In fact, one volunteer producer, a first-generation immigrant from Hong Kong, had already covered many of these issues in episodes concerning parenting and intercultural conflict in the school system, and had developed language training segments for each episode. For this individual, involvement in *Chinatown Today* was both a means of encouraging cross-cultural communication between Anglos, Chinese Canadians, and new immigrant communities and a forum for her own participation in grass-roots expression and activism (interview with the author, 18 June 1997). According to one of the show's supervising producers, this second feature of *Chinatown Today*, as a forum for community participation, is the underlying purpose for his involvement in the series. He describes the role of *Chinatown Today*, and community television in general, as one of 'enablement,' whereby members of the community are encouraged to use the media to identify, express, and meet their needs rather than waiting for the social structure to do so for them (interview with the author, 14 June 1997). For several of the volunteer producers (VP) I spoke with, this form of 'enablement' was, in fact, the central rationale for their participation in community television. For these individuals, many of whom are second-generation Chinese Canadians, the series provided an opportunity to learn more about their own experiences of living between two cultural worlds:

VP 1 : I didn't know anything about the community. The Chinese-Canadian community – my community, my parent's background. So my reason for joining was to learn more about the community and myself. I'm not here to learn television skills. I started to hang around here [community channel] to learn from *these* people. Some people are trying to reach out to the outside communities, but for me there are enough problems within the community and that's what I'm interested in working on. All the mainstream Chinese media are from Hong Kong, and that's the main voice you hear. But you've got people like my parents who came here twenty-five years ago when there were about ten thousand people and most were living in Chinatown and then later you've got people from Taiwan, and now Hong Kong, with money, and they don't know anything about our history. What do they know about the Chinese Exclusion Act or wartime internments? They don't have a tie yet to the Chinese-*Canadian* community.

(interview with the author, 12 June 1997)

VP 2 : I got involved with *Chinatown Today* because for me, and for quite a few Chinese who've been here for a long time, we have this question of identity – if you come over from another country you already know who you are – you know you're Chinese. Whereas if you've lived here a long time, everything's meshed so that you can't tell the difference. You get comments like 'You're a banana,' that's where you're yellow on the outside but white on the inside. Or you hear 'bamboo,' which means you're hollow on the inside ... Being Chinese Canadian in Canada doesn't mean that much to me, but being Chinese Canadian in Vancouver does because there's more of us and there's more of a division between us ... This show exposes me to a lot of different people – it's an extension of my own life ... I want to promote a better understanding, or empathy, that would be a better word, of the community.

(interview with the author, 19 June 1997)

It is this capacity of community television to incorporate grass-roots participation in the production process that has allowed one broadcasting avenue to explore and represent the lived culture of Vancouver more fully than those in the mainstream. And it is not just isolated interest groups or ethnic communities who use the channel to give voice to their experiences and concerns. Community television in the Vancouver regional district generates more than 3,000 hours of programming annually, and the range in genres varies from documentary, informational series, and cultural performances to arts and entertainment and magazine shows. In fact, one producer I spoke with had even developed a children's program and a weekly locally inspired sitcom at the Vancouver studio. This individual had purposely developed these ideas within the community channel because the levels of access and experimentation allowed there could not be found in any other broadcasting structure (interview with the author, 20 June 1997).

Community television is able to deal with alternative issues and experiment with innovative story ideas and styles because it is a non-profit medium. Put simply, community television can address marginalized voices because it does not have to concern itself with maximizing audiences and pitching content to a mainstream construction of locality. In fact, as mentioned earlier, Vancouver community television's parent company, Rogers Cable, largely left the channel to its own devices because corporate executives assumed that no one watched the community channel anyway. A change in attitude, and control, was swift in coming when Rogers conducted its first audience survey in late 1996 and found that close to 600,000 viewers were tuning in to the community channel every week. The timing of the Rogers survey coincided with CRTC hearings over the continued necessity for protecting community television into the next decade. In March 1997, the CRTC announced that new cable companies entering the market would no longer need to provide a community channel in their basic service package and that the national regulator would no longer protect existing community channels. According to the CRTC:

This policy reflects the Commission's belief that opportunities for local expression would continue to be provided in the absence of a regulatory requirement. In the Commission's view, after more than twenty-five years of operation, the community channel has achieved a level of maturity and success such that it no longer needs to be mandated. *Apart from its benefits to the public through local reflection, the community channel provides cable operators with a highly effective medium to establish a local presence and to promote a positive corporate image for themselves.*

(CRTC 1997a: 48, emphasis added)

Rogers Cable had apparently expected the CRTC's final decision, and in January 1997 began a complete restructuring of its community channels across the country.

What became immediately evident in the case of Vancouver community programming was that Rogers was less concerned with 'local reflection' than it was with the ability to use the channel to 'promote a positive corporate image' for the company. With the knowledge that 600,000 people were watching the community channel, Rogers saw an opportunity to develop a standardized national schedule that would allow for promotion of the cable company and its related entertainment and communications services, such as video rental chains, across Canada. Consequently, Rogers closed five community television facilities in the Vancouver regional district, leaving one neighbourhood studio for metropolitan Vancouver.[13] Not only did Vancouver lose its essential neighbourhood focus, but much of its regular programming was cancelled to make room for new standardized magazine shows that would appear across Canada with a local focus and an emphasis on marketing Rogers products and services. The flagship example of this type of program was the weekly talk show *Plugged In*, which appeared across Canada as *Plugged In Vancouver*, *Plugged In Ottawa*, *Plugged In Toronto*, and so on.[14] By the time this study had ended, the future of programs such as *Chinatown Today* and documentaries like *Silent Winter* was extremely uncertain. In the midst of shuffling the schedule according to the company's national advertising needs there was talk of collapsing several multicultural programs into a weekly South Asian hour, which provided some interesting implications for impending struggles for content domination between the Indian and Southeast Asian communities. What appeared certain, however, was that the term 'community' would no longer be solely defined at the local level. One program coordinator described the situation as follows:

We are one of the most powerful marketing points that they [Rogers] have. Not because of what we do as a community channel but because of our position on the dial. The company saw our potential to advertise their other services, so that's what you're going to see at the top and bottom of every hour – their marketing efforts. We now have a brand name, we're Rogers Community TV across the country. My concern right now is how much stuff is going to be dictated from above for a national sense of the channel versus what the local needs are. Right now they're using the channel a bit as a political football. Who are we really serving here? ... We have the resources, and at this point they're not letting people in the local offices set the standard. We're being pulled in all different ways. It used to be centralized in Burnaby, which was bad enough for us. But now it's centralized in Ottawa, which is really out there.

(interview with the author, 27 April 1997)

The parallels between Vancouver community television and the regional CBC studios provide an interesting glimpse of the current moment in Canadian television broadcasting. The move away from regulatory support or commitment to a public-service mandate for television, one that addresses the issues of culture and community, indicates that the move towards a global consumer model of broadcasting is not resulting in a 'disappearance of the national' in television programming as much as a 'disappearance of the local.'

The Global Cultural Economy, or Where Is Here?

As the foregoing discussion indicates, it is no longer sufficient to talk in nostalgic terms about the representation of some neatly bounded and defined notion of a local or national community. The case of Vancouver illustrates how the local and the global are inextricably bound by a new form of community. However, what does remain at stake is the question of where and how the new cultural forms emanating from this particular global-local nexus will find representation in the current media environment. While Vancouver independent producers and CBC managers have had some time to adjust to the diminishing opportunities for developing local cultural expression within television programming, this is an entirely new experience for producers in community television, who have always seen the local as their particular cultural terrain. And, although all of the producers I spoke with accept that the globalization of media culture is inevitable, almost all stated that the turn to international audiences is happening during a time when people most need to understand the changes they are facing directly within their local and national communities. As one community television producer stated, '[Global culture] is like global capital. It *lives on the surface* – there's no commitment to the place, the people, the towns' (interview with the author, 27 April 1997, emphasis added). Perhaps it is because of their own commitment to working at the local level to describe global interconnections that volunteer producers at Vancouver community television were best able to articulate the perceived importance of a medium for local expression:

VP 1: As everyone looks at the global, less people are taking care of people at the local level. We have to put more effort and attention on them than ever before.

(interview with the author, 18 June 1997)

VP 2: We've got too little Canadian content as it is. Actually, forget Canadian content. How about Vancouver content? The local is a reality check: Look, here I am. I want to be in touch with who I am.

(interview with the author, 12 June 1997)

It is this last comment – the perceived link between place and identity that remains at the core of the debate within the cultural development model of Canadian broadcasting and communications policies. Implicit within this statement is that the turn to the global media environment somehow diminishes or erases this connection. Therefore, the next chapter examines the nature of international media productions and co-productions and the reasons underlying concerns of cultural erasure or homogenization within the new global cultural economy.

Chapter 4

Going Global: The Disappearing Domestic Audience

This is the television and film business. This isn't community theatre that we're doing.

Vancouver television producer, 1997

The new reality of international media is driven more by market opportunity than by national identity.

Steven Ross, former head of Time-Warner, 1995

As the above comments suggest, in the new global media landscape economic contingencies are winning out in the ongoing struggle between market forces and national cultural development goals. As we see dwindling financial and political support for national public broadcasting institutions around the world, producers in countries with relatively small domestic markets, such as Canada, have found it necessary to turn their attention to international audiences and co-production partners to piece together the requisite funding to tell their stories. Within the growing body of scholarship on media globalization, debates over the role of the rapid increase in international television flows have emphasized the potential for either cultural homogenization or fragmentation at both the national and global levels. For some, the globalization of the electronic media does not inevitably translate into the dissolution of national communities and identifications through the formation of a uniform global cultural order but, rather, contributes to increasingly complex formations of supranational and subnational community affiliations as cultural forms and symbols are no longer territorially fixed (A. Smith 1990). Although not always explicitly stated, opposing concerns over potential cultural homogenization in a global media arena often convey a subtext that homogenization equals *Ameri-*

canization. Given Hollywood's disproportionate international presence, this is not a surprising inference. However, thus far little attention has been given to the ways in which emergent television production practices *outside the United States* have contributed to the global circulation of American-inflected television texts.

This chapter examines the growing trend towards international television co-productions and joint ventures and addresses the cultural ramifications of producing for the global market. It begins with a consideration of the rationale underlying the various forms of international media co-ventures and then examines the cultural negotiations producers must engage in when developing a project with a foreign partner or even when just selling an existing idea or program to an international broadcaster. Specific attention is given to the debate over the potential for cultural homogeneity as producers attempt to universalize the particular, or culturally specific, narratives and styles of their local and national communities to increase their global resale value. As the Vancouver case study shows, the global audience is not a vague or nebulous construction in the imaginations of international producers and media corporations. In fact, the preferred *global* audience for most international producers, given its sheer size as a single, English-language target market with a high percentage of domestic television ownership, is the American audience (Alvarado 1996: 68). As a result of their geographic and cultural proximity to Hollywood, Canadian producers have thus become particularly attractive co-production partners for media companies around the world. The final section examines how the tensions between cultural homogeneity and cultural fragmentation are played out in terms of domestic audience expectations. As this section illustrates, Canadian audiences, despite their engagement with and enjoyment of American television, continue to show support for programs that represent their own particular sociocultural circumstances and sense of place at both the local and the national levels. The implication here is that global media production is detrimental to a sense of national and local community only to the extent that it supplants, rather than merely supplements, domestic media offerings.

Turning towards the Global: The Rationale behind International Co-productions

Canadian television producers and broadcasters have long been reconciled to the fact that international sales of domestic media programming are a key component of both profitability and the capacity to generate revenue for future productions. Over the past decade, however, the international media market has become increasingly important to the production as well as the distribution of domestic television programs. International joint ventures (IJVs) with foreign production partners are now, in fact, often the preferred mode of production for countries with potentially small domestic audiences and, with forty-four international co-production treaties, Canada has become one of the leading nations in formalizing production agreements with television producers around the world. While the majority of these agreements are with European nations, Canada has more recently signed treaties with various countries in South America, Africa, and throughout Southeast Asia.

The economic benefits of IJVs are readily apparent. An international media partnership allows producers to share the financial risk of project development and provides both parties with access to one another's government cultural subsidies and tax incentives. And, perhaps most importantly, a formal co-production allows a television program to qualify as domestic content in both countries and thereby assures access to markets where cultural protection barriers exist. IJVs vary in structure, content, and the extent to which a production will be accepted as a domestic property. Of the numerous contractual forms that fall under the umbrella term of international joint venture, official co-productions, co-ventures, and twinning packages are the predominant types of international television production agreements.

Official co-production agreements are the preferred format for producers who wish to gain unimpeded access to another country's market and simultaneously reap the benefits of national subsidies both at home and abroad. For a project to qualify as an official co-production, both countries must be prepared to make a relatively equal financial and creative investment in it. While exact contributions vary with every agreement, it is generally expected that both countries will supply a lead actor to the project and, in the case of the Canadian contribution, will invest at least 30 per cent in the total production budget. Co-ventures, on the other hand, are the least restrictive in terms of relative contributions to the project, and under new, stricter, government guidelines, have more difficulty in qualifying for domestic subsidies and tax incentives in Canada. Co-ventures are developed between producers in countries that do not have a formalized co-production treaty, and the primary goal is to share the costs and financial risks of the production process. Twinning packages fall in between the two other forms of IJVs and consist of an agreement in which the producers in both countries develop and produce comparable yet distinct domestic projects and then partner them so that each will receive airtime in the other's broadcast market (Hoskins and McFadyen 1993).

International co-productions evolved in the early 1950s as the European nations attempted to revitalize a postwar film industry by sharing costs and resources and gaining access to larger audiences (Taylor 1995). In the early stages of proliferating international joint ventures across Europe (and later in North and South America) media researchers often presupposed that foreign television partnerships would develop along the lines of geolinguistic compatibility and would lead to the development of new cultural blocs or regions of media development. However, as Paul Attallah (1996: 181) points out, the current global television landscape shows that the types of IJVs and frequency of co-production agreements depend less on cultural and linguistic similarities than they do on congruent regulatory environments in the participant countries. This is clearly evidenced by the recurring patterns in Canadian co-productions. While some might suppose that Britain would be a natural co-production partner for any Canadian television project, there are, in fact, few such agreements between Canadian and British producers. Instead, because Britain does not have a domestic content quota system, most agreements between the two countries tend to be in the form of twinning packages (ibid.: 180). Interestingly, the French are the most important and frequent co-production partners for Anglo-Canadian producers. Like Canada, France has a centralized broadcasting and regulatory system complete with a domestic point and quota structure. This particular co-production treaty became especially valuable for Canadian producers when, in 1992, France formally designated all Franco-Canadian television productions developed in English as European works. Consequently, these Canadian co-productions now qualify as domestic content throughout the European Union (Collins 1994: 395). As for co-ventures, the third category of IJVs, Canadian partnerships in these areas tend to be with American producers, as there is no formal co-production treaty between the two countries. The benefits of co-ventures for Canadian producers stem from cost-sharing the production budget, while for the American producers, the goal is to cede a minimum of creative control to ensure sufficient Canadian content (CanCon) points to permit access to the Canadian market as domestic content. As a result, the majority of these co-venture projects are derivative of American formulas, stories, and settings and often resemble the type of service productions in which Vancouver becomes a locations setting rather than the site of culturally specific stories.

However, it is often the proximity to and understanding of the American production system that makes Canada such an attractive co-production partner for countries around the world. These factors, combined with the market importance of English-language productions, afford the possibility that a co-production project with a Canadian producer may provide a door to the American market. And for American producers, a co-venture with a Canadian producer may similarly offer an avenue into the more restrictive markets in the European Union. What makes Canadian projects particularly appealing to European media buyers and distributors, however, is the fact that they portray the popular conceptions of North America while remaining subtly distinct from American television. According to one media consultant from the Netherlands, 'Canadian features with universal themes translate well in Europe because "Canadian sensibilities" are more European than American' (quoted in Armstrong 1996: 3). This reference to a different Canadian 'sensibility' was also frequently invoked by the producers with whom I spoke in Vancouver. As an elusive cultural identification, it was often described as a sense of marginality both within the nation and internationally – a way of seeing the world from the periphery, as a former colony of Britain and as a perceived cultural satellite of the United States. While the ways in which this negative sense of identity (describing oneself by what one is not) translates into television programs will be further explored later in the chapter, the above commentary provides insight into the success of Canadian television productions in the international market. In fact, after the United States, Canada is the largest exporter of television programming worldwide. In 1995, Canadian-produced television programs and movies generated $1.4 billion in international sales, an increase of 175 per cent from 1993 – a volume of growth that producers believe will increase as the number of international co-production treaties continues to grow (Winsor 1997: A7).

While the success of Canadian television exports in the international marketplace bodes well for the continued participation of Canadian producers in the industry, the accompanying comment about the appeal of Canadian stories with 'universal themes' brings into question how and whether distinctly 'Canadian' stories will be produced in the global cultural economy. As Sinclair, Jacka, and Cunningham (1996) observe, participation in co-productions and international media trade markets changes the target audience for domestic producers. Herein, the 'primary audience which regulates the flow of peripheral programming internationally' becomes the foreign media buyers and distributors who enter into agreements where 'rough-and-ready genre expectations are in play' (19–20). And as commentary from one international sales director at MIPCOM (one of the largest annual international media-buying conventions) indicates, the world's audiences have already been divided into psychographic genre zones as far as television sales are concerned. For example, according to Nathalie D'Sousa, police series are particularly popular in Germany, while the 'environmentally conscious Scandinavians' tend to be interested in ecological documentaries (quoted in Rice-Barker 1996: 24). The implication is that if Canadian producers concentrate their attentions on the export market, then the interests of foreign audiences as defined by media buyers, rather than the interests of domestic audiences, will determine the types of programs that are produced.

This dilemma sheds light on the central tension in the growing trend towards international co-productions and the emphasis on the global audience market. While IJVs and international sales are crucial to small-market producers seeking development funding in an environment of diminishing government support for domestic production, the concomitant loss of cultural specificity can be the first sacrifice in negotiating control over the development of programming. While examples of generic 'Europudding'-type programs abound,[1] a recent miniseries about one of the most Canadian of all institutions, the Hudson's Bay Company, provides an illuminating case. When producer Michael Levine decided to produce a television miniseries based on the book by Canadian political commentator Peter C. Newman, he realized from the beginning that the project's success would depend on a patchwork of international financing. Thus, with investment from British and American production companies, the story of Canada's penultimate trading post (and future department store) downplayed any focus on its national role and instead emphasized its roots in imperial Britain:

> Now, we could take it and we could plant the entire story in Montreal and on Hudson's Bay and in Winnipeg, and we could tell it from a Canadian viewpoint in a way that I could guarantee that absolutely nobody would have bought it ... The way to do it is to focus on the Orkneys and the Scots and the money men in London and the British Royal Family, so you see an

international story ... That's the dilemma of export, because the minute
you export, by definition you are speaking to universals.

(quoted in Saunders 1997: C1, C3)

This perceived need to universalize the culturally particular became a
recurrent commentary in my conversations with Vancouver television
producers, in that the push to internationalize has reconciled most
producers to accept a level of homogeneity in their future development
plans. It is within this context that questions of representing the specificities of place and community become particularly problematic; as
one producer asks, 'My question is, are we going to be able to do
anything that's Canadian, or is it going to be this kind of nowhere
land?' (Martyn Burke quoted in Saunders 1997: C3).

Negotiating Culture in the Global Economy: Producers Look for the Universal in the Particular

According to Waters (1995), under the processes of globalization, material and economic exchanges tend to bind social relations to the local
while symbolic exchanges in the form of information, culture, and
entertainment 'liberate relationships from spatial referents' as they
'appeal to human fundamentals that can often claim universal significance' (9). The differentiation of 'place' and 'space' takes on new dimensions in debates over postmodernity and the dilemmas of
cultural fragmentation or homogenization. As mentioned in the first
chapter, Harvey emphasizes the fact that 'place' (local culture and
community), with all of its symbolic manifestations, becomes increasingly important to people living in a world of complex global cultural
flows. Indeed, the translation of the sociocultural specificities of the
quotidian experiences, social struggles, and contestations within the
immediate community (place) into the symbolic arena of television
narratives has been a fundamental goal of nation-building broadcasting policies in Canada. Within the context of Vancouver, this 'de-
spatialization' of cultural production, depicted by Waters above, assumes
two forms. In the first instance, stories that represent the particularities
of place are able to achieve universal resonance because of the global
restructuring of the community, while in the second instance some
stories purposely de-emphasize place, obscuring its specificities in order to appeal to universal 'human fundamentals.'

An example that represents the first form of de-spatialization of cultural production was cited in a conversation with an independent filmmaker who had produced a movie about the intergenerational cultural conflicts facing a Chinese-Canadian family in Vancouver. Although the film, which later aired on Canadian television, explicitly referenced the site of the city as the framework for the story about a young Chinese woman's struggle to navigate between two cultural worlds, the production resonated with audiences in urban centres across North America:

> When we screened [the movie] in New York, people came up to me and they thought we had shot it in San Francisco. It was distinctive; it was about the Asian immigrant experience in Vancouver, but as I said people in New York thought it could be San Francisco. The story had universal themes that were carried through. Of course, people in Vancouver look at it and know right away. The landmarks are so distinctive, that comes through. But it's also subtle, there's definitely a sense of West Coast feel to the film ... All of the actors were Canadian, the writer-director was Canadian, the producer was Canadian. Everyone who saw it in Vancouver knew it was a Vancouver-made film and everyone who saw it in Toronto knew it was a made-in-Vancouver film.
>
> (interview with the author, 22 July 1997)

As this particular example illustrates, the symbolic exchanges that are transforming globalizing cities are contributing to new forms of community and cultural interaction that are simultaneously place specific as well as universally recognizable to people in other global urban centres. In this respect, media content can 'liberate relationships from spatial referents' without denying the socio-cultural dimensions of the place of origin. For this particular movie, the producer wanted an international audience for a recognizable Vancouver story and was not willing to sacrifice the storyline to placate distributors. Concessions that would erase the specificity of the city did not need to be made, given the fact that the culturally particular elements of the film explored universal themes of the immigrant experience. However, these types of productions tend to be the exception rather than the rule in the global cultural economy. In the case of television and film productions intended for the global market, and especially in the case of IJVs, the second form of de-spatialization – whereby the particularities of place must be de-emphasized in favour of universal themes and representations – is usually most evident.

Hoskins, McFadyen, and Finn (1994) explain this form of de-spatialization as a consequence of the 'cultural discount' that marks media content that is too culturally specific: '[a] particular program rooted in one culture and thus attractive in that environment, will have diminished appeal elsewhere as viewers find it difficult to identify with the styles, values, beliefs, institutions and behavioural patterns of the material in question' (367). As the economic wording of the term indicates, international media buyers are not willing to pay top dollar for programs that carry a cultural discount, if they are even willing to buy them at all. Therefore, in an effort to avoid the cultural discount, most international co-productions aim at a form of universalism that homogenizes television content in such a way that stories take place in the 'nowhere land' described earlier by producer Martyn Burke. In fact, even members of the large private Canadian production companies, such as Michael MacMillan of pre-merger Atlantis, contend that culturally specific domestic programming will be scarce if IJVs become the only available means of television production: 'In the world of international deals, the homogenization of program content is inevitable. We're not supposed to talk about that but it's happening, and only government support will ensure that our own stories keep getting told' (quoted in Zemans 1995: 154–5). For some producers, however, the major concern is not that domestic stories will be watered down to meet an international buyer's criteria, but rather that they will not even be proposed or developed. As CBC producer Mark Starowicz underlines, 'the decision-making point is at the buy-in. We don't change our stories, we murder them in the crib' (quoted in Saunders 1997: C3). Following Starowicz's argument, the question that begs to be asked is, If Canadians are not telling their own stories, then whose stories are they telling? The implication is that the trend in international co-productions is to tell generic, or formula, stories that follow the trends of whatever is currently popular or appealing to the preferred audience market: the United States. In fact, the concept of a 'nowhere land' in television production is somewhat of a misnomer. Most stories have to exist in a time and place and, in the case of IJVs, that context is often a [re]presentation of an American city.

Highlander and *Poltergeist: The Legacy* are two (of many) international television co-productions that highlight the generic processes of global production strategies. Based on the 1986 feature film starring Sean Connery and Christopher Lambert, *Highlander: The Series* is a Canada (Filmline International)–France (Gaumont Television) co-production that features the travails of immortals battling for supremacy, while *Polter-*

geist, also a Canada (Trilogy Entertainment Group)–France co-production, traces the activities of a group of supernatural sleuths who attempt to eradicate otherworldly evil forces from the natural realm. Both series fulfil the requirements for domestic government support through equal investment, use of lead actors from each country, and location of production (Vancouver – and sometimes Paris for *Highlander*). However, unless supernatural forces are integral Canadian or French cultural signifiers, neither program draws upon national narratives or social processes. Moreover, despite their physical production location, the actual setting for both series is the United States – Vancouver becomes Seattle in *Highlander* and San Francisco in *Poltergeist*. The story structures also follow the recognizable American formula wherein good prevails over evil within the hour, which facilitates international distribution and syndication sales to American television networks.

It is in this respect that American television and movies are able to maintain a hegemonic presence in the global cultural economy. The United States has 'written the "grammar" of international television' (Morley and Robins 1995: 223) to the extent that audiences around the world recognize and accept the American mode of television production; moreover, foreign producers seek to reproduce that style as the international common denominator for global (preferably American) audiences. The result is not that audiences naturally prefer American television, or that these programs inculcate an American value system, but that American (or American-style) television programs begin to dominate international markets. As Sinclair, Jacka, and Cunningham (1996) explain, 'The cultural imperialism theory failed to see that, more fundamental than its supposed ideological influence, the legacy of the USA in world television development was in the implantation of its systemic model for television as a medium' (9). With an increase in global competition in television productions aimed at the American market, many Canadian writers and producers are, in fact, bypassing the middle ground offered by IJVs and attempting entry directly into American network or cable television. The goal of gaining access to the American market, whether through an IJV or a direct sale to a U.S. network, fundamentally changes the content and style of a Canadian program.

'Nowhere Land' or Somewhere U.S.A.?

The business is and will continue to be, in my estimation, driven by the American market. Hollywood created movies and television and will

continue to dominate them, irrespective of our international co-production treaties and the globalization of the business. Scarcely anything gets
made without a U.S. sale. Doesn't matter how small.

Vancouver television producer
(interview with the author, 7 August 1997)

The extent to which cultural specificity is lost in an IJV is largely
dependent on the countries involved in the production partnership. As
stated earlier, Canada tends to be a preferred partner because of the
North American style and sensibility that is brought to the project. Here
the emphasis is on developing a North American style without producing a completely American story. In other words, foreign producers see
their Canadian partners as willing to negotiate on cultural points to the
extent that both countries are able to maintain a semblance of references
to their specific national contexts even when following a generically
American story formula. As French producer and director Michael
Mitrani explains, this is not the case when dealing directly with American producers and broadcasters: 'Co-productions with Americans in-
variably suffer from identity problems ... The American determines the
script. There are no compromises' (quoted in Hoskins and McFadyen
1993: 231). In any international joint venture involving the United States,
the American production team will enter the agreement from a position
of power. American producers are in a unique position among most
Western countries as they can usually recoup or absorb their production
costs wholly within their domestic market. Thus the desirability of
gaining access to the American audience tends to make an IJV with a
U.S. partner appear more beneficial to the foreign producers than to
their American counterparts. As a consequence, 'locals go as suppli-
cants' (Morley and Robins 1995: 117) when pitching story ideas or co-
venture proposals to American production companies and broadcasters.

My conversation with one independent television producer in
Vancouver provides an illustration of the differences between co-
productions with European partners and co-ventures with American
producers and broadcasters. This particular producer was not only one
of the first individuals to sell a Canadian story as a movie of the week
(MOW) directly to an American network (CBS), but was also one of the
first producers to enter into an official co-production agreement with a
British partner. In the case of the British co-production, which was a
children's story, the cultural negotiations were apparently quite minor.
The primary point of contention, at the time of our interview, was

whether or not the lead character should be an aspiring Little League baseball player when the sport is not overly popular with young people in England. The agreement with CBS, however, demanded a complete overhaul of the script for the MOW. In its original version, this particular project was a reality-based story of a woman murdered in Vancouver. Along with the rights to the story, the producer had also secured releases for interviews with all parties involved in the case and had approval to use their real names and details from the legal proceedings. This attention to detail proved to be somewhat unnecessary as, in the end, CBS insisted that the names, nationalities, and even personality traits of the main characters be changed to suit the network's formula for 'true-crime' MOWs. Consequently, the story was placed in 'small-town America' (filmed in Vancouver), and any psychological complexities of the main characters were eliminated so that the generic 'good guys' could be distinguished from the 'bad guys.' According to this producer, the network was steadfast in following formulas that appealed to its preconceived perception of the American audience:

> I was told a long time ago that this is American television. The audience is rural Ohio or Indiana – the Midwest – especially the CBS audience. And they homogenize things for that audience. They don't care. American network television doesn't even really do authentic or historical stuff about their own culture. If you want to get into stuff like that you'll go to the cable companies – Turner, Showtime, HBO, A&E.
>
> (interview with the author, 7 August 1997)

These American cable stations may have a greater appetite for unique or specialized programming, but as my interviews with other Vancouver producers underlined, they are not that far removed from the networks in their expectations of formula, style, and the American audience.

One producer who had recently completed a historical television documentary for A&E described the American television industry as a risk-averse environment in which the commodity form of production and audience marketing dictated adherence to genre and style expectations:

> There's a real formula to television. Especially American television. Different networks have different formulas ... There's a real structure and approach and level that storytelling takes place on and it's just got to be *that*. It's a product, it really is. A conscious business decision. They want people

to turn to their channel and recognize a look, a kind of show, a voice, an approach. It's their brand ... For A&E we had to make certain changes in the process of rewriting, polishing, and all that. It was really interesting; there were certain things that were very American. The kinds of things that I can't imagine a Canadian wanting changed. For instance, you have to be really clear, you really have to hit your audience over the head. And this is A&E, not Fox, right? It's supposedly for the educated television watcher. And our show was not stupid. The writing is pretty good for TV ... We had to show what the stereotypical pictures in people's heads would be. There were a couple of things like that. To me it was very American because that's how Americans are, I find, especially in TV. They have this idea of history and they don't want to hear anything else. They don't want to hear maybe what really happened or even learn about it. They just want to assume this is what it is and it's all these superficial stereotypes. Their news is like that. Their self-censorship is like that ... There's just no way that if we were doing it for CBC that that comment would come back. It's partly that we have higher expectations of our audiences. Here, we don't assume that people will flip the channel if something is unrecognizable for half a second. That's literally what it was ... It's a type of mentality that they're in the market, really competitive, and people sit with their remotes in their hands and you can't afford to have any chances, any time where you're increasing the odds that they'll look at something else. They're a business and that's first. So whether we might have done it differently because it would be nicer that way, or have a better pace or feel when the explanations came later – to them it was a business concern.

(interview with the author, 10 July 1997)

In a similar vein, another local producer shared her experiences in trying to negotiate around the restrictive codes of American television that dictated the detailed conventions of the medium down to the last minutiae of timing and cueing the audience's attention:

There are certain formulaic kinds of things for all American television shows and movies. This happens then and then this happens next and then that, and so on. For example, you have to have a music cue every twenty seconds, whether there is drama or not. And if there is drama, then you have to accentuate it. I remember running into that because I wanted to make that American sale. It's absolutely critical. In post-production on my first one – it was a courtroom drama and we were on a tight close-up of one person. And it was a very dramatic part of the script. It was riveting. And we had to put music cues in it. Now, really! We fought with the distribution people over that. They said, 'Well, you have to have that. It's been silent for 45 seconds.'

(interview with the author, 19 August 1997)

Although the above comments appear to indicate primarily the stylistic differences between Canadian and American television programming, they actually speak to the divergent sensibilities between the two countries, as referred to by producers throughout the course of this study, and the negotiation of these sensibilities in television programs. The combination of a culture defined by a consistent questioning of what it means to be 'Canadian' and a broadcasting structural history rooted in the realism of the documentary format has resulted in a television style that encourages open-ended ambiguity and risk-taking in both narrative content and form. A brief examination of some Canadian programs that were not able to gain access to the American television marketplace illuminates these distinctions and also foregrounds the rationale of producers who call for increased support of public broadcasting in the form of the Canadian Broadcasting Corporation.

According to Canadian filmmaker and television producer and director Anne Wheeler, domestic productions stray from the American television model to the extent that they not only address the ambiguities and complexities of national sociocultural discourse but also do so in a manner that is devoid of music cues, easy explanations, and dichotomies of good and evil: 'The population of the planet is tuned to American programming. The challenge is to get into the American market without making American films ... I believe we have our own way of telling stories. Our most accomplished filmmakers come from a documentary background ... Whether through fiction or fantasy, we try to tell the story through real people' (quoted in Beginnings 1996: 31).

Canadian television programs and MOWs are, indeed, marked by a sensibility for presenting controversial and often disturbing depictions of social issues and problems in a non-glamorous, albeit fictional, form. Even humour and satire tend to take a look at the darker side of the Canadian condition through the perspectives of realistic characters, and often without the benefit of a laugh track. Much of the decoding work is left to the audiences, and in Canada many of the television programs that have attracted the largest audiences have dealt with uncomfortable issues, including youth crime (*Little Criminals*), incest

(*Liar, Liar*), mistreatment of Native people (*Where the Spirit Lives*), and abuse in Catholic orphanages (*The Boys of St Vincent*).

Given the restrictive framework of American television, and the accompanying fear of alienating advertisers, it is not surprising that Canadian producers have had a difficult time selling the above programs to the American networks. What is considered prime-time viewing in Canada is seen as a risky encounter with taboo subjects in the United States. In the case of *Where the Spirit Lives*, a CBC MOW about the physical abuse of Native children placed by the government in parochial schools, producer Keith Ross Leckie found that he could not sell it even to the more highbrow Public Broadcasting Service (PBS), an American network committed to public service, education, and quality programming: 'They liked the script but said their audience wasn't interested in Native issues so they wanted to make it a regular orphanage; they said they couldn't show any abuse or even imply abuse of children, so that would have to come out; and they said it couldn't be negative toward a religious organization' (quoted in Leger 1996: 16).

Little Criminals and *Liar, Liar* met with similar reactions from the American networks and PBS, despite the fact that they were sold to, and well received in, several other countries including England, Brazil, Italy, Malaysia, South Africa, and several Scandinavian countries.[2] *Little Criminals*, with its realistic portrayal of Vancouver youth crime with all its accompanying harshness and profanity, was not of interest to any American network or broadcaster. In fact, the show's producer doubted the show would ever have been developed through a co-production, co-venture, or even through a private Canadian broadcaster: 'CBC is the only broadcaster in the world who would have done this film and financed it' (quoted in Leger 1997: 28). As *Little Criminals* scriptwriter Dennis Foon elaborated,

> CBC was involved from the get-go and gave us full support to make it a credible piece of art and drama. We had artistic freedom we wouldn't have had at another broadcaster. When you have several broadcasters or coproducers everyone wants to have a say. We were protected from that. The people involved in this project were committed to telling the emotional truth and getting across its political message while engaging viewers ... We made a choice early on not to make it commercial. We knew it would hurt foreign sales.
>
> (ibid.)

The ability to produce programs like *Little Criminals* and *Liar, Liar*, and their consequent popularity with Canadian audiences, underlines the role that television plays in exploring the sociocultural specificities of place and the capacity of the medium to negotiate and 'construct collective memories and identities' (Morley and Robins 1995: 91). It is this particular capacity that many local producers worried could be lost in the trend towards audience market expansion in the global cultural economy.

It is also, however, important to understand the rationale underlying the American broadcasters' disinclination to buy and air these types of programs. While much of this reluctance signifies the cultural disjunctures between the two countries, it also illustrates the divergent motivations of market-oriented and public-service broadcasting institutions. In the United States, the commercial imperative of private broadcasting results in a risk-averse environment in which the fear of offending advertisers leads network executives to construct an image of the audience that falls towards the more conservative, or 'rural Ohio/Midwest,' side as explained earlier by one television producer. The CBC, conversely, has been able to take greater risks in programming as it has traditionally relied on advertising for only 30 per cent of its production revenue. Moreover, Canadians have learned the grammar of CBC television and are thus more accustomed to television that tends to break the rules of the American model. It is also not implausible that the American networks have shown a lack of understanding, or acuity, with respect to their own audiences' tastes and critical viewing skills.[3] When, after profitable international sales and high domestic audience ratings, *Liar, Liar* was eventually sold to CBS, the MOW received the highest week-night ratings the network had registered in eighteen months. It was the top-rated show of the night and the fourth highest of that week (M.J. Miller 1996: 473). According to Ivan Fecan, former CBC vice-president of English television,

> They [CBS] scratched their heads about it and said, 'Well, you've broken all the rules. You tell a story that's a lot blunter than we'd ever tell it, you don't have anybody who is known to an American audience in it, in the court scenes your lawyers wear "costumes";[4] this violates every single development rule we have and yet you've done better than we have for four months. What's going on here?'
>
> (ibid.)

Aside from a few successful sales, including *Liar, Liar*, culturally specific Canadian stories remain difficult to sell to the American network broadcasters. Despite the positive audience response to such alternative fare, there has not been a subsequent flurry of production activity to develop programs that similarly address the intricacies of American social and political issues in a forthright manner. Perhaps American network executives perceive these successes as flukes, or they are only willing to take a risk on them once they have seen evidence of their success in other markets. Whatever the reasoning behind the American reluctance to purchase culturally particular foreign (even Canadian), rather than universal, programming, Canadian producers rarely develop such projects with a U.S. sale at the forefront of their budgeting decisions. Rather, for these types of programs, a future sale to an American network is fortuitous, while support from Canadian broadcasters, and specifically the CBC, is essential.

It is therefore not surprising that it is usually only those producers who are most committed, or driven, to developing domestic stories who do not dilute the specificity of cultural narratives to appease a co-production partner or to enter the U.S. market. And with decreased federal support to the CBC, and virtually non-existent funding for independent regional producers, such television content is becoming a relative rarity within Canada. In the face of mounting frustrations with the domestic funding environment, most of the local producers with whom I spoke expressed a greater openness to dealing directly with the American networks or cable stations, even if it meant a concomitant loss of control over the direction of the style and content of a story idea:

ST: Why are you going directly to the American market rather than working through an international co-production or through the Canadian broadcasters?

IP: Money. They pay for it. If they like it they say, 'Here,' and you agree on a budget and that's it. And the money's all coming from one place and it's decent money ... It's a one-stop shop, as opposed to Canada, where you get a licence fee for 15 per cent, then try the Cable Production Fund, then Telefilm, then B.C. Film, and then you still might need another broadcaster. This whole financing puzzle that you have to put together – bureaucracy, paperwork – which, fair enough, they can't just give you money, but it's just so much simpler with the States. And the budget ends up being more with the exchange. It bumps it up 25–30 per cent. And they like that too. That's one reason they like working with Canadian producers – they get more value for their money.

(interview with author, 10 July 1997).

Past success with American sales and co-ventures, therefore, tends to encourage independent producers to continue to seek direct access to the U.S. market by universalizing their projects. The comparative ease with which agreements and funding arrangements are finalized with American broadcasters, as opposed to the circuitous process of acquiring funding in Canada, has encouraged some producers to opt out of the domestic television sphere altogether.

In the midst of this increasing move of production away from the regional and the national the question of the Canadian audience itself remains. It is often assumed that, because Canadians watch a disproportionate amount of American television, they are not interested in, or do not enjoy, domestic alternatives. However, as audience numbers for quality domestic television programs indicate, Canadians appreciate seeing their stories and everyday lives represented to them in dramatic form and are vocal supporters of domestic television that provides them with a sense of collectivity and shared experience in both a universal and a particular context. It is not that there are not enough Canadians watching domestic programming when it resonates with their feeling of place and community but rather that there are never enough potential Canadians watching to make it profitable for many producers to neglect the international market. Consequently, Canadians become a marginal market within the larger global media economy.

Bringing It Home: The Canadian Audience for Domestic Television

To speak of a *Canadian* audience is not unproblematic, particularly given the salience of regionalism, ethnicity, and other intersecting forms of cultural identification within the Canadian national context. However, to the extent that Canadian broadcasters rationalize their programming decisions within the discourse of national audience share, reach, and ratings, it is difficult – and remiss – to ignore the ways in which the audience's voice is constructed within the domestic television industry's larger production strategies. In the absence of in-depth ethnographic research into the ways in which Canadians interpret and contribute to the processes of generating meaning from available television texts, this section explores Canadians' attitudes and responses to national and American programming as reflected in industry research reports and public participation in broadcasting debates and lobby efforts. Together, the implications from these forms of audience representation correspond with the work of media scholars (e.g., Silj 1988) who argue that, when given a choice, audiences will select domestic television content over American when it is available and of equal production quality.

As mentioned in the first chapter, all national public-service broadcasting institutions are compelled to develop programming that appeals to audiences as publics or citizens rather than as markets or consumers (Ang 1991). Consequently, programming is *supposed* to resonate with the countervailing sociocultural issues of the community rather than cater to popular acceptance of the formulaic genre productions that characterize private television networks. In this respect, these institutions, with the loftiest of goals, are intended to provide a service resembling an electronic public sphere that allows for ritual participation in the continual construction and reconstruction of the definition of the larger national community. The attainment of this goal has been particularly challenging for the CBC given the private-public structure of the institution. For Canada's national public broadcaster the audience, of necessity, has always been constructed as both a public and a market simultaneously.[5]

Despite this contradictory view of the audience, or perhaps because of it, the CBC conducts some of the most extensive quantitative and qualitative audience research of any Canadian broadcaster. In addition to commissioning audience ratings research for all television programs, the corporation also relies on focus groups and a regular audience survey panel that provides detailed comments on CBC programs every week. The CBC also sends out viewing questionnaires to approximately one thousand Anglo-Canadians throughout the year. In 1991, the CBC completed its most comprehensive audience study of the decade. In the corporation's internal report, *How People Use Television*, the CBC research department examined Canadians' engagement with and enjoyment of domestic public and private television programs as well as American programming. Not surprisingly, the study found that Canadians watch a disproportionately greater number of American entertainment programs than domestic dramas. However, at the same time, 62 per cent of respondents reported that 'U.S.-made programs had too great an influence' on Canadian life. This number had increased by

4 per cent from a similar study conducted five years earlier (CBC Research 1991: 11).

Although the CBC found it had an 'audience reach' (the number of viewers who watch at least one minute of programming a week) of 80 per cent, a substantial majority of the audience members interviewed (70 per cent) described the public broadcaster as less entertaining, more formal, and less regionally attuned than the Canadian private broadcasters. However, when the questions turned to entertainment programming, viewers stated that the substantive portion of Canadian drama and comedy programs they watched were CBC productions. This is not an unexpected finding considering that the Canadian private broadcasters produce very few domestic dramas. More intriguing, however, were the findings that when quality Canadian alternatives to American programs were available they received a higher rating on the CBC's 'Enjoyment Index.' For instance, the CBC drama *Street Legal*, a dramatic series about a group of lawyers in a small storefront office in Toronto, was rated as 'more enjoyable' to Canadian audiences than the American international mega-hit *Dallas* (ibid.: 84).[6] The final audience portrait painted by *How People Use Television* is one in which Canadians appear to want quality drama programs that are entertaining *and* that speak to the sociocultural specificity of their community at both the national and the regional levels. In the meantime, American television programs fill the void left by the dearth of domestic alternatives. In this respect, the conclusions of the CBC study underline Straubhaar's description of 'cultural proximity,' through which he argues that audiences 'first seek the pleasure of recognition of their own culture in their programme choices, and that programmes will be produced to satisfy this demand, relative to the wealth of the market' (quoted in Sinclair, Jacka, and Cunningham 1996: 14). In the case of Canadian television, there is audience demand for 'culturally proximate' programs; however, as noted earlier, the potential number of viewers does not constitute a 'wealthy market' for most producers.

Canadians are not unaware of their lack of market appeal to most independent and private producers, and while their support for domestic television may not be reflected adequately within the discourse of ratings, it is effectively voiced in public participation and protests in debates concerning cutbacks to the CBC. Thus, while CBC television may not dominate the viewing schedules of most Canadians, the broadcaster is still seen as the primary institution that supports domestic social and cultural expression as constructed in popular programming.

This recognition is evidenced in several public acts of support for the CBC throughout the last few years of funding cutbacks and implied threats of privatizing the national broadcaster. Most notable among these actions during the course of my study were the 'Keep the Promise' campaign, initiated by the lobby group Friends of Canadian Broadcasting, and the CBC 'unity train' organized by a grass-roots coalition called Cavalcade of Concerned Citizens.[7] In the spring of 1997, during yet another round of cutbacks that would amount to more than $400 million in lost revenue for the CBC, the Friends of Canadian Broadcasting held public meetings across the country to protest further destruction of the broadcaster's production capabilities. Timed to coincide with the upcoming federal election, signs and stickers reading 'CBC: Keep the Promise' covered lawns, apartment windows, and car bumpers throughout Vancouver and other Canadian cities. In late April of that year, Cavalcade organized a cross-country railway journey that picked up Canadians from east to west to congregate in support of the CBC on Parliament Hill in Ottawa one month before the election. Although these efforts did not prevent the final round of cutbacks to the corporation, the symbolism of thousands of Canadians riding the unity train was not lost on federal politicians. The use of the railway was not only a salient symbol of Confederation but also served as a reminder that the Canadian Pacific Railway was the first producer and disseminator of radio programming that later became the responsibility of the CBC – a resonant signifier of Canadian unity and cultural sovereignty.

This is not to say that Canadians show their support for domestic cultural production only through grand acts in times of crisis. There are, in fact, several television programs that receive extraordinarily high ratings (in Canadian terms) and vociferous support through the public hearings process mandated by the Canadian Radio-television and Telecommunications Commission (CTRC). This has been particularly apparent in the case of comedy programming and, most notably, in the fight for a second window for two of the most popular domestic programs – *The Royal Canadian Air Farce* and *This Hour Has 22 Minutes*. Both programs are sketch comedies that draw on the Canadian variety show tradition steeped in political and social satire of power structures, whether in the form of the federal and provincial governments, the United States, or the legacy of British colonial rule. In audience terms, these comedies reaffirm a collective (negative) sense of Canadian identity *vis-à-vis* Britain and the United States to the extent that a person must have 'insider' understanding of the points of reference inscribed within the cultural codes to get the joke. In October 1997, just a few months after the voyage of the unity train, the privately owned Baton Broadcasting Corporation and the Canadian Association of Broadcasters (CAB) brought a grievance before the CRTC protesting the CBC's use of its specialty channel, CBC Newsworld, as a second window for the two comedies. At the time, *Air Farce* and *22 Minutes* were generating audiences of over 1 million and 1.3 million, respectively, each week during their first airings on the CBC main network (CBC audience researcher, interview with the author, 15 July 1997). Later in the week, the same episodes would capture equally large audiences in their second airing on CBC Newsworld. Their scheduling, which coincided with the rerun hour of American syndicated programming on the private stations, was thus drawing audiences away from the commercial broadcasters. However, this was not the rationale that Baton and CAB used to bring the CRTC into a content and licensing debate over CBC Newsworld. Rather, the private broadcasters argued that airing comedies on a specialty news channel was a violation of the mandate and licensing requirements of specialty programming as defined within CRTC regulations. The CBC countered their grievance by stating that since both programs were satires of news and current events they did not violate the 'news-only' licensing requirement of Newsworld.

The *Air Farce/22 Minutes* dispute is of specific interest for two reasons. First, because of the technicalities of broadcast licensing regulations and despite its role as the national 'guardian' of Canadian content, the CRTC found itself in the ironic position of having to side with private broadcasters airing American programs. Second, as all hearings before the CRTC are required to be publicized to the extent that all Canadians may respond or 'intervene' with their opinions on the matter under consideration, the *Air Farce/22 Minutes* case received close to record responses from the public with 1,274 interventions filed in support of the CBC. Nevertheless, the CRTC denied the CBC's claim and concluded that,

> The Commission acknowledges the well-earned success of *Air Farce* and *This Hour*, and the tremendous popularity that these comedy programs enjoy among Canadians. It also notes the immense support for the CBC's application to broadcast this type of programming on both the main network and on CBC Newsworld. A majority of the Commission, how-

ever, is not convinced that such programs are a suitable component of a news specialty service such as CBC Newsworld, and is concerned that their inclusion in the service could have unwelcome implications and consequences for the Canadian specialty services industry.

(CRTC 1997b: 2–3)

Although the CBC, and those Canadians who filed interventions on its behalf, lost that particular round with the CRTC, the response to the *Air Farce/22 Minutes* dispute underlined both the popularity of particular domestic programs and the importance of the public forum on cultural issues to the Canadian psyche. When asked for their input on matters of culture and broadcasting, Canadians will respond *en masse*.

This level of public participation resurfaced in January 1999 when CBC Newsworld held a call-in town forum in which CBC executives responded to questions and comments from Canadians across the country concerning their views about and requests from the corporation. The level of response was so overwhelming that Newsworld added an hour to the program to accommodate the number of callers. This was in addition to an equivalent two-hour forum that had taken place earlier that day on CBC radio. In summary, the vast majority of people phoning in expressed their belief that the CBC was essential to the continued depiction of Canadian stories and experiences on television, although these comments were tempered by repeated statements that the CBC did not do an adequate job of including regions outside central Canada in its drama programming. However, there was a strong reiteration of support for the CBC comedy shows *Air Farce* and *22 Minutes*, both of which were seen to draw on the shared narratives of the national experience and were lauded for living up to the spirit of the corporation's mandate (CBC Newsworld 1999).

The extent to which Canadians participate in the cultural realm illustrates the sense of importance that is accorded to the continued support for domestic storytelling on the nation's television screens. Moreover, the success of specific shows, particularly comedy, underlines the broadaster's capacity to produce popular programs that contribute to a shared sense of community. The following chapter examines this matter through an analysis of the program *This Hour Has 22 Minutes*, which is not only one of the most highly rated programs on Canadian television but was also the most frequently mentioned show among the producers I interviewed when asked which programs they felt most represented a sense of community through television.

As the *22 Minutes* case study indicates, this series, and satire in general, is especially effective at addressing the particularities of both place and space in the nation as they draw on shared references that demand a level of specific sociocultural knowledge and experience. As the callers to Newsworld emphasized, region and a sense of place matter to Canadians. Satires such as *22 Minutes* resonate with people across the country because, rather than glossing over regional tensions through a veneer of centrally defined 'national culture,' this particular brand of Canadian comedy speaks directly to the sense of marginalization that pervades the Canadian experience both within and outside the nation's borders.

The ability to continue to produce stories connected to the sociocultural specificities of place, however, will largely depend on the future of public-service broadcasting and cultural development policies in a global media arena. If the domestic audience continues to be constructed as a marginal *market*, and funding for national broadcasting continues to decrease, television producers will be more motivated to pursue international co-production agreements that provide access to global audiences. As the preceding discussion illustrates, IJVs have contradictory implications in the debate over cultural homogenization within the context of media globalization. The tensions between the particular and the universal illuminate the intersection between the economic and the symbolic dimensions of contemporary global television production. Programs that experiment with genre boundaries and formulas and invoke people, events, and issues that are inextricably tied to specific local communities may carry too high a perceived cultural discount to suit the tastes of global television buyers. The likelihood that these types of productions may not resonate culturally beyond the boundaries of the region or nation constitutes too high a risk for private broadcasters, and distributors, who seek to maximize audiences, and thereby profits. Conversely, programs that adhere to genre expectations – usually corresponding to the formulas and grammar of American television – and speak to universal, non–place-specific themes, are seen to be safer bets in the international marketplace. These globally generic programs ensure, in the minds of sellers and buyers, a degree of cultural recognition and accessibility for international audiences. Their reception need not be one of critical artistic acclaim. Rather, the primary asset of a generic or culturally 'universal' program is its reduced capacity for risk in a risk-averse industry. As the global continues to infuse the local, some of the cultural particularities of local places are univer-

sally resonant in their translation into television programming. Therefore, a central question now facing global television scholars is whether
or not stories that are *too* particular to the sociocultural experiences of
small nations will be diluted in the cultural and economic negotiations
between international co-production partners – if they are produced
and aired at all.

Marginal Amusements: Television Comedy and the Salience of Place in the Canadian Sensibility

My assistant is from England, and she said to me, 'You know, it's funny but I find Canadians sneaky.' I've never imagined Canadians as being sneaky, but now I think she's exactly right. It's the colonial experience. You try and get your way. You can't get your way by direct means so you get it how you can. And whether you get it by whining, snide comments, or by humour, you just do it. When you're facing power which is way beyond what you have, you do what you have to do ... Being Canadian is like being at the back of the class all the time. Making snide comments but at the same time getting good grades and having the teachers like you and you get away with it. You're sort of polite; you're sort of funny; you're not a geek – it's not like you can't do athletics or your grades are bad – but you're slightly sneaky, pretty snide, but you're also polite and well-behaved. They can't really get you on that; you're not overtly bad. The teacher's most likely to make you the class monitor when she walks out. It's sort of like our position in the U.N. [laughing].

Vancouver locations manager and independent producer
describing the Canadian penchant for satire, 1997

While it appears that the locality of Vancouver is slowly being erased from the cultural production map of Canadian broadcasting, on the other side of the country a much smaller coastal province is proving that regional programming can thrive and capture the national imagination under the right circumstances. In 1996, there were no indigenous dramas in production in Vancouver. However, the CBC studio in Halifax, Nova Scotia, was exceeding its production capacity in developing programs for the national broadcaster. CBC Halifax is not only home to the country's second-most-popular program, *This Hour Has 22 Minutes*, it is also a co-production partner with Sullivan Enterprises, the producer of several nationally and internationally popular programs including the regionally specific *Anne of Green Gables* and *Road to Avonlea* series. Independent producers in Nova Scotia, and throughout the Maritimes, have defied the traditional network conception that 'good' television can only be produced in Toronto and have therefore successfully developed programs that are inextricably tied to the sensibilities of place and yet resonate nationally.

The rationale behind the current success of regional television in Nova Scotia mirrors that of the heyday of domestic television production in Vancouver during the 1960s and 1970s. In both cases, the CBC network expended the necessary resources in terms of scheduling, financing, and local creative control to enable the regional production teams to develop programs that simultaneously depicted the sensibilities of the local community's experiences and achieved an intersubjective resonance that affirmed a sense of community at both the regional and the national levels among Canadians across the country. The level to which the experience of place translates into the success of current Maritime television cannot be overemphasized, for as Michael Donovan, head of Salter Street Films (the producer of *This Hour Has 22 Minutes*), explains, 'The programs are dependent on their location. They could not be produced in Toronto or Vancouver without materially altering the product. The content is formed by the context. And the context is formed by the people' (quoted in Vardy 1996: 21).[1]

This chapter examines how place, identity, and community formations are constructed and represented within the framework of the weekly comedy series *This Hour Has 22 Minutes*. As previously mentioned, *22 Minutes* was cited by almost all producers who participated in this study as one of the programs that exemplified the national popularity of domestic television and further underlined the importance of representing regional voices to the national community. The discussion begins with a consideration of the relationships between identity, comedy, and the various experiences of cultural, economic, and political marginalization within the Canadian context. Here it is argued that the Canadian penchant for irony and satire is a manifestation of a form of resistance against power centres both within and beyond the borders of the nation. The fact that *22 Minutes* is produced in the Maritimes – one of the most marginalized regions of the country – highlights the relevance of place in this consideration. An analysis of selected excerpts from the series illuminates the ways in which spheres of power are confronted and how that resistance speaks to the common experiences of marginality throughout Canada.

Canadian Comedy and the Politics of Resistance in the Margins

When Canadians speak of the popularity and success of domestic television comedy they are usually describing sketch comedies characterized by a long national history of satire and parody. Unlike in the United States, there have been few successful situation comedies on Canadian television. This is partially attributable to the nature of the television economy of comedy production wherein hundreds of pilots are produced while only a few succeed in gaining a regular and sustained network airing. Given the limited production budgets in Canadian television, the 'failure rate' of the situation comedy is too great a risk for most producers and broadcasters (Ivan Fecan, quoted in Wyatt 1993). The few Canadian situation comedies that have made it to the nation's television screens have largely been derivative of American formulas but with far less invested in production quality. Consequently, their season runs have usually been shortlived.[2]

Sketch comedy, conversely, has enjoyed a tradition of success that dates back to the first years of Canadian television and the popularity of the variety show. From a simplistic standpoint, the popularity and longevity of Canadian sketch comedy could be explained by the relatively inexpensive nature of the genre in comparison to the situation comedy. However, media scholars have convincingly argued that, economic considerations aside, sketch comedy operates on a cultural level that captures the Canadian imagination by speaking to the common experiences of postcolonial nation building. Rasporich (1996) underlines this phenomenon in tracing the nation's comedic roots to a time before television, and to the popularity of satire in Canadian literature – in particular, the works of Stephen Leacock, whose humour epitomized the Canadian tendency to find amusement in striking out at authority: 'an ambivalent ironic stance, born of imperial squeezes of Mother England and the United States' (85–6).

Indeed, it has been through comedy, and specifically satire and parody, that Canadians have negotiated a negative sense of identity, defining themselves through who they are not. In television this has translated into a dearth of the 'pervasive, jokey humour' of plot devices that are used to resolve the everyday 'situation' of situation comedy in favour of a 'mimetic' form of domestic humour (M.J. Miller 1987) that imitates, parodies, and pokes fun at the two imperial powers that cast such long shadows over the Canadian identity project. As Mary Walsh, the creator of *22 Minutes*, explains, 'Sitcom work is impossible because we Canadians are a complaining lot. And you can't be complaining in a sitcom' (quoted in Bawden 1994: SW5). The format of sketch comedy, as opposed to sitcoms, accommodates the complaining nature of Canadian culture by cloaking resentment at those in power in the guise of parody and satire. In this respect, humour both exposes and defuses the political and economic structures that maintain the centre-margin relationship nationally and internationally. In brief, it accords a sense of power to those who feel alienated from spheres of power.

In terms of television programming, the Canadian sketch comedy hails from the 1950s and the work of Wayne and Shuster, who defined the domestic form of the genre for more than three decades. In their weekly CBC variety show, Johnny Wayne and Frank Shuster parodied the sacred cows of British high culture and American politics and thereby laid the foundation for all succeeding Canadian sketch comedies that perfected the art of critiquing culture from the perspective of the knowledgeable outsider. Notable examples include *SCTV* (1970s–1980s satire of North American television), *Kids in the Hall* (1990s satire of dominant North American social and cultural values), and *Royal Canadian Air Farce* and *This Hour Has 22 Minutes* (contemporary social and political satire). As the pioneers of Canadian television sketch comedy, Wayne and Shuster exemplified the fact that those who observe and stand at the receiving end of power relationships are most capable of mimicking and critiquing power in the form of parody and satire. Their roles as informed political and cultural spectators eventually led to continental success as regulars on *The Ed Sullivan Show* and as writers for several other American comedies.[3] However, their most notable contribution to Canadian television was to establish satire as one of the country's national cultural bonds.

As a form of cultural bonding, satire, and its relationship to power and marginality, corresponds with the discussion of Canadian identity, postmodernism, and the importance of hierarchies of 'others' introduced in the first chapter. Within this framework, Hutcheon's (1991) study of Canadian cultural productions and performances, and the struggle between dominant and marginal discourses, emphasizes the role of irony as the key voice of both postmodern theory and the Canadian experience:

Obsessed, still, with articulating its identity Canada often speaks with a doubled voice, with the forked tongue of irony. Although usually seen as either a defensive or an offensive rhetorical weapon, irony – even in the simple sense of saying one thing and meaning another – is also a mode of 'speech' (in any medium) that allows speakers to address and at the same time slyly confront an 'official' discourse: that is to work within a dominant tradition but also to challenge it – without being utterly co-opted by it.

(1)

Following Hutcheon's argument, irony becomes the mode from which marginalized groups (whether defined by region, gender, ethnicity, race, or class) can stand in opposition to dominant cultures. In her words, 'irony allows people to speak from the margins and thereby decentres "centrisms"' (19). Marginalization, from this perspective, has received substantial attention as an integral component of conceptualizing forms of self-consciousness, group identity and community. Drawing upon Gramsci's articulation of 'critical elaboration,' Jonathan Rutherford (1990: 20) posits that identity, 'is the consciousness of what one really is, and [consists] in "knowing thyself" as a product of the historical process to date which has deposited an infinity of traces, without leaving an inventory. Identity marks the conjuncture of our past with the social, cultural and economic relations we live within ... Making our identities can only be understood within the context of this articulation, in the intersection of our everyday lives with the economic and political relations of subordination and domination.'

Consequently, identity formation, particularly within the context of a community, lies in the space of negotiation between commonality and difference circumscribed by relations of power: the centre *vis-à-vis* the periphery. The relationship between centres of power and the margins should be viewed as a process of mutual identification for, as Rutherford continues, the margins contribute to the definition of the centre by continually drawing attention to the issues of difference or 'marking what the centre lacks': '[I]t is in its nature as a supplement to the centre that the margin is also a place of resistance. The assertion of its existence threatens to deconstruct those forms of knowledge that constitute the subjectivities, discourses and institutions of the dominant hegemonic formations' (ibid.: 22).

This is precisely the role of satire, particularly from the regional vantage point, that serves as the interregional bond between the various provinces that constitute the national community in Canada.

Despite their divisions and cultural differences, the regions share in recognizable forms of marginalization resulting from perceptions of subordination to, and domination by, the powers of central Canada, the United States, and the legacy of Britain's imperial past. This continuation of the theme of negative identity manifests itself in the Canadian experience as a form of unity through shared subjection to common political, historical, and economic processes. Lianne McLarty (1988) refers to this as a position whereby the margins create a form of unified self-consciousness of 'Canadian-ness' as a form of difference from definitions of the United States, especially as they are played out in the realm of popular culture. Without diminishing her argument, the following analysis of *This Hour Has 22 Minutes* illustrates that the creative process within the margins not only presents a site of resistance against the United States but further generates oppositional constructions and readings of the struggle to define Canada from within its own borders – namely, resistance against 'official culture' imposed by the centre. The series represents the spirit of regional broadcasting policy as a means of representing difference and contributing to the ongoing project of confronting, transforming, and sustaining the boundaries of the national community through the stage of television culture.

These connections between irony and marginalization, and their representation within the genre of satire, reaffirm the tension between inclusion and exclusion that underlies the maintenance of collective identities. To expand upon Hutcheon's discussion of irony: the comprehension of the double-coded nature of satire assumes a set of shared values and a common cultural context. To 'get the joke' a person must have an insider's knowledge of the points of reference inscribed within the cultural codes. It is not surprising, therefore, that satirical sketch comedy was seen to be most representative of the nation-building goals of Canadian broadcasting policies since, '[P]ared down to its essence, humour is a socio-cultural and group phenomenon, and the humourist a spokesperson for a group that shares common language, experience, attitudes, and value systems. The successful joker is in complicity with the audience, reflecting the group back to itself, affirming its identity.' (Rasporich 1996: 84).

It is through this shared complicity against official definitions of the Canadian national narrative that *This Hour Has 22 Minutes* reaffirms the group's identity by implicitly writing the regional voice into the centralized forces of national broadcasting.

This Hour Has 22 Minutes: **The Newfies Strike Back**

If we accept that parody and satire are most adroit when performed by those who stand outside the spheres of power, then it is only fitting that one of Canada's most successful television sketch comedies should be the creation of a comedy troupe from Newfoundland. Newfoundland is not only one of the more marginalized provinces in the country it is also the most reluctant member, after Quebec. 'The Rock,' as it is popularly referred to by inhabitants, was the last province to join the country, and 48 per cent of Newfoundlanders voted against a confederation agreement with Canada in 1948. The first fifty years of inclusion in the national fold have not been particularly easy for the province at the northern tip of the Atlantic Maritime region. With a small population inhabiting a large outcropping of rock surrounded by ocean, Newfoundland has supported itself through a precarious fishing-based industry and regional equalization payments – a form of national welfare subsidized by the wealthier provinces. The combination of underpopulation, isolation, and poverty placed Newfoundland in the unfortunate position of being the most ridiculed province in the country. The 'Newfie joke' is a continuing national tradition that has provided Canadians from other regions with a source of superior sentiment that could be seen as masking their own feelings of subordination in relation to central Canada and the United States. As popular culture critics Geoff Pevere and Greig Dymond (1996) explain, the ensuing sense of exclusion emanating from the experience of being the poor relation has provided Newfoundlanders with a keen and critical perspective of the country: 'Separated from the rest of Canada by a combination of factors which include geography, history, politics, economics and culture, Newfoundland represents the virtual and actual outer limits of the Canadian experience. If one of the defining characteristics of Canadian popular culture is a sense of continental marginality, then the Newfoundland experience exists on the margins of marginality. The outsider's outsider. Alienation squared' (30).

Alienation has, in fact, contributed to a rich and lively regional culture of music and storytelling that owes as much to the province's proximity and historic links to Ireland and Celtic traditions, as it does to its peripheral location within Canada. At the edge of the country, both physically and psychologically, Newfoundland and the other Atlantic provinces are perfectly poised to paint a satirical portrait of the rest of the country.

It is within this regional context that the members of the comedy troupe that would eventually develop *This Hour Has 22 Minutes* honed their keen sense of political and cultural observation that translated into two successful sketch comedies on the national CBC network. *CODCO*, the predecessor of *22 Minutes*, whetted the Canadian audience's appetite for the biting social satire that emanated from the sentiment of Maritime alienation. Mary Walsh, one of the founding members of *CODCO* and the creator of *22 Minutes*, remembers growing up among relatives who were reluctant to consider themselves as Canadians after the province entered Confederation. Indeed, she attributes the success of their material to this sense of marginality within the country:

> I felt alienated from Canada. I learned a great deal of resentment for Canada and all things Canadian. Newfoundlanders went from being England's doormat to being Canada's laughing stock. Canadians do not know who they are. Newfoundlanders always knew who Canadians were: People who thought they were better than us. But what makes Canadians constantly think they're not as good as the buddy [Americans] next door? Why are we so ashamed of what shaped us? We have an identity. We're us. We have different voices.
>
> (quoted in Adilman 1993: D2)[4]

Walsh and three other Newfoundland compatriots formed *CODCO* in 1973 and travelled the region performing sketch comedy revues, based on the sociocultural experiences of their community, until their act was developed into a weekly television series in the late 1980s. The name of the show signifies both the region's primary resource – cod fishing – and the ramifications of national resource policies that led to the depletion of cod stocks and ensuing regional poverty.

While *CODCO* focused on parodying the social and political setting of Newfoundland, *22 Minutes* expanded its material to encompass the dual forms of alienation that define the shared Canadian experience: regionalism and continentalism.[5] In developing *22 Minutes*, original *CODCO* members Mary Walsh and Cathy Jones joined younger Newfoundland comedians Rick Mercer and Greg Thomey to develop a more incisive political satire that depicted a growing sense of belonging to Canada and insecurity relative to the United States. As the show's two primary political satirists, Walsh and Mercer explain how this 'outsider's outsider' perspective resonates with national audiences and accounts for the recent success of Canadian comedy writers in general:

Mercer: I don't think there's a lot funny about being Canadian. I think one of the reasons why all of those [comedy writers] are successful is they know what's really funny about being an American. We speak the same, we look the same. Yet we're very different, so we have a good bead on America. And I think Newfoundlanders feel the same way about Canada. We're similar but we have this attitude that we're way out on the edge.

Walsh: We're off the edge. We're not attached. We didn't even become attached until 1949 so we still carry all that baggage with us, having been a country – that sense of Canada being another country. There are Canadians and then there are Newfoundlanders.

Interviewer: Do you define yourselves as Newfoundlanders first and Canadians second?

Walsh: I do, though I feel much more Canadian as I get to be more middle-aged.

Mercer: I've always felt very much Canadian and part of Canada. That's probably my generation. But even if you're travelling in other countries, you say you're a Newfoundlander, and they look at you like they don't know where that is and you say, 'Oh, I'm a Canadian.' If, like Quebec, we had seven million people here, we'd have the exact duplicate of that situation. I'm sure we'd have a Bloc Newfoundland.

(quoted in The Creative Land 1994: 38)

While it is the specificity of Maritime history and socio-economic experiences that inform the regional sensibility of *This Hour Has 22 Minutes*, it is also the shared sentiment of multiple locations of belonging (city, region, nation) that enables the series to speak to Canadians across the country. As such, regionalism, which is often seen as a fragmenting force, in this respect becomes a mutually recognized discourse that offers a moment of unity or collectivity against commonly perceived centres of power. As the following analysis suggests, it is the ability to

articulate the prevalence of regional alienation that actually draws together a national audience.

Speaking from the Margins: An Analysis of
This Hour Has 22 Minutes

To examine irony and satire within the context of critical-cultural approaches to television is an interesting task. Often, the goal of cultural
studies analysis is to shed light on the myriad ways that television
contributes to dominant, or common sense, renderings of the social
landscape; however, irony works in an apparently antithetical manner
to subvert these forms of representation. In brief, programs like *This
Hour Has 22 Minutes* consciously attempt to disrupt the preferred constructions of dominant, established, social and political discourses and
thereby challenge rather than reinforce the status quo. Therefore, while
all television programs are multivocal to the extent that they incorporate the various contradictions within a given society, the satirical form
of *22 Minutes* contains the boundaries of interpretation to a preferred
discourse that invites a resistant reading of the nation as text. The
following analysis illustrates this process through a consideration of
selected episodes that speak to issues of place within the Canadian
national context. Drawing on Jeremy Butler's (1994) framework of ideological criticism, this analysis examines the ways in which the voices of
marginalization challenge centralized power structures by explicating
(1) the privileged discourses within the television text; (2) the social and
economic interests served by those discourses; and (3) the ways in
which the discourses of the television text address and relate to the
discourses of the viewer. Given that the weekly series satirizes a broad
range of social and political issues, the discussion is limited to selected
episodes and recurring characters that address issues of community
and understandings of place that are relevant to this study. These topical considerations specifically include regional tensions within the nation and representations of Canada's postcolonial positioning within
the continental and global arenas.[6]

The series *This Hour Has 22 Minutes* is based on the premise and
structure of the nightly national newscast. As such, the *mise-en-scène* is
that of the news studio in which the show's four characters report the
'news' to a live audience in the Halifax CBC studios. Included in the
newscast are several excursions to press conferences, on-location reporting, editorial commentary, and simulated satellite interviews with

news 'sources' that provide the substance of the material for the various weekly sketches. The show's title is itself a play on the name of the acclaimed and controversial 1960s CBC series *This Hour Has Seven Days*, a weekly current affairs program that incorporated elements of docudrama and event re-enactments to explore the social and political circumstances of the time. By changing the 'seven days' to '22 minutes,' the cast and creators underline the commercial imperative of television in the 1990s, wherein a half-hour is reduced by at least eight minutes, if not more, for advertising breaks. The title concomitantly signifies the end of the golden age of Canadian public-service broadcasting when programs like *This Hour Has Seven Days* were able to experiment with various forms of presenting 'reality' in news form with little concession to business interests.

The premise for *22 Minutes* is not, however, primarily a satire of broadcast news programs. Rather, the *mise-en-scène* of the newscast provides the avenue from which to satirize society and, especially, those in power. The iconography of on-the-scene reporting that characterizes broadcast news reaches a new height of verisimilitude on *22 Minutes* when the show's 'reporters' actually attend real press conferences and interview actual Canadian politicians. Liberated from the strategic practices of real journalism, such as perceptions of objectivity, fairness, or balance, the cast of *22 Minutes* is able to confront the Canadian political elite and, as will be shown, hold them accountable for their role in any perceived social, political, and economic mis-step. Canada's political figures not only willingly participate in their own degradation but often ask to appear on the show because of its popularity across the country. Their ability to appear as 'good sports' is a perceived source of political capital, but as cast member Rick Mercer once remarked, 'I think they really believe it's a good thing for them to do but sometimes you can see in their eyes that they'd rather be having surgery' (quoted in Wyatt 1997: D18).

While all politicians are equal fodder for potential vilification, those who fall to the right of centre are particularly vulnerable to satirical treatment by the *22 Minutes* troupe. In this respect, the most privileged discourse of the sketch comedy series is one that prefers the ideals of the social welfare system that once played a larger role in the Canadian political system. Unlike commercial television news, *22 Minutes* attempts to serve the economic interests of middle- and lower-class Canadians and the social interests of those who are marginalized by race, gender, or sexuality, rather than of people in positions of economic and political power. As Rick Mercer acknowledged in two separate interviews, the show's sociocultural sensibility is rooted in the Atlantic regional experience:

> I guess it's being from the Maritimes. We see things differently there from central Canada. We're not reverential at all. I mean they are politicians.
>
> (quoted in Bawden 1998: E1)

> Nova Scotia is now the socialist bastion of Canada, probably the last socialist bastion in all of North America, like Sweden.
>
> (quoted in Wyatt 1997: D18)

It is from within this sensibility that the show is able to resonate and intersect with the discourses of the so-called average Canadian viewer. In their personae as reporters, Walsh, Mercer, Thomey, and Jones assume the *vox populi* and not only forthrightly say to politicians what Canadian citizens would like to say themselves but also what they would like to hear real journalists ask of those in power.[7] Even for viewers who disagree with the show's political leanings, the ability to see the country's politicians taken to task in a national forum provides an experience similar to the enjoyment of a spectator sport.[8]

Of the *22 Minutes* cast members, Mary Walsh and Rick Mercer (prior to his departure from the show) were the central political satirists, and it was Walsh's roving reporter character, Marg Delahunty, who dealt the most powerful cuts to any politician who appeared to be drifting into the neoconservative realm that targeted the Canadian social safety net. Marg, who has been best described as 'a Zellers nightmare: violet eyeshadow, orange lipstick, big glasses, gold-plate jewelry' (Johnson 1996: 46), in the seemingly innocent guise of a matronly middle-aged aunt, confronts politicians in the middle of media scrums and questions them at length but rarely allows them a response to her political commentary. In one such episode, Marg Delahunty pushes her way through real reporters on the parliamentary beat to address then federal finance minister Paul Martin after she has woken from a nightmare in which she has found herself in bed with the politician:

> [Marg with microphone in Martin's face]: Well, Paul Martin: the Canadian Bill Clinton. That's what your friends are calling you. Can you imagine what the rest of us are saying about you? Now don't get me wrong. Working like a trojan horse, you've never been so popular. Look at the

work you've done. You've reduced government spending by 30.5 million spoondalicks and you've kept unemployment way up there – the highest it's been since the Great Depression. I wonder if you're ever confused sometimes? Do you have a kind of political dyslexia because I thought the people were saying, 'More jobs, less cuts?' But never mind the political stuff. Do you feel any heat between us – man-woman stuff. I was afraid I was falling into that women love a tyrant – all girls love to be spanked – that kind of thing, you know. You know when Prime Minister Chrétien retires, God love him, I always imagined I'd make a stunning PM. Course that would be difficult where I'm not a Liberal but then neither are you and nobody seems to mind at all.

(aired 3 March 1997)

Canadian audiences, who know the context, understand that the flirting and reference to Bill Clinton have nothing to do with a sex scandal; rather, like criticisms of Clinton, they are allusions to the Liberal party's continuing popularity despite the reversal of the small 'l' liberal agenda on which it was elected to power. Marg's flirting tone softens the blow she deals to Martin as she alludes to his revealing his true conservative agenda once the 'trojan horse' entered the House of Commons. The audience is able to revel in the finance minister's discomfort as he is only able to smile for the cameras while Marg speaks over any comment he attempts to make.

Mary Walsh, however, saves her most stringent barbs for those politicians who forthrightly promote a right-of-centre political agenda. Thus, in a similar confrontation with Mike Harris, then Ontario's Conservative premier, Walsh's Marg Delahunty becomes 'Marg, Princess Warrior.' Here, Marg, clad in a red-velvet warrior mini-skirt as a flashier version of her namesake, Xena, marches up the steps of the provincial legislature to the accompaniment of theme music and narration:

[Intro.: Voice-over. Video of flames and riot police in slow motion]: In a time of a new millennium, of deficit cutters and demagogues [photo of Mike Harris appears], a land in turmoil cried out for a hero. She was Marg, Princess Warrior: iron willed, true of heart, vaccinated in the arm with a gramophone needle. Her vocal quest for justice would save the universe. She could talk a dog off a meat truck.

[Marg with her arm around Mike Harris]: 'No, no, no and again, no.' That's what they seem to be saying. Now you know me, I'm not one to accentuate the negative but that's what they're saying. Now one thing that they're not saying is – they're not calling you and your cohorts 'Satan's spawn,' some kind of heartless, demonic, vicious, authoritarian philistine – oh no, it's still a Mike-a-palooza out there, let me assure you. Most of Ontario voters still believe that the sun, the moon, and the Chevron signs shine right out of your back passage. All they're saying is 'slow down, where's the fire?' Why not carry on with all those election promises to cruelly harass the poor and the powerless? Now, Mike, I tell ya, your people have spoken. If you ignore them it's at your own peril. Now I want you to go in there [the Legislative Assembly] and I want you to do the right thing. And I'm telling you, Mike, don't make me come back and smite ya. 'Cause I will, my darling, I'll smite ya. I'll grind you under my warrior's heel utterly and finally. Now it's nothing personal, Mike. 'Cause let's face it, you are kind of cute for a premier but it is my job [raising sword] for I am Marg, Princess Warrior.

(aired 10 March 1997)

Sketches such as these underscore the way in which levels of community overlap within Canada. Despite the size of the country, the relatively small and dispersed population is familiar with the current central sociopolitical issues in almost every province. Consequently, audiences in Saskatchewan will not only be familiar with Mike Harris's policies in Ontario but can read them both as an indication of the perceived central-Canadian propensity to dominate the national news and as a political program that defies the established notions of dominant Canadian ideologies – namely, the social safety net of a welfare state. It is difficult to imagine a similar level of interstate awareness in a larger and more heavily populated country, such as the United States, where audiences in Massachusetts are probably unlikely to be well versed in the state of governance in New Mexico. The fact that these sketches are able to resonate with viewers across Canada, a country with a far less vocal sense of nationalism than the United States, indicates that regional diversity and loyalty to place need not be discordant with a sense of national community.

Indeed, the salience of regionalism is a central motif that threads together much of the satire in 22 Minutes. Not only are the sociocultural specificities of each province prime targets for parody in the series but so is the concept of regional loyalty and, particularly, regional distinctness itself. In a regular segment, 'streeters and rants,' troupe member Rick Mercer, until his recent departure from the show, provided a weekly monologue that attacked current bids for power by institutions, politicians, and even provinces. Shot in grainy black and white on the wharves of Halifax, Mercer's 'rants' were framed again in the *vox populi* as he walked in front of freighters and through empty warehouses speaking directly to the camera, often in extreme close-up, to deliver his spin on the subject he found most annoying at that moment. As the following rants about demands for special regional recognition from both Quebec and British Columbia illustrate, Mercer's position as an underdog Newfoundlander provides him with a vantage point to deconstruct the relative positioning of regional powers within the national community:

Did I miss something somewhere? Lucien Bouchard lost the referendum. Look up 'loser' and there's Lucien. And even though he lost, he says there is no way Quebec will ever negotiate with Canada. Instead, he's gonna keep having referendum after referendum until he finally gets his own way. He's like a ten-year-old having a temper tantrum in the middle of Toys 'R Us. And instead of hauling him out and putting him in the car, Chrétien is starting to fill up the cart. Distinct culture, constitutional veto, Hot Wheels, Tonka, Nerf gun, Dinky toys, whatever it takes. But, nope, nothing is good enough for Lucien. It's every toy in the shop or nothing. Hey, Jean, if you don't watch it, you're gonna spoil that youngster, and we're gonna have to live with it. Lucien, you lost, you're a loser, and losers negotiate. Everyone wants Quebec to stay in Canada and sooner or later you're gonna have to take yes for an answer. But if this bawling doesn't stop soon, next thing you know, instead of unity rallies, the rest of Canada is gonna be saying, 'That's it, I'm taking off the belt,' and then you'll really have something to cry about. The car gets pulled over and you'll be walking home with an arse the colour of the Maple Leaf.

(first aired 4 December 1995)

Now, I don't want the people of British Columbia to take this the wrong way. God love ya. You got a lot going for you. You got the beautiful mountains, great weather, you can swim in your ocean without having to freeze to death. The people I've met from there are nice enough. But, boys, oh, boys, I hate to be the one telling you, but over the last couple of weeks, you've been starting to sound a lot like Quebec. Look, somebody had to tell you. First you wanted a constitutional veto. You couldn't believe you weren't given the veto. Give us the veto, you said. So then they gave you the veto, and what happens? You said, I can't believe they gave us a veto.

You've never been so insulted in all your lives. And now? Now you want
more or something 'bad' is going to happen. Please, please, on behalf of
the rest of the country, I'm begging you, stop now before it's too late.
You're on a very slippery slope. Can demands for distinct society be far
behind? And, sure, you're already distinct. You've got the most stable
economy in the entire country. What am I saying? You've got an economy.
That's as distinct as you're gonna get in Canada. Where I come from,
people are more worried about becoming an extinct society. You think
you're feeling left out? Imagine how Prince Edward Island feels. Everything the average Canadian knows about P.E.I. comes from *Road to Avonlea*
and, sure, they make that in Ontario. You got everything going for you.
You're better off than most. But, please, one problem child at a time.

(first aired 18 December 1995)

In the tone of the 'regular guy' talking with intimate friends, Mercer's
rants evoke the previously mentioned 'spoiled child in the national
family' invective levied against British Columbia whenever one region
claims to be more 'distinct' than the others. This tone appeals to the
sentiment of viewers across the country, as every region has claimed to
be unfairly disadvantaged at one time or another.

All regions are prey to the *22 Minutes* troupe members' satirical
portraits, including their own maritime community. In fact, some of the
show's most popular recurring characters are self-parodies of Canadian
Newfie jokes that draw on derogative associations to isolation and
inbreeding and references to national 'welfare bums.' Examples include
the Quinlan Quintuplets (of which there are only four) – a family of
dim-witted con artists dressed in lumberjack shirts and fishermen's
toques who are continually inventing bizarre get-rich-quick schemes –
and Jerry Boyle, the disreputable leader – and only member – of the
Newfoundland Separation Foundation (NSF – a play on 'non-sufficient
funds'), who spends his days attempting to elicit money in the guise of
campaign fund-raising. These characters and vignettes provide a particularly interesting use of irony. At one level, they appear to contribute
to the ongoing malignment of maritimers, but at another level, the joke
is on those Canadians who perpetuate the Newfie joke, as the segment
creators are Newfoundlanders who provide the country's most popular
and insightful social and political satire every week. In this respect, the
double coding is such that the *22 Minutes* troupe is able to simultaneously control the region's deprecation while exposing the fallacies
thereof.

Although no region or community is spared the troupe's satirical eye, the most regular and scathing parodies and rants are aimed at the power centres that elicit a regionally shared connotation of marginalization: Ontario (read as Toronto and Ottawa), the monarchy (as representatives of the remnants of colonialism), and the United States (the constant power spectre to the south). Toronto, or the 'centre of the universe' as it is disparagingly referred to in many provinces, is a regular target in the show's weekly 'news' segments, and the off-the-cuff comments by the 'anchors' imply a complicit agreement with the viewers that everyone feels similarly alienated from or antagonistic to the city. For example, when the Ontario provincial government implemented its plans to amalgamate surrounding municipalities into metropolitan Toronto and thereby create a megacity, the 22 *Minutes* coverage announced that while this would be beneficial to the economic management of the region, 'the problem [would be] that there will be more Toronto' (aired 10 March 1997). Similar sentiments are expressed in a segment where Native commentator 'Joe Crow' (Cathy Jones) talks about the implications of a potentially sovereign Quebec: 'Hard about separation now, eh? These days it's like listening to "Achy, Breaky Heart" – it makes everyone groan like the Great Gassy Elk. Now on the other hand, if Toronto wanted to leave we'd be over there all weekend helping them pack' (aired 21 October 1996). The undertones of hostility towards Toronto, in both the program and the larger Canadian imagination, are manifestations of the resentment towards those who bear disproportionate levels of power and influence, whether real or symbolic.

The symbolic power of the British monarchy is also regularly mocked in 22 *Minutes* segments, with the implication that a non-elected, and foreign, body should bear little role in the affairs of a sovereign country. When an electronic billboard in London's Piccadilly Circus displayed a 'Save the Seals' statement to boycott Canadian goods as a means of protest against northern seal hunting, the 22 *Minutes* anchors 'announced' that a similar billboard in Ottawa had displayed a response stating, 'Save the Mad Cow. But get her off our money' (aired 9 December 1996). This sketch draws on current debate in Canada over whether the nation should follow Australia's example, move closer to the status of a republic, and shed the last vestiges of colonialism that accompany Commonwealth status. Unlike Australia, however, the monarchy provides a contradictory presence in the Canadian context. While Canadian audiences enjoy satirical barbs against Britain, there remains a prevalent sentiment that Commonwealth status provides a measure of utility as a cultural buffer from the United States. And, indeed, it is the United States that receives the most severe satirical treatment, to the most popular response, in the sketch comedy.

The proximity, and influence, of the United States has provided Canadians with their strongest rallying point around the Maple Leaf. The oppositional form of identity that derives from 'not being American' has provided Canadians with the most efficacious 'other' with which to overcome regional fragmentation and form the national imagined community. The political and cultural insecurity that accompanies the seemingly insubstantial border between the two countries provides perhaps the greatest sense of marginalization for most Anglo-Canadians. In comedy, this sense of marginalization and negative identity is demonstrated through a resistant humour that illustrates what Cornelius Castoriadis (1990) refers to as 'the apparent incapacity to constitute oneself as oneself without excluding the other – and the apparent inability to exclude the other without devaluing and, ultimately, hating him' (quoted in Morley and Robins 1995: 22). In *22 Minutes*, the United States becomes a favourite target of mockery as a means to address Canadian feelings of political, economic, and cultural subordination and to reinforce a sense of difference.

Much of the Canadian 'inferiority complex' emanates from the perception that the world's most powerful nation appears to have little understanding or knowledge of its neighbour to the north and, moreover, sees Canada as a political satellite populated with like-minded citizens. Thus 'difference' from Americans has become an important part of the Canadian psyche and is a popular theme in *22 Minutes* sketches, and particularly in Rick Mercer's rants:

> When I was in grade four I woke up and heard Peter Gzowski say that the Canadian dollar was worth seventy-five cents. I freaked out, took everything I had, eight bucks in change, and bought forty-six fudgesticks at recess. I was hedging my bets against inflation. I panicked. I suffered. Half the fudgesticks melted, and I ended up with an ice cream headache. And now, twenty years later, the dollar's back down, the debt's up, and everyone's freaking out because the *Wall Street Journal* says we're an honorary member of the Third World. The pain is coming back. Okay, let's not be rash. Stay off the fudgesticks. We're the Third World? Says who? The *Wall Street Journal*. And where in the world do they live? New York City, one of the biggest sewers on the face of the earth. My advice to the crowd south of the border: people who live in glass outhouses shouldn't throw stones. Otherwise, we'll just start flinging them right back at ya.

We'll go toe to toe with the Yanks on guns, crime, Florida, air, water, medicare, and the biggest advantage that we've got of them all: at least we're not Americans.

(first aired 23 January 1995)

Mercer's rants explicate how humour serves as a form of passive aggression or resistance against dominant cultures. Going one step further, in 1996, when the Canadian government refused to sever economic ties to Cuba despite threats of American trade retaliation, he used his rants to celebrate actual political resistance against the United States. The Canadian government's resolute stand on the Cuban issue was an overwhelmingly popular decision both politically and culturally in Canada. Mercer's weekly rants echoed popular sentiment that the Cuban dispute highlighted the cultural divide between Canadians and Americans in their respective antagonism, or lack thereof, towards Communism. Cuba thus became a signifier of Canadian difference and political autonomy:

There's a lot of arguments out there for and against trade with Cuba. But the best one for increasing it so far is that the United States wants us to stop. In their self-appointed overzealous mission as defenders of freedom, they have finally reached the point where they've decided that sovereign nations like Canada are only free to do what America tells them to do. Yah, if the United States was a thirty-five-year-old male, he'd be in a mental hospital – for his sake, for our sake, and for the sake of the whole neighbourhood. And the diagnosis? Below-average intelligence, suffers from delusions of grandeur, medicate heavily. Unfortunately, America is too big to get the restraints on, and they're not in a very good mood. Of course they're not. If I looked that stupid I'd be pissed off too. America stopped trade with Cuba to teach them a lesson in 1961. And now, thirty-five years later, Cuba's trading with everyone else to teach America a lesson. Businesses are springing up left, right, and centre and not one of them is American. Castro the Commie is becoming Castro the Capitalist. He's open for business and Canadians have every right to be there. Because, hey, Canada's a free country, and freedom's not just another word for doing what America tells ya.

(aired 11 March 1996)

Lloyd Axworthy, Canada's last true liberal, headed to Cuba last week. And good for him. It's supposed to be very nice this time of year. Actually, I'm glad he went, because the thought of a Canadian cabinet minister

lunching with Fidel Castro had the Americans so mad, they didn't
know whether to swallow or spit. Now Lloyd says he only talked to Fidel
about increasing trade and human rights. I say, do it one better. I say, we
take a page from Lucien Bouchard's book and talk about sovereignty-
association, not between Canada and Quebec, but between Canada and
Cuba. We could call it 'Canuba.' When you think about it, 'Canuba'
sounds more Canadian than 'Canada.' Now, granted, there's a few bugs to
work out. Like we're the True North Strong and Free, and they're neither.
But come on, Canadians love a beach. And we can offer a lot to Cuba.
We're already their largest trading partner, we've got a strong currency,
we're in NAFTA, and we still believe in universal health care and education. And the best thing is that on the pissing-off-America scale, this
would be a ten. And when they complained, we could say, 'Ah, shut up,
we've got you surrounded.'

(aired 27 January 1997)

These 'rants' also illustrate a common form of intersubjective national
irony as they underline the relatively inferior role Canada plays in
tangible global political and economic processes while simultaneously
critiquing the American propensity to overstate its role as an international power broker.[9] Another prevalent strand of this form of irony
manifests itself in a converse manner, in which Canadian difference is
demonstrated from a position of intangible power: the perception of
intellectual or educational superiority to the American other. This particular form of irony, wherein Americans are portrayed as holding a
disproportionate degree of global power in relation to their comprehension of world history and other cultures, is a long-standing feature of
Canadian satirical resistance to American hegemony as well as a staple
of 22 Minutes sketch material.

This latter means of establishing difference through satirical form
began with Rick Mercer's 'coverage' of former President Clinton's
re-election and man-on-the-street interviews with Americans on location in Washington, D.C. The American presidential election provided
Mercer with substantial comedic material with which to compare the
Canadian and American political and cultural systems. His first rant in
front of the White House exemplifies the paradigm of the 'more
knowledgeable Canadian' described above:

When you walk around Washington, D.C., you can't help but be in total
awe of the place. It's the epicentre of the last great superpower left standing, and boy, do they know it. But Canadians should feel proud of them,

happy for them. Because America is our neighbour, our ally, our trading partner, and our friend. Still, sometimes you'd like to give them such a smack! But we can't. If we tried, let's face it, they would kill us. And therein lies the problem. Pierre Trudeau said it was a lot like a relationship between an elephant and a mouse. Brian Mulroney, to give him the benefit of the doubt, felt that Canada could influence America more from the inside. Therefore, he devoted most of his public life trying to get the mouse up inside the elephant. And, let's face it, that's a period in our country's history we'd all like to forget. So what are we gonna do? Well, for starters, we have to think differently. We have to erase this whole elephant/mouse analogy from our minds. America is not an elephant. For one thing, elephants never forget, whereas Americans don't know much to begin with. Ninety per cent of them can't pick out their hometown on an unmarked map. We're bigger than they are and we're on top. If we were in prison, they'd be our bitch. Our role is to remind them of the little things like that, over and over and over again. And if they get mad with us, we'll just have to take our name off the map and feel safe in knowing that they will never find us.

(aired 11 November 1996)

This appeal to the Canadian discourse that 'Americans don't know much,' and particularly about their northern neighbour, became a recurring theme throughout Mercer's visit to Washington. In his persona as 'reporter' J.B. Dickson, Mercer used the favoured and most subversive form of Canadian satire *vis-à-vis* the Americans by encouraging them to show their lack of knowledge about Canada through their own words. Herein, 'J.B.' would stop Capitol Hill employees on their way to work and ask their opinion as to whether the upcoming meetings between President Clinton and Prime Minister Chrétien should be called the 'Clinton-Chrétien Summit' or the 'Chrétien-Clinton Summit.' However, playing on the assumption that even Washington insiders would not know the name of the Canadian prime minister, Mercer substituted the names of Canadian media personalities Ralph Benmergui and Peter Gzowski in the place of Chrétien. To reinforce the punch-line, after none of the selected interviewees corrected the prime minister's name, the segment closed with 'J.B.'s' response to one individual who chose the Benmergui–Clinton Summit option:

J.B. Dickson: Oh, alphabetical. Very diplomatic.
Interviewee: That's why I work in Washington.

(aired 4 November 1996)

The Washington segments, and particularly the on-the-spot interviews with Americans in positions requiring at least primary knowledge of Canada, were so popular with the *22 Minutes* audiences that they became a weekly segment called 'Talking to Americans.' Mercer's future 'reports' included trips to Harvard where faculty and students were asked their views on nonsensical 'facts' such as the cruelty of the seal hunt in the prairie province of Saskatchewan, and return visits to Washington where people were asked to congratulate Canada on achieving nationhood the previous week. Shortly before his departure from *This Hour Has 22 Minutes* in 2001, Rick Mercer completed a one-hour episode of 'Talking to Americans.' The special attracted 2.7 million viewers and still ranks as one of the highest-rated programs on the CBC network.

The implications of this brief analysis of *This Hour Has 22 Minutes* should not leave the impression that a sense of national community in Canada is attained only at the satirical expense of the United States. Rather, at a broader level, this sketch comedy illustrates how common points of identification – in a national sense – are constituted through the dialectical relationship between discourses of difference and commonality in the Canadian experience. Thus, despite sociocultural differences among the regions, a shared narrative based on the experiences of life in the periphery provides moments of community that are able to find expression in the virtual geography of television. Life in the margins provides a way of seeing the world, and particularly one's relationship to centres of power, which resonates across the regions and forms a larger sense of community without denying the specificities of the local. This is perhaps an insight into that intangible 'Canadian sensibility' described by many of the producers in this study – the idea that, regardless of the subject matter, a domestic television production cannot help but be informed by the creator's experience and sense of place at both the local and national levels.

As previously mentioned, it is often easiest to see these moments of intersubjectivity in a comedy program because of the culturally specific nature of the genre. Indeed, comedies are usually the least globally marketable programs because of the need for audiences of 'insiders' who will be receptive to the cultural codes of the text.[10] However, comedy should not be seen as the only televisual format that bridges the cultural gaps of regional diversity in Canada. As seen in examples of popular drama mentioned in the preceding chapter, television that explicitly references the experiences of the places in the margins generates some of the country's largest and most responsive audiences. It is in this respect that regional television production exemplifies the ways in which the periphery is, in fact, a place of resistance to both the power centres of central Canada and the United States. Therefore, the idea of a national cultural community is not an anachronism in a global media environment. What this study does indicate, however, is that there remains a precarious balance to be achieved between fostering indigenous television stories – without imposing a notion of official culture – and providing the requisite support for producers in a diverse domestic market that is perceived as numerically insignificant in global market terms.

Chapter 6

Regimes of Community in 'Hollywood North': Reproducing Local and Global Cultures in a Televisual World

The central premise underlying the preceding chapters, and reinforced in the book's title, *On Location*, is that the national, regional, and global community formations illuminated on our television screens are social constructions to the extent that they are the products of a series of complex negotiations between policy makers, funding agencies, and the creative minds that reinterpret diverse, and often competing, conceptualizations of place in the process of cultural storytelling. It is a truism to state that television does *not* provide a mirror of any society. If this were the case, we would see far greater diversity in the range of issues, events, and social subjectivities played back to us every time we sat in front of our television sets. Rather, the televisual world is one of partial representations of the social, political, and economic realms we inhabit. It is necessarily selective, and, therefore, the processes of inclusion and exclusion in televisual storytelling privilege certain definitions of communal life while marginalizing alternative lived realities. Thus, before turning to some final reflections on the present condition, and possible future, of Canadian television in a global media environment, it is worth revisiting the contested nature of community definition as it collides with the realm of televisual production. In the following section, I return to questions posed in the first chapter: What is a community? Who defines the boundaries of a community? How are communities formed in a global media environment? The intent here is not to impose definitive answers but rather to interrogate our preconceptions about the construction of community in a mediated world. To do so, I contextualize the discussion within the Foucauldian conceptualization of discursive regimes and the production of knowledge. The emphasis is on the means by which the various media-related institutions are able to construct preferred ways of *knowing* the meanings of national, global, and local spheres – a form of power that limits the constructions of alternative definitions and productions of community formations.

Discourses of Community in Media Culture

It is relatively straightforward, in a cartographical sense, to identify the various levels of community, be they national, local, or regional, in the formally recognized boundaries that physically demarcate territories. It is, however, a far more challenging task to understand the ways that the lived experiences within these spatial organizations translate into the symbolic senses of belonging that underpin the formation of diverse cultural identifications. It is the latter of these two dimensions of community that has provided the central problematic for this book and for much of the contemporary scholarship on the role played by the media in processes of cultural globalization. Within this perspective, the images and narratives of media culture that travel across physical borders provide the building blocks for competing forms of cultural belonging that increasingly complicate, or defy, the sociocultural specificities of space and place. The history of Canadian broadcasting illustrates the persistence of faith in the capacity of the media to encourage symbolic socialization into the *idea* of the nation that will then, it is hoped, correspond with the political entity that is the nation-state. This relationship between media representations of community and the development of a national self-consciousness, as formulated in broadcasting policy and implemented in production practices, focuses our attention on the implications of the constructed nature of the 'National Symbolic' (Lauren Berlant, quoted in Morley 2000: 107) in two significant ways. First, it highlights the fact that essentialized identities do not develop, in primordial fashion, by mere virtue of national citizenship. Rather, the sentiment of national belonging must be continually fought for and fostered through the creation of a 'discourse of nation.' The media play a central role in disseminating the preferred definitions of nation and national belonging. Second, the investment, both politically and economically, in developing media forms that support the dominant definition of the nation testifies to the primacy of this particular regime of community identification over all others, whether based on region, locality, or ethnicity. In brief, governance of the nation-state places primacy on the nation as the site of cultural identity in a manner that attempts to subsume competing forms of cultural self-consciousness.

The history of Canadian broadcasting policy illustrates the changing discursive boundaries of the nation to be reproduced in mediated cultural form. National public broadcasting in Canada was, from its inception, designed to defend against the perception of cultural domination by the United States. At this particular historical moment, the dominant discourse of nation was one of unity in diversity, the idea that the definition of a Canadian community had to recognize and portray, in broadcast form, cultural *difference* among the regions that nonetheless coexisted as a politically integrated community. This discursive regime of nation came into question as such differences, epitomized by the rise of Quebec nationalism, were seen to destabilize the governance of the nation-state. Thus a new discourse of nation, one that emphasized a singular national identity that could overcome regional discontent, was produced and remains the dominant voice in broadcasting practices to this day. These strategic deployments of specific discourses of nation in Canadian broadcasting policy attune us to the ways in which national institutions – specifically, the assemblage of media policy, funding, and network broadcasting agencies – help to produce the object that they speak of: the nation. The centrist (or Toronto-centric) vision of Canada that would come to define the national regime in English CBC television production parallels that of other national public broadcasters. As Stuart Hall reminds us, the BBC – the predominant broadcasting model for most Commonwealth nations – did not provide a mirror to a British national self-consciousness but instead was 'an instrument, an apparatus, a "machine" through which the nation was constituted. It produced the nation which it addressed: it constituted its audience by the ways in which it represented them' (quoted in Morley 2000: 108).

As Clive Barnett (1999: 375) argues, this is a common feature of broadcasting institutions within most social-democratic systems in that they function as 'sites of national cultural policy aimed at inculcating a particular model of cultural citizenship.' Invoking Foucault's conceptualization of governmentality, Barnett illustrates that the formation of cultural policies that attempt to mandate a discourse of nation through regulatory control are mechanisms of power that seek to 'shape the daily life of a population ... [and] regulate dispositions at an actual distance' (ibid.: 381).[1] This power to govern the definition of 'national' programming, as illustrated in the CBC's production policies regarding the regional television centres, was cited most often by the Vancouver production community as a primary source of frustration in developing local stories for inclusion at the national network level. It is within this tension over the development of 'national' stories that we see the conflicting discursive regimes of community definition. As my conversations with Vancouver television producers indicate, for those living and working in the periphery, the local is a place that is consistently informed and constituted by regional, national, and global processes. Unlike the discursive regime of nation in broadcasting policy – one that depends on fixing boundaries against the external Other – local cultural production recognizes that the various spheres of community suffuse one another; they are inseparable from one another and mutually form the sociocultural specificity of places.

The experiences of those living in the margins of the nation-state, as seen in the practices of community television producers and the stories and commentaries of such regional productions as *This Hour Has 22 Minutes*, provide a unique vantage point from which to construct 'counter-narratives of the nation that continually evoke and erase its totalizing boundaries – both actual and conceptual ...' Such counter-narratives 'disturb those ideological manoeuvres through which "imagined communities" are given essentialist identities' (Bhabha 1994: 149). At its most basic level, the Vancouver case study underlines the necessity of reassessing our perceptions about questions of cultural identity and the role of national broadcasting institutions in a global media arena. By recognizing the discursive nature of community definition, we are alerted to the fact that representations can change with changes in policy discourses. The lessons of television production in Vancouver indicate that cultural *difference* is an integral component of any sense of national self-consciousness and that in a world of flows – of images, peoples, and ideas – multiple sites of identity and allegiance cohabit the physical space of the nation. This seemingly new world of global disjunctures and interconnections has, in fact, led to the argument that we need to transfer our attention from media policies that emphasize the nation-state perspective to a policy that addresses the more ambiguous term of 'community,' in general:

> The rescaling of economic processes and regulatory regimes is associated with the fragmentation of both the national public spheres and the singular liberal subjectivities with which they have been normatively associated. The multiplication of cultural public spheres therefore means that 'there is no longer a general subject of culture' ... The internationalization

of economic processes, and the fragmentation and multiplication of public spheres, reterritorializes the normative individual subject of the nation into a series of differently scaled networks of representation and participation. Mass mediated public spheres increasingly address individuals not as members of a whole nation, but as a series of multiple, minoritized subjects. ... The government of culture, in short, is no longer institutionally or spatially contained within the nation-state.

(Barnett 1999: 376).

Does this particular call for a new discourse of community in cultural policy require us to dispense with the nation as a regime of community in reconceptualizing broadcasting in a global media environment? I would argue no. In brief, national representations still matter and, as the creation of 'Hollywood North' exemplifies, these may be lost in the global cultural shuffle to reach international audience markets. Rather, it is imperative to reformulate the discursive regime of the nation as one which is inclusive of alterity in its articulation of community.

Missed Opportunities or Opportunities Not to Be Missed? Concluding Thoughts on 'Hollywood North'

The history of Canadian broadcasting has been characterized as a story of 'missed opportunities' (Raboy 1990), of which the most notable loss has been that of diverse regional voices in the development of a broadcasting system that interprets and represents the nation to itself from a centralized viewpoint. As the centre replicates itself on Canadian television screens, it is perhaps not surprising that a regionally fragmented community has become an avid audience for American television programming. Positioned as outsiders in both televisual landscapes, Canadians on the periphery have opted for the one that will, at minimum, provide the epitome of production quality and investment.

The members of the first task forces on national broadcasting policy foresaw the current situation as the logical conclusion of a broadcasting system that imposed, or attempted to construct, a sense of national identity rather than fostering a sentiment of national belonging through interregional communication. From the early days of radio programming, policy makers were attuned to the importance of local community in the Canadian hierarchy of allegiances to places. And, indeed, from *The Beachcombers* in the 1970s to today's *This Hour Has 22 Minutes*, it has been those television programs that are informed by the regional sensibility that have garnered some of the most enthusiastic audiences at a national level. In this respect, the first broadcasting commission reports were decades ahead of current research findings in their assumptions that people would overwhelmingly choose media content indicative of their own lived experiences, given proximate quality, over that of another society.

Today, as Canada continues to wrestle with questions of cultural sovereignty and nation building, there are many who argue that national public broadcasting institutions – indeed, nation-states themselves – are becoming increasingly irrelevant in an era of instantaneous global electronic communications. In the eyes of globalization enthusiasts, technology has not only rendered a seemingly borderless world but also promises unlimited avenues for diverse international cultural representations through satellite broadcasting and the proliferation of specialty cable television channels. Conversely, as nationalist sentiments rage and turmoil continues in global hotspots, we are constantly and dramatically reminded that the concept of a nation-state, and the means with which to express a national sense of self, remain desired goals in communities around the world. In brief, 'place' still matters. Thus, to reiterate earlier thoughts, we should hesitate to celebrate the arrival of a global culture that is defined in terms of the nation-state writ large, and should continue to scrutinize community formations and available access to global media channels.

This study has begun to interrogate some of the assumptions underlying the relationship between popular media and the local-global cultural nexus through the case study of the Vancouver television production community. Initial implications from this analysis indicate that many Canadian television producers are eager to develop stories that draw upon the sociocultural specificities of place, and that Canadian audiences appear to support such efforts. Moreover, inclusion and representation of these stories at the national level remain crucial to producers and audiences alike. In order to understand the confluence of economic and political discourses and practices that have impeded achieving the initial cultural goals of national broadcasting policy, this study has attempted to 'make visible the processes through which certain forms of culture become dominant ... through situating the object of analysis within the system of production' (Kellner 1995: 42). What emerges is a picture in which the contradictions between the market and cultural development models of broadcasting collide with geographical power struggles over the allocation of production resources and the right to determine the definition of the nation. In the case of the Vancouver independent production community, the turn towards international partnerships and a global audience is both a means of resistance to federal definitions of the national culture and a strategy with which to accommodate the financial requisites of the industry. The parallels between the cultural negotiations at both the domestic and the global levels of television production become particularly evident when placed within the context of the tension between market and cultural goals. In other words, overarching terms such as 'national' or 'domestic culture' and 'cultural globalization' – as they pertain to television broadcasting – subsume the inherent tensions between what are, in fact, four simultaneously congruent and contradictory processes: national, domestic culture; national, domestic markets; cultural globalization; and economic globalization.

Drawing upon conclusions from the Vancouver case study, the remaining discussion recommends a clearer conceptualization of these contradictions in future Canadian broadcasting policies and practices. The first section addresses what might be seen as the tangible processes of national television culture – namely, the restructuring of the industry in a manner that reconciles the national broadcasting mandate with its initial goals of interregional communication. The second section speaks to the need to reconceptualize the more intangible relationships between cultures, places, and their symbolic representations in the virtual geography of global television.

Rethinking 'Canadian' Content in the New Millennium

American television has been described as a contradictory institution in the sense that it provides a venue for creative, and even artistic, social expression while remaining primarily a business and, therefore, a profit-oriented industry (Meehan 1994). These contradictions are even more pronounced in the private-public structure of Canadian television, where artistry and profit concerns rest in an uneasy balance with national cultural goals. Thus, while content regulations and federal funding measures are seen as integral components to support culturally relevant television programming for a small domestic market, success in terms of sustained access to national networks remains measured in the market terms of ratings and audience numbers. Given the fact that there will never be sufficient numbers of Canadians to motivate private broadcasters to invest independently in domestic television production, policy makers have compromised the boundaries of content stipulations to accommodate the economic interests of the industry. Consequently, the citizenship of key creative personnel, rather than the nature of the actual content, determines whether or not a television program is sufficiently Canadian. If culture is defined in market terms, then these regulations can be viewed as a success, for they have contributed to the sustained employment of Canadians in a competitive global industry and have provided a measurement device for the public funding of productions that have, in turn, generated international sales. In fact, as Canada is now the world's second-largest exporter of television programming, many industry insiders have announced the ultimate achievement of national broadcasting policy goals and question whether content regulations remain necessary to the newly matured industry. Indeed, the former head of the CRTC, Keith Spicer, announced in 1993 that such was the commercial success of Canadian television that the CRTC itself could become obsolete in the twenty-first century.

However, if culture is defined in symbolic terms, whereby television provides an arena within which to tell the stories that negotiate the sociocultural boundaries of the national community, then the current regulatory structure remains short of achieving the ultimate goals of national broadcasting policies. As the interviews with Vancouver producers indicate, the ability to translate domestic content regulation incentives into profitable television productions necessitates the dilution of cultural specificity of content. After all, larger audiences can only be be found beyond Canada's borders, and therefore the universalization of symbolic culture is seen as the only means to attain maximum profit returns.

The nation's public broadcaster, the CBC, was intentionally developed to mitigate the culturally homogenizing forces of a commercial television industry. However, the corporation's own private-public structure, in combination with its centralized, bureaucratic decision-making apparatus and successive funding cutbacks, has been unequal to the task of providing a truly alternative avenue for domestic cultural expression. This is not to say that the CBC has failed to contribute to the development of culturally relevant programming. As this study has shown, the few quality programs that have resonated with Canadian audiences have generally been CBC productions or co-productions. Therefore, the implication is that a renewed, and more solid, commitment to the initial mandate of the public broadcaster is crucial to sustaining the Canadian cultural presence in television production. This entails a detailed questioning of the private-public structure of the corporation as well as a reassessment of the role of regional production in the network schedule.

The CBC's broadcasting licence came up for renewal in March 1999 and, as required for national broadcasting, the CRTC held community hearings across the country in order to assess the public's opinions on the future of the corporation. The overwhelming public turnout to the meetings throughout the nation indicated that the CBC remains an important symbolic institution to many Canadians. This revitalization of public discourse on the current state of national broadcasting presents us with new opportunities that are not to be missed. As the Vancouver case study indicates, the globalization of the television industry is a contradictory process. At one level, it has provided an arena in which independent regional producers have been able to free themselves from the constraints of 'official culture' and compensate for their exclusion from the central funding agencies that support indigenous production. On another level, the global market imposes its own version of official culture in that creative and economic capital must be invested in stories that resonate beyond the nation's borders. And, as the conclusions generated from the cultural negotiations of international joint ventures indicate, such productions must be particularly compatible with the grammar and formulas of the American television industry. Thus, attention needs to be refocused on the CBC and the means by which to ensure that the national public broadcaster has cultural relevance in the new millennium.

The first and most important finding implicit in the Vancouver case study is that the interwined private-public strands in Canada's broadcasting industry structure must be disentangled. This means not the dismantling of regulatory and funding agencies but rather the separation of the two broadcasting spheres so that both may pursue the logical goals of their respective infrastructures. Regulations remain imperative to the objectives of domestic cultural production. Even community television – established to serve as the most accessible broadcast arena to local interests – will be used as a marketing tool by the private sector if protective regulations are removed. However, regulations must be revised to differentiate between market and cultural development goals. Independent producers and private broadcasters who seek to pursue opportunities in the global marketplace could see reduced domestic content regulations in the purchase or production of non-news programming. However, this liberation from the yoke of national broadcasting policy does not come without a price. The successes evidenced by global Canadian productions indicate that some profits could easily be transferred, in the form of licence fees or production taxes, to the development of a completely public CBC structure. Also, independent producers who chose to work with broadcasters following this option would face reduced eligibility for superfund subsidization. In return, private broadcasters would benefit from the CBC's departure from the competitive, and limited, pool of Canadian advertising dollars. This is, admittedly, an optimistic scenario given the contemporary neoliberal turn in economic and political governance internationally. A minimum commitment to long-term funding allocations for the subsidized component of the CBC would at least allow the national public broadcaster to develop long-range, coherent production strategies. This could alleviate the instability of current year-by-year scheduling decisions that have, thus far, worked against the sustained development of culturally relevant television series.

A truly public CBC would also require substantial restructuring if it were to become the primary platform for Canadian productions. If nothing else, the statements of Vancouver's production community indicate that the centre cannot hold the whole together. Instead, a system of regional production or 'multiple points of entry,' such as that outlined in Sauvageau's recommendations, would facilitate the goals of interregional communication that formed the basis of the first task force on broadcasting policy. As out-of-house production agreements with companies such as Salter Street (the co-producers of *22 Minutes*) illustrate, regional sensibilities speak to the sociocultural experiences of Canadians across the country and are best created outside of the centres of political and cultural power.

Finally, Canadian content regulations must be revised to reflect the spirit of broadcasting policies. Content, not citizenship alone, should determine the appropriate level of funding and access to the public broadcaster. This is the most complex aspect of broadcast restructuring, as defining culture in the measurement of a quantifiable point system has always been a central problematic in Canadian policy and practice. Following the conclusions of the Vancouver study, I would caution against parochial constructions of 'authentic' Canadian culture of the 'Mounties and moose' variety. Rather, content regulations need only stipulate that stories must draw on the sociocultural specificities of places within the nation. In brief, 'place' must be acknowledged rather than erased for content to qualify as 'national.' Moreover, the explicit reference to place in domestic television production should not be seen as mutually exclusive of global cultural forces. One of the most important conclusions to be drawn from the Vancouver context is that the local continually intersects with the global. It is the specific negotiations within this local-global nexus that provide the particularities of place and the material for stories about this site of community. Consequently, 'national' broadcasting should not be an attempt to construct an imagined community in the traditional and nostalgic sense of a bounded locale somehow insulated from international forces. Canada was born from, and continues to develop within, a context of competing levels of community – local, regional, continental, and international. It is in this respect that the cultural challenges and opportunities facing the globalization of the Canadian broadcasting industry provide a valuable model from which to examine similar processes in other national contexts.

Unfortunately, the idealism of my suggestions here appears increasingly unfeasible given recent developments in the politics of broadcast financing in Canada. More than ever it is evident that the industry side of television funding is prevailing over the goals of cultural development. In February 2003, the federal government handed down a budget that announced a veritable spending spree in the national public sector. A financial surplus in the federal coffers precipitated a long-overdue reinvestment of billions of dollars in health care, education, and other areas that had suffered in the austerity measures introduced over the past decade. Anticipating a share of the benefits of the surplus, many people working in the television industry were dealt a surprising blow when the new budget instead announced a 25 per cent cut to the CTF. Since its establishment in 1996, the CTF had been allocated $100 million per year (on a year-by-year basis) to subsidize domestic television development. It was estimated that the budget reduction to $75 million for the next two years would translate into a loss of 390 hours of television programming, a cut in production activity by $83 million, and sixty fewer new productions for 2003–4 (Adams and Posner 2003). To add insult to injury, the federal budget simultaneously included an increase of 5 per cent (from 11 to 16 per cent) in production tax credits to foreign film and television producers shooting in Canada. Although this boded well for ensuring the continued attraction of runaway American production, the concomitant loss of CTF subsidies implied that local producers would have to devote greater energy to service work on American projects in order to earn enough money for their own productions. The catch was, of course, that this would further reduce the time available for them to develop domestic dramas at all.

Not surprisingly, the budget decisions whipped the Canadian television industry into a frenzy. *Da Vinci's Inquest* producer Laszlo Barna's outrage reflected the shock waves rippling throughout the production community: '[The two-year $150-million allocation to the CTF shows] utter disregard for indigenous productions. If you just do the math, indigenous production is being cut by $50 million. Where on earth are our cultural priorities? How can it be, in this time particularly, when there is money on the table? It's a two-year commitment, but for less. I'm very disappointed' (quoted in Posner and Adams 2003).

The budget proclamation preceded the CTF committee's adjudication of subsidy applications by a matter of weeks. The end result was that the CTF was forced to reject 64 per cent of the applications submitted. CBC-TV's chief programmer, Slawko Klymkiw, emphasized the extent of the damage to domestic production when he announced that the public broadcaster had received funding for only 25 per cent of its project requests compared to a success rate of 91 per cent in 2002 (Funding Cuts 2003). Following the CTF decisions, a critical mass of Canada's leading actors, union leaders, and producers converged on Ottawa to meet with members of Parliament and protest the cuts to the television industry superfunds. Actor Paul Gross, of *Due South* fame, summed up seventy years of broadcasting history in his statement to federal MPs: 'Television drama is the most powerful cultural medium in contemporary society. To maintain our identity as a nation it's essential that a range of Canadian stories be on our TVs. Instead, Canadians are being fed an overwhelming diet of U.S. drama programming' (Canada NewsWire 2003). One month after these lobby efforts, the ministers of Finance and Heritage agreed to restore $12.5 million to the CTF.[2] This measure is less promising than it sounds since it is only one-half of the amount cut from the superfund; moreover, the replacement money is not a new allocation but rather money borrowed from the CTF's 2004–5 budget (CFTPA 2003). Consequently, the future of sustained funding support for domestic television remains precarious.

The perpetual emphasis on the industry component of television, as an economic engine and purveyor of jobs, over the symbolic dimensions of television as a storytelling medium has long-term implications for the Canadian broadcasting community. The trend towards government divestment from domestic television funding means that producers must increasingly approach their projects from a market perspective, with audience size and profits becoming the central considerations in the television drama development process. The recent restructuring strategies of one of Canada's largest media companies – Alliance Atlantis Communications Inc. – provides a telling glimpse into a future where market concerns are the predominant drivers of production decisions. In 2001, Alliance Atlantis bought Salter Street Films for $80 million in stocks and cash. In December 2003, the company announced that it would be closing Salter Street Films, as well as most of its other production holdings, aside from the highly successful American-situated *CSI-Crime Scene Investigation* franchise. The decision had nothing to do with program quality or audience popularity in regard to Salter Street productions. Indeed, most of Salter Street's programs, including *This Hour Has 22 Minutes*, remained among the most highly rated Canadian television programs, and the company had just won an Academy Award for co-producing Michael Moore's biting political satire *Bowling for Columbine*.[3] Rather, the Alliance Atlantis decision was based purely on the bottom line. As Judson Martin, chief financial officer of Alliance Atlantis, explained, the company's main obligation was to its shareholders, and as drama production became more cost intensive and less profitable, it behooved the company to refocus its strategies: 'The high-cost, low-margin, prime-time drama business is not a good business now, and hasn't been for some time' (quoted in Blackwell 2003: B7). Consequently, with the exception of *CSI*, Alliance Atlantis has decided to move out of television production and concentrate on broadcasting and film distribution. If Alliance Atlantis, which for all intents and purposes already operates primarily out of Los Angeles and is quite heavily invested in American network television production, does not find quality television drama to be a marketable enterprise, it is highly doubtful that smaller private Canadian companies will continue to develop this sector without government incentive structures in place. As an industry leader, Alliance Atlantis's decision carries an ominous message for television producers in small-market countries: it is not a matter of whether you are good enough but of whether you are profitable enough.

In light of the Alliance Atlantis case and the ongoing crisis in government funding for domestic broadcasting production, it would be easy to conclude that the door is closing on opportunities to foster the development of television programs that speak to the diversity of cultural experiences and communities in Canada. However, it is too early for such pessimism and, as is always the case in this country, just when people begin to predict the end of domestic television, another task force or committee will arise to reassert the centrality of the medium to Canadian nationhood. Such was the case in June 2003 when the Standing Committee on Canadian Heritage presented its 872-page report on the state of Canadian broadcasting, *Our Cultural Sovereignty: The Second Century of Canadian Broadcasting.* What is most striking about this report is that its suggestions for the brave new world of broadcasting in the new millennium are substantially to return to the preliminary assumptions that established the parameters of national broadcasting in the early 1930s. After two years of consultation with members of the broadcasting industry, input from Canadian citizens from across the country, the submission of 200 briefs, and testimony from 350 witnesses, the committee's report put forth ninety-seven recommendations for strengthening the role of television as a cultural institution. Paramount among these was a renewed commitment to the representation of local communities within a globalizing world: 'Based on this experience, it is the Committee's conviction that the Canadian public wants a more transparent, democratic and vibrant broadcasting system – one that reflects local communities as well as the world around them' (Heritage Committee 2003). Many of the committee's recommendations parallel the findings from my fieldwork experience in Vancouver and my own suggestions for the future of domestic television. Indeed, the report goes one step further and calls for 'a local initiatives fund to promote community and local broadcasting – a fund that would give voice and power to local communities' (ibid.). Following are several of the key recommendations that correspond to the conclusions generated by my project:

(rec. 5.10) That the Canadian Television Fund be recognized by the government as an essential component of the Canadian broadcasting system. This recognition must include increased and stable long-term funding. The CRTC should be directed to oblige licensees, with the exception of small cable operators, to contribute to the CTF.

(rec. 6.1)   That the CBC be provided with increased and stable multi-year funding (3 to 5 years) so that it may adequately fulfill its mandate.

(rec. 6.3)   That the CBC deliver a strategic plan to Parliament detailing resource requirements for the delivery of local, regional, Canadian programming and new media initiatives.

(rec. 7.8)   That the Broadcasting Act be amended to recognize not-for-profit

broadcasters as an integral component of the Canadian broadcasting system.

(rec. 9.2)   That the government develop a community, local and regional
broadcasting policy in consultation with key broadcasting industry
stakeholders.

(rec. 9.8)   That the Department of Canadian Heritage create a Local Broadcasting Initiative Program (LBIP) to assist in the provision of radio
and television programming at the community, local and regional
levels.

(ibid.)[4]

As a rhetorical statement, *Cultural Sovereignty* is a compelling document. It demonstrates that, in a globalizing world, televisual representations of the nation – as an entity made up of local communities – still
matter to so-called ordinary citizens and cultural producers alike. Furthermore, it reinforces the feasibility of creating a broadcasting environment that fosters these cultural ends. The question that remains is
whether or not we are willing to make a political and economic commitment to this venture.

This book began with a proposition that the nations of the European
Union would have done well to examine more closely the Canadian
communications context as they developed their policy of 'television
without frontiers.' In this examination of the relationship among geography, community, and broadcasting, it is hoped that, at a minimum,
the case of the Vancouver television industry illustrates that the establishment of a global cultural market does not inevitably translate into
the development of a global cultural community. Broadcasting policies
that attempt to erase the specificities of locality, region, and nation
cannot create a continental cultural community where none has existed
before. This new form of continental 'official culture' promises to reproduce the forms of the generic, non-resonant television programming
that is coming to dominate the Canadian televisual landscape. To the
extent that nations around the world are experiencing the ramifications
of a borderless, electronic media community, we can see that the particularities of cultural-geographic experience are inherently universal
to some degree. Consequently, the global media environment should
provide an arena wherein the various spheres of collective identity can
be negotiated, rather than erased, in the realm of television culture.

Appendix: Main Characteristics of an International City

(Panayotis Soldatos in Smith and Cohn 1994: 655)

(Particular points of interest to Vancouver, not previously mentioned, are elaborated in bold below.)

A The city has a geographically international exposure.

B It is receiving, from abroad, foreign capital, manpower, and services and is engaged in various economic and trade transactions.

C It is hosting foreign and/or international institutions (MNCs, banks, consulates, trade commissions, and tourist offices). **Several international banks have offices in Vancouver, with the Hong Kong Bank of Canada being predominant. The Canadian Department of Finance has also recognized Vancouver as an international banking centre.**

D Its firms and other economic institutions are present abroad.

E It has direct transportation links with foreign countries.

F It is significantly engaged in social communications activities with foreign countries (tourism, student exchanges, trade missions) and has a strong telecommunications network. **All four universities in Vancouver sponsor student exchanges with countries in Southeast Asia, and the province also sponsors student exchanges at the high school level. The Vancouver Board of Trade is actively involved in international trade missions.**

G It has an outward-looking supporting services network (convention halls, office and research parks, and hotel facilities).

H Its mass media have an international presence and/or audience abroad.
 The *Vancouver Sun* and the *Hong Kong Standard* participate in a joint venture to produce and distribute the *Asia Pacific Report* quarterly. Both countries have news correspondents based in one another's regions and have audiences abroad. The Hong Kong–based newspaper *Sing Tao* has operated in Vancouver since 1983, and the Hong Kong–based *Ming Tao* began operations there in 1993. In 1992, developer Thomas Fung began Fairchild Television, a Chinese program broadcaster based in Vancouver with a national audience.

I It hosts, regularly, major international events (exhibitions, festivals, sports events).

J It is the locus of national, regional, or local institutions with an international scope, reputation, or impact (international relations' clubs, international local chamber of commerce, universities, and research centres).
 All four Vancouver universities have Asian research institutions as well as numerous other international research centres.

K Its public or private institutions have agreements of cooperation with foreign or international institutions (sister cities agreements, economic cooperation agreements).
 Vancouver has five sister cities and eight cities with which it holds a select relationship status. Los Angeles is the only non-Asian sister city with which Vancouver maintains formal and regular political, cultural, and economic accords.

L Its local government has the requisite administrative apparatus to conduct city paradiplomacy.

M Its population make-up has an international composition.
 While individuals from Hong Kong, China, and Taiwan form the largest immigration base in Vancouver, the city also has a large Indian population, and by 1996, 12 per cent of Vancouver's immigrants came from India.

Notes

Chapter 1 Local Cultures and Global Quests: Imagining the Nation in Canadian Broadcasting

1 According to Philip Resnick, there are two kinds of nations: 'those fostered from above, from the state, and those that have grown from below, from civil society. English Canada is the first kind of nation while Quebec is the second kind' (quoted in Laxer 1992: 202). Herein, the relatively homogeneous cultural and linguistic composition of Quebec has fostered an independent momentum in terms of protecting regional identity from the political threat posed by the dominant Anglo-Canadian culture. English Canada, on the other hand, is far more reliant on the federal system to unite the far-flung and ethnically diverse population into a cohesive nation in the sociological sense. These differences are readily apparent in the differences between French and English broadcasting. Quebec's more cohesive sense of itself as a cultural community has led to the development of a thriving television industry with audiences who are incredibly loyal to programs that foreground the sociocultural specificities of their locale. French domestic dramas consistently win their time slots over imported programs, and the province has a French star system akin to that of Hollywood and unheard of in English Canada. According to one commentator, 'In Quebec ... broadcasters show original homegrown drama not because they're required to, but because the viewers demand it!' (quoted in Dalfen 2003).

2 Regionalism finds its first explicit mention in the 1968 Broadcasting Act, with emphasis given to the division between anglophones and francophones. Here, two vague stipulations are mandated for the simultaneous

protection of national sovereignty and the representation of regional interests:

2(g) the national broadcasting service should
  (iii) be in English and French, serving the special needs of geographic regions, and actively contributing to the flow and exchange of cultural regional information and entertainment, and
  (iv) contribute to the development of national unity and provide for a continuing expression of Canadian identity.

The priorities given to the aspect of national identity over regional expression are clearly evidenced in the drastic budget reductions at the CBC in 1990. Regional television suffered a loss of $46 million under the restructuring of the corporation. At the same time, only $12 million was cut from the national network. The eventual result was the loss of all regional programming except for 'essential daily regional news and information programming' (CBC 1990). The process of restructuring preceded the passage of a new Broadcasting Act by a mere few months. The new act mandated that

3(m) the programming provided by the Corporation should
  (ii) reflect Canada and its regions to national audiences, while serving the special needs of those regions.

3 Given the diverse ethnic composition of the Canadian provinces outside of Quebec, it is somewhat problematic to refer to them as Anglo Canada or English Canada. In keeping with current academic reference, I use the term English Canada in discussing the phenomenon of *Anglo* regionalism. In this respect I am following Angus's (1997) example where English Canada is defined by the primary use of English in provincial education, commerce, and government.
4 Murdock (1989) concedes the acuity of the cultural studies argument that most political economy analyses are reductionist in their overemphasis on the simple base-superstructure relationship between culture and economics (and Marx's assertion that the economic determines in the *last instance*). However, he presents a strong argument for recognizing that, as far as media production is concerned, we need to acknowledge that the economic often determines in the 'first instance': 'the role played by economics in structuring the operations of the cultural field, in organizing the processes through which discourses are converted into media products ...

"determination" not as a fixed one-to-one relation between economic dynamics and cultural forms but as a process ... of setting limits ... and of encouraging and preferring certain options over others' (440).

5 Bennett (1992) argues that broadcasting policy is another area that has received inadequate consideration within cultural studies approaches to media analysis. He gives particular attention to the Canadian and Australian contexts, in which postcolonial settler societies that 'have been on the wrong end of colonial or imperialist relationships' have a greater need to bring culture into the sphere of policy (36). In this respect, analysing broadcasting policies within these parameters is a requisite to understanding the relationship between culture and power both within and between nations.

6 Expo 86 provides an interesting contrast to Expo 67. While both world fairs were centennials – the first Expo commemorated the country's hundredth year and the second celebrated Vancouver's hundredth year – Expo 86 was described as a thinly veiled 'American theme park' (Ames 1993). What is also interesting about Expo 67 is that it was one of the few moments of strongly expressed nationalism. Even the patriation of the constitution from Britain in 1982, which was expected to contribute to nationalist sentiment, was largely marked by Anglo-regional antagonisms and Quebec's refusal to ratify the new agreement.

7 The discussion in Bourdieu and Wacquant (1992) of the relationship between the habitus and the field is instructive for my discussions with the Vancouver producers. In this respect, they are all well versed in the 'rules of the game' in the field of international television production and the different strategies that must be designed to accommodate national and international broadcasters and distributors. Yet they also bring the cultural contexts of their individual habitus, whether regionally or nationally inflected, to the stories that are up for negotiation within the field.

8 Postmodernism, as a defining term for current cultural processes, is an area of contested debate within scholarly discourse. Throughout this work I use the concept as it has been incorporated in current literature about the instability of a national Canadian identity rather than as a descriptive label for an era that many scholars simply refer to as the latest stage of advanced capitalism.

9 As Feldthusen (1993) argues, these definitions of Canadian content are 'merely acts of faith,' to the extent that policy makers hope a program will 'reflect' Canadian culture because a Canadian produced it. More often than not, producers attempt to *de-Canadianize* their programs (i.e., make Canadian cities look like American cities, cast famous American actors,

etc.) so that they can sell them internationally. This is especially true in the case of international co-productions, which count as Canadian content if there is a 40 to 50 per cent Canadian investment in the project.

10 Brenda Longfellow's 1994 analysis of that most marginalized of all Canadian media forms – film – underlines that the concept of identity as a state of becoming rather than being has been a consistent theme in most contemporary Canadian feature films: 'the narrative is constructed as a search for an identity in the spaces between official Canadian culture and the experiences of transnationalism, immigration, and exile' (quoted in Magder 1995: 178).

11 Mark Starowicz argues that the problem with the dominant presence of American programming is that Canadians learn more about American social issues and problems than they do about domestic issues. In his opinion, the lack of Canadian drama programs denies the development of a public sphere within which to discuss Canadian society: 'When Canadian TV sets are dealing with race, it's almost always on programs like *Hill Street Blues*, or *Cosby*, or *Miami Vice*. But the 300,000 blacks in Toronto are from Caribbean cultures, and have little in common with American blacks ... The Canadian dynamics, in fact, the entire dramatis personae, are different. We do have racism, we are debating how to adjust our school system ... We need reality on our televisions. But our problems and the solutions are not those we are watching on our screens' (quoted in Audley 1994: 339–40).

12 Many works dealing with the terms 'localization' and 'globalization' fail to ever define these terms (see, for example, the range of articles in Nederveen Pieterse and Parekh 1995). In the larger literature of globalization, 'local' can be defined as anything from a city to a neighbourhood to a clan or a subculture. 'Local' sometimes seems equated with the nation, which is interesting given that this site is seen as the weak link under globalizing forces. Region is another problematic location; it can be a territory within a nation or a combination of nations (or ethnic groups) united by geolinguistic or political-economic interests. Some clarification is needed here, as these terms have long-standing definitions in the Canadian context. Therefore, for the purposes of this study, 'local' is used in relation to the city (Vancouver), 'region' is used within the customary Canadian terminology (here it is the West) except when referring to Vancouver's strategic moves towards 'city-state' status, which distances it from other locations within the province (thereby creating a new sense of 'region').

Chapter 2 Constructing the Global City: Contextualizing
'Hollywood North'

1 Not all of these programs remain in production in Vancouver. *Sliders* and
Strange Luck were both cancelled by Fox after their first seasons, and *The
X-Files* moved to Los Angeles in 1998, partially in response to lead actor
David Duchovny's ongoing complaints about Vancouver's weather. None-
theless, seventeen American television series continued to call Vancouver
their permanent production home in 2002.

2 Not all American and other foreign producers go out of their way to erase
Vancouver's identifying characteristics. Joel Schumacher, the director of
Cousins, was apparently unconcerned when Canadian flags would appear
in shots or when the B.C. rapid transit Sky Train would go by in the
background. Schumacher felt he was telling a story that was not place
specific and that minor Canadian references would not prove to be a
detriment to the movie (author interview with a locations manager, 8 July
1997). Similarly, Jackie Chan's *Rumble in the Bronx*, which as the title implies is set in New York, was not overly cautious about excluding Canadian landmarks or even the ocean and mountain backgrounds from
several shots. As one locations manager explained: 'That show was very
chaotic. The way that Hong Kong filmmakers make their movies is very
quick and fast ... and they shoot double the amount of film that the Americans shoot. Their setups are quick – they just run and do it, do it, do it.
They could've shot without showing the mountains but by then they were
just like, "Ah, it doesn't matter anymore." That was part of the cheesiness
that everyone loved' (interview with the author, 27 June 1997).

3 As Stephen Miller (1994) documents, there were only three feature films,
one television movie, and one series produced in Vancouver in 1978. Of
these, one of the features was Canadian and the television series was one
of the CBC's most successful programs, *The Beachcombers*, which is discussed in more detail in chapter 3.

4 Perhaps the most problematic example of the commodification of culture
in *The Shooting Gallery* is a photograph of a group of First Nations people
dressed in traditional clothes and performing in a ceremonial dance,
accompanied by text reading, 'The tribes with legends and totems. Proud
people willing to share their heritage with you.'

5 Chris Carter's reference to his series as 'product' is an interesting and
prevalent description of television as a commodity form. Several of the
independent producers also referred to their work as product, particularly

when discussing audiences and the American and global market for film and television.

6 As one locations manager noted, 'The minute you start yelling "Bring the film industry home," it's too late. It's like Detroit declaring, "Bring the car industry home"' (interview with the author, 27 June 1997). Members of the B.C. Film Commission described a visit from Jack Valenti in 1996 where, upon seeing the rapid development of both the industry and the commission, he appeared nervous at the city's success: 'He was kind of, "Looks good. Looks a little bit too good"' (interview with the author, 13 August 1997).

7 Both the municipal and the provincial governments give high priority and attention to the locations and service industry. Never was this more evident than in the summer of 1997 when a garbage collectors' strike coincided with a strike by actors on the series *Police Academy* who were demanding pay equity with their American counterparts. While health department officials declared an impending epidemic, the government refused to negotiate with the garbage collectors or order them back to work as an essential service. The actors, however, were immediately declared an essential service and ordered back to work in defiance of their union's objectives.

8 B.C. Pavilion Corporation, the Crown corporation that owns The Bridge Studios, announced in 2002 that it would sell the studio and several of its other properties to private interests over a two-year transition period. The argument was proffered that the Vancouver television and film industry had matured to the extent that this form of provincial government support was no longer vital to the industry's future development. Private ownership of The Bridge Studios has raised concern among domestic producers who depended on revenues generated from the facility (Edwards 2002).

9 Discussions and proclamations of Vancouver's status as a 'world-class' city abound in the city's news media. This particular quotation comes from an article that compiles a list of the factors that highlight the city's global stature. The article is titled 'WC City: Artists! Writers! Moguls! Eco-Heroes! Accidents Waiting to Happen! Vancouver's Claims to Global Fame' (Glave and Sutherland 1995).

10 Vancouver's Downtown Eastside corridor is the poorest neighbourhood in the city. As a result of increasing poverty and marginalization, the rates of crime, transience, and drug use are among the highest in the country. Intravenous drug use has become so prevalent that Vancouver's Downtown Eastside alone now has the highest rate of HIV infection in the Western hemisphere, according to the World Health Organization.

11 It is estimated that $1 billion entered Canada annually through Hong Kong immigration during the past decade (Cernetig 1997: C6).

12 The superfund that this individual is referring to is the Canadian Television Fund (CTF), which is addressed in greater detail in chapter 3.

13 Indian director Subhash Ghai stands in contrast to Danny Hui. One of Bollywood's biggest directors, Ghai chose Vancouver as one of the two primary locations for his movie *Abroad* in 1996. The movie specifically deals with the stories of Indians who have left their country for Canada. Although Ghai once said he would never do a film in another country because his 'characters don't belong there,' he was impressed by Vancouver and even implied that he might stage the movie's premiere there: 'It's been very unfortunate that I've been missing this beautiful city most of my life. Vancouver has a very different feel from any other city I've visited, and I think a better quality of life ... If we shoot here we should show it here; I think the Indian community would like that' (quoted in Birnie 1996: E3). It is important to note that there is a sizeable and prominent South Asian community in Vancouver. This fact may be obscured by the emphasis on the Southeast Asian, and particularly Hong Kong, diaspora in this book. This emphasis is not intended to downplay the number and diversity of other ethnic communities in the province. Rather, the foregrounding of Southeast Asia follows from the dominant public dialogues and government economic and cultural strategies at play during the time of my study. One issue that is particularly worth mentioning is the extent to which second- and third-generation Indian youth are attempting to enter into the prolific Bombay – now Mumbai – film community ('Bollywood') as an alternative to the more exclusionary Hollywood system. There has been a proliferation of dance and music schools in the province that aim to train young people to perform in Indian musical films. This cultural phenomenon would make a fascinating study in itself.

14 Wayne Sterloff, president of B.C. Film (a provincial funding organization not to be confused with the B.C. Film Commission), has long been vocal in protesting the regional inequity in the federal government's allocation of financial resources for television and film production. He has repeatedly pointed out that the government quickly invested in the development of production companies and indigenous production when Ontario was overwhelmed by the American locations industry but has consistently refused to do the same in British Columbia: 'You go to the federal government and you say "God, we're part of the country. Don't you think this treatment is unfair to our filmmakers?" And they say "No, B.C. is all about servicing U.S. productions. We don't have to give them anything." And

it's not just the federal government, it's the CFTPA [Canadian Film and Television Production Association] as well. It's completely unfair' (quoted in Caddell 1996: 7).

15 One CEO of a large private broadcasting company also pointed out that western producers have always had a 'frontier mentality' in developing cooperative strategies to accommodate the lack of support from central-Canadian funding programs and government agencies (interview with the author, 27 July 1997). Several producers I spoke with described how members of the local production community will volunteer their time and equipment or reduce their fees during down time in the service industry, to help friends working on Canadian television stories and movies. As for the aforementioned production house, Pacific Motion Pictures (PMP), recent changes in ownership may actually indicate a renewed change of focus from the local to the global production arena. Founded in 1989, PMP grew within a decade to become one of the largest independent television and movie production companies in Canada, with production budgets totalling over $300 million. In 1998, PMP was bought by the Canadian post-production house Rainmaker Entertainment Group but was sold back to its initial owners nine months later as part of an overall streamlining plan. Within a year, PMP was sold to Sextant Entertainment Group Inc., a production and distribution company that explicitly emphasizes its concentration in 'international markets and fiscal responsibility' through 'co-productions and co-financing' (Sextant 2000). Indeed, one of the most attractive features of PMP for Sextant was not the role it played in the domestic production community but the fact that the company had 'established relationships with Hollywood decision makers that are unparalleled in this part of the world' (Sextant executive vice-president Michelle Gahagan quoted in Business Editors 2000). Although it should not be presumed that Sextant's global outlook precludes any possibility for investment in domestic production, it is worth noting that the company, as part of a larger holding, was forced to shuffle its board of directors to satisfy foreign ownership restrictions when it applied to the CRTC for a licence to broadcast The Hallmark Channel [Canada] (CRTC 2002).

16 *The Littlest Hobo* was a long-running Canadian series about a German shepherd dog that travelled across the country helping people out of difficult situations. It could be described as a low-budget *Lassie*. *Exotica* is one of the more accessible movies by writer/director Atom Egoyan. While Egoyan's films are generally highly regarded and have become recognized internationally, they are often included in the general description of Canadian films as being too dark or artsy.

**Chapter 3 The Politics of 'Space' and 'Place': Mandating 'National'
Identity in Canadian Media Policy**

1 In his book *When Television Was Young: Primetime Canada 1952–1967*, Paul
Rutherford (1990) provides an excellent overview of the history and context of the 'golden age' of Canadian television. The book provides a comprehensive analysis of the development and content of television dramas
aired from the introduction of television to the implementation of the 1968
Broadcasting Act.

2 The fact that a series can be considered a 'hit' with an audience of 1 million viewers underlines the size of the potential audience in Canada in
comparison to the United States where one ratings point is equivalent to
approximately 980,000 households (Levin 1998: 9B). Audience considerations are examined further in chapter 4.

3 *The Beachcombers* was incredibly popular with international audiences, the
Germans in particular. Tourism from Europe increased rapidly during the
run of the series. This phenomenon has occurred to an even greater extent
with Japanese tourism to Prince Edward Island in response to the *Anne of
Green Gables* book and television series. The orphan Anne has become a
folk hero in Japan, and thousands of tourists flock to P.E.I. annually to
visit 'Anne's' house. Recently, a new ritual has developed, with several
Japanese couples wishing to renew their marriage vows at the farmhouse
where author Lucy Maud Montgomery was married (Mulligan 1998: 13:8).

4 Unlike its television counterpart, CBC radio has a large and loyal following across Canada. The success of CBC radio is usually attributed to the
fact that it is a non-commercial medium and produces many of its programs within the regions, thus creating a strong sense of interregional
connection among CBC radio listeners. The fact that the corporation's
television arm developed according to a centralized, private-public model
is seen as the central obstacle to its ability to achieve the same resonance
with Canadians.

5 According to Sauvageau, the reluctance to allow regional production
centres to predominate in the system was primarily a result of network
politics – Toronto had become accustomed to its role as the central decision-making office for English-Canadian programming and had no intention of relinquishing that power (interview with the author, 26 October
1993).

6 The cancelling of *The Beachcombers* remains a contentious point to this day.
The fact that Toronto cancelled the series while it was still generating
significant audience numbers is seen by many producers I spoke with as

proof of network disdain for regional television productions. There appeared to be a prevalent attitude that Toronto had merely been waiting for the opportunity to end the show and found that rationale under the 'restructuring' strategy of the CBC in the early 1990s. However, there was one program on CBC television that all regional managers indicated as a similar success because of, rather than in spite of, its regional emphasis: *On the Road Again*. Although this program is produced out of Toronto, it provides a cross-country glimpse of out-of-the way Canadian towns, and is consequently often compared to programs on CBC radio. As one regional manager (RM) describes the show, then in its fifteenth year,

RM: It started as a farm show – you know – looking at hog reports and all that, and gradually developed into a lifestyle program and then became a real quirky look at rural community life, which nobody was looking at in a way other than news. The only time you go to Hagersville is when there's a tire fire, or a wheat post when there's a drought – there's always a disaster or something. The idea of 'Why would anyone go there? Who really lives there?' Well, most of the population. It was just an idea whose time had come. I learned so many things about rural Canada, working on that show. It was quirky and funny, and some of the people we profiled, had they lived in the city, they would've been institutionalized. Completely nuts, but because they lived in the country it was okay, they could spread out. The hermit who lives in a badger hole in Upper Arm, Saskatchewan, is a great story for us, but in the city he'd be on a park bench with a shopping cart. It was a clever way of going about tapping into parts of this country and certain stories that people don't know about and, in fact, don't know they want to know about. And it's been extremely popular with the critics as well as the viewers. That's the happiest marriage I think I've found in terms of the mandate, the viewership, everything altogether and the critics on board. No one ever says anything bad about *On the Road Again*. It really works for the CBC, and no other network would do something like that. That always reminded me of CBC radio – a television version of *Morningside* [Canada's longest-running and most popular national radio program, now discontinued]. That's part of what we have to do.

(interview with the author, 30 July 1997)

7 One independent producer, who also underlined the ways that the Atlantic provinces have maintained a distinct 'cultural label' through their accents and storytelling tradition, provided a different perspective on the

distinctiveness of West Coast culture from his vantage of moving to Vancouver from Montreal. In this person's opinion, there was a very definite way of speaking and an accent to West Coaster's English that they played down to get work on American television and movie productions: 'What I noticed was that the actors had affected a sort of broadcasting English so that it wasn't the kind of "oots" or "owts" or "ahts." It was very subtle for the most part, but clearly, with experience, you could tell that they had practised so that they would seem flawless on American television shows ... then those actors go on to act in Canadian films, like ours for example, and they continue to wash out that accent' (interview with the author, 22 July 1997).

8 This problem was exacerbated in 1999 when the CRTC removed requirements that specified the types of drama programming to be produced and aired and instead formulated the general term 'priority programming,' which was supposed to be broadcast eight hours a week in the 'peak-viewing period (7:00 p.m. to 11:00 p.m.).' The term encompasses both information and general entertainment programming. As a result, programs that are cheaper to produce, such as reality programming, become a priority for private broadcasters. Industry figures indicate that this change in the regulations has led to a decrease in the number of Canadian drama series produced from twelve in 1999–2000 to five in 2002–3 (Adams 2003). Readers will notice that I do not place the same degree of emphasis on private broadcasters, such as CTV and CanWest Global, as I do on community television and the CBC throughout this book. This is because of the scheduling and production practices of the private broadcasters. They are not required to produce dramatic series in-house but instead form agreements with independent producers through purchasing, licensing, and broadcast schedule agreements. And, as indicated, they attempt to limit even the purchase of domestic drama to the bare minimum requirements. Consequently, it is these independent producers who are the focus of sustained consideration throughout this work.

9 This was exemplified in the 1996 bidding war for the first new television licence in Vancouver in more than twenty years. Baton Broadcasting Corporation's (BBC) winning bid to open Vancouver Television (CIVT) was predicated on a promise to commit to several hours of local weekly drama and variety programming that would air both regionally and nationally. The sentiment among the independent production community at the time was that Baton would fulfil the necessary minimum of its contract during the first two-year review period and then fall back on importing American programming once it had secured its first five-year

licence. During the first year, the producers' concerns appeared justified – at that point, Baton had developed only one prime-time drama and a few variety/talk shows.

10 In 1997, Alliance and Atlantis each spent more than $120 million on television drama production, with the majority invested in Ontario (Independent Production 1997: 23). More interesting is the fact that both companies sought to increase their presence in the United States and began to develop most of their projects out of Los Angeles (independent producer, interview with the author, 22 July 1997). Operating now as Alliance Atlantis Communications Inc., the company is a major player in both the continental and the global television production industries.

11 The CBC eventually picked up *These Arms of Mine* for the 2000–1 network prime-time season. The producers of the series promoted the program for its depictions of everyday life in urban Vancouver: '[E]xperience a world rarely seen on television – the one many of us actually live in.' Despite the fact that the series developed a loyal fan base and won a Gemini award, the CBC cancelled it in March 2001.

12 Susan Morgan, the head of CBC dramatic series, emphasized that the network was very much in control of the development process of *Da Vinci's Inquest*. Without providing specific details, she stated that, 'Creatively we are typically very involved and we certainly were with this particular contract. [Scripts were developed and submitted, followed by meetings between the network and the show's creators, with critical feedback from the CBC.] Much talking, arguing, agreeing and laughing ensued, followed by the writers undertaking a second draft, and so on' (quoted in The Gatekeepers 1997: 33).

13 Volunteers at the Vancouver East community television station successfully negotiated an agreement with Rogers in which the cable company agreed to donate the studio's existing production equipment to the staff producers and to continue to pay their operating expenses until January 1997. At that point, the former Vancouver East community station officially became an independent, non-profit organization called Independent Community Television Co-operative (ICTV). ICTV continues to produce the series *East Side Story* and is active in grass-roots community movements within the neighbourhood.

14 Not long after I completed this project, Shaw Communications Inc. took over Rogers's cable programming and service territory in British Columbia. Shaw continued Rogers's practice of using the community channel as a marketing outlet for its products and services.

Chapter 4 Going Global: The Disappearing Domestic Audience

1 As the members of the European Union negotiated cultural policy goals in *Television without Frontiers*, they sought to avoid programs that would hide or erase national cultural differences by appealing to a formulaic genre that could be defined as uniformly European in character. The term 'Euro-pudding' came to define this hodge-podge type of production that would attempt to characterize cultural elements of all the nations and thereby resonate with none.

2 *Degrassi High*, an internationally acclaimed Canadian youth series, faced similar problems with PBS. Although PBS bought the series, several of the more realistic or controversial themes were edited or removed from selected episodes. A notable example was an episode in which one of the lead characters was having an abortion. At the end of the episode, a right-to-life protestor pushes a 'fetus doll' into the young girl's face. This was edited out of the PBS broadcast despite the fact that the image would become a recurring theme in future episodes. As M.J. Miller (1996: 336) notes, there is a perception among Canadian producers that 'As a country we are a lot more open or we can talk more honestly to our audience.'

3 The creators of the British adult-animation series *Bob and Margaret* met with similar responses from U.S. broadcasters who wanted to make the program more accessible to Americans by changing several key creative aspects of the series. According to the creator of the series:

> I find there's lots of Americans that will say, 'Well, I like it, but the American public won't' ... They'll always talk as if everyone else is stupid, and they're the only ones that can appreciate something differ-ent ... As we talked to them about the episodes, we got the feeling that they kept wanting more and more American characters involved. It just started to sound ridiculous, like the whole of London was occupied with Americans ... They were talking about making Bob and Margaret live in Minnesota! ... so we just panicked, really.
>
> (quoted in Doherty 1998: B4)

   In the end, the British creators formed a co-production agreement with the Canadian animation company Nelvana, which was more than willing to leave the initial concept intact.

4 The 'costumes' that are being referred to are the black barristers' and solicitors' robes that Canadian lawyers are required to wear when appear-

ing at various levels of the Canadian court system. It is a part of British judiciary protocol and remains a part of the Canadian system.

5 The CBC relies on advertising for 30 per cent of its revenue, with the remainder provided through federal appropriations. The corporation must continually take into account advertisers' images of the *desired* audience in its production decisions, as it is uncertain how much funding will be provided by the government from year to year.

6 In *East of 'Dallas,'* Silj similarly found that *Dallas* lost Peruvian audiences to a popular locally produced comedy program.

7 Between December 1996 and May 1997 there were several high-profile grass-roots campaigns organized to protest continuing funding cuts to the CBC and demand multi-year stable funding for the public broadcaster. All of these were planned to coincide with the forthcoming federal budget and preparations for the next federal election. The 'Keep the Promise' campaign was organized by a veteran lobby group,' The Friends of Canadian Broadcasting. 'Keep the Promise' included the organizing of public town hall meetings, petitions, and the distribution of lawn signs to residences within selected federal ridings. The lawn signs read: 'The CBC Promise. Keep it.' The other two major campaigns were organized entirely by non-partisan Canadian residents. Of these, the Cavalcade of Concerned Citizens' CBC Unity Train and the Ours to Keep coalition were the most visible. Ours to Keep was founded by a lawyer in Ontario, and the coalition soon grew to include chapters across the country. This group's mandate was to collect 1 million signatures calling for greater government support of the CBC on a petition that would be discussed at a national press conference, attended by all chapter leaders, in Toronto in May 1997. Cavalcade's Unity Train, mentioned in this chapter, was a potently symbolic effort in which the group's members were able to negotiate special rates with Via Rail and [the now defunct] Canadian Airlines to pick up interested Canadians from Vancouver to Halifax and several points north and south with plans to congregate in a protest rally on Parliament Hill in Ottawa on 2 May 1997. While all three coalitions emphasized the important role that the CBC played in fostering a sense of national unity, Cavalcade and Ours to Keep also brought the issues of regional representation and the recent losses of regional programming to the forefront of their campaigns. As one public statement from Cavalcade states, 'We believe the budgetary cuts to the CBC are dismantling the Corporation's ability to maintain its regional voices. Without vigorous and vibrant regional voices there will be no need for the CBC' (Coordinator's Communique 1997). Members of these two organizations even donated their own money to

organize their regional chapters and campaigns. The heads of the Saskatchewan chapter of Ours to Keep underlined the depth of national response to the downsizing of the CBC in their statement that the federal government had 'received more mail and phone calls on this issue than any other since taking office' (Baker and Boyd 1997).

Chapter 5 Marginal Amusements: Television Comedy and the Salience of Place in the Canadian Sensibility

1 The success of out-of-house production through the development of track-record production companies such as Salter Street Films Ltd underscores the viability of creating quality regional domestic programming without relying on more insular CBC in-house production teams. Salter Street is unique as an independent company, however, in that its executives are committed to developing Canadian stories despite their interest in international sales. The fact that these producers are able to develop regionally inflected programs is largely the result of the strength of the CBC's current interest in co-producing and airing their projects.

2 Pevere and Dymond (1996) provide an excellent overview of the numerous failed Canadian sitcoms from the 1960s to the 1990s. Examples of the derivative American formula range from *The Trouble with Tracey* (a 1970s version of *I Love Lucy*) to *Snow Job* (a 1980s version of *Three's Company* set in a ski resort). As an interesting counterpoint, most Canadian sketch comedies have enjoyed high ratings, and some, such as *The Royal Canadian Air Farce*, have survived the transition from radio to television – resulting in a thirty-year run in national broadcasting.

3 Over the last decade, much has been written about the significant Canadian presence in American sitcom writing teams, from the days of *The Smothers Brothers* to *The Simpsons* and *Seinfeld*. *Saturday Night Live*'s Canadian executive producer, Lorne Michaels, is said to have intentionally 'loaded' his creative staff with Canadian writers because they were 'first-rate mimics, and they were unparalleled at the art of parody' (Pevere and Dymond 1996: 195).

4 The use of Maritimes vernacular – such as the terms 'buddy' and 'spoondalicks'– is a defining feature of the troupe's comedy. No attempts are made to erase the regional idiom, and some of the terms have seeped into the larger national vocabulary.

5 *CODCO* was, at times, so regionally specific that many of the jokes did not translate across regional boundaries. Overall, however, the program sustained a national audience.

6 The episodes selected for consideration aired during the 1996–7 television season. The original air dates are provided for any repeat broadcasts during this period.

7 The troupe's comedic interventions into Canadian politics have led many in the national media to refer to *22 Minutes* as the country's 'unofficial opposition' party in Parliament (e.g., Johnson 1996).

8 Regardless of socio-economic background or political affiliation, national polls indicate that most Canadians favour continued, if not increased, federal support for public education and national health care.

9 'Intersubjectivity' is the term used to describe those moments of shared understanding or connotation that affirm membership in a cultural community.

10 It was reported that, when the sketch comedy *The Royal Canadian Air Farce* was sold to border American PBS stations in 1997, 'all Canadian political references not known across the border would be stripped' from the selected episodes. This is particularly interesting given that national political satire is the dominant feature of the series. Nevertheless, it was said that the episodes would 'still be topical and show their Canadianness' (Air Farce Wings Southward 1997: C6).

Chapter 6 Regimes of Community in 'Hollywood North': Reproducing Local and Global Cultures in a Televisual World

1 Barnett astutely criticizes the emphasis on Foucault's conception of disciplinary practices as the primary focus of most analyses of cultural policy in media studies. He rightly concludes that Foucault's later work on governance is more relevant to the practice of policy formation and implementation. The micro-focus on discipline is inadequate to the task of showing how policy translates into power from a distance and it neglects the agency of those regulated to resist the imposition of discursive boundaries.

2 It is worth noting the political context in which the cuts to the CTF took place. Finance Minister John Manley and Heritage Minister Sheila Copps were competing for the leadership of the Liberal party, and members of the production community believed that they were 'playing politics with the issue' of broadcast funding (Thorne 2003). There is also significance to their respective portfolios – as former industry minister, Manley has a very different perspective on television from Copps. The fissures between their respective mandates is illustrative of the industry-culture divisions in television as an institutional apparatus.

3 *This Hour Has 22 Minutes* survived the closure of Salter Street Films as 'it is not produced on Salter Street's premises' (Blackwell 2003).
4 The committee's report also called for a return to a single Department of Communication to alleviate the tensions between industrial and cultural goals caused by the splitting of jurisdiction over broadcasting between the Departments of Industry and Heritage.

References

Abbas, A. 1997. *Hong Kong: Culture and the Politics of Disappearance*. Minneapolis: University of Minneapolis Press.

Abu-Laban, Y. 1997. Ethnic Politics in a Globalizing Metropolis: The Case of Vancouver. In T.L. Thomas, ed., *The Politics of the City: A Canadian Perspective*, 77–95. Toronto: ITP Nelson.

Adams, J. 2003. Group Calls for CRTC to Tighten TV Rules. *Globe and Mail*. 18 March: http://www.globeandmail.com/ Retrieved 4 May 2003.

Adams, J., and M. Posner. 2003. Federal Budget: Film Tax Breaks Rise Despite U.S. Anger. *Globe and Mail*, 19 February: http://globeandmail.com/ Retrieved 4 May 2003.

Adilman, S. 1993. A Hilarious Hymn to Canada. *Toronto Star*, 8 December: D2.

Air Farce Wings Southward. 1997. *Vancouver Sun*, 31 May: C6.

Alvarado, M. 1996. Selling Television. In A. Moran, ed., *Film Policy: International, National and Regional Perspectives*, 62–71. London: Routledge.

Ames, M. 1993. The Canadianization of an American Fair: The Case of Expo 86. In D.H. Flaherty and F.E. Manning, eds, *The Beaver Bites Back? American Popular Culture in Canada*, 237–46. Montreal and Kingston: McGill-Queen's University Press.

Anderson, B. 1991. *Imagined Communities*. London: Verso.

Ang, I. 1991. *Desperately Seeking the Audience*. London: Routledge.

Angus, I. 1997. *A Border Within: National Identity, Cultural Plurality, and Wilderness*. Montreal and Kingston: McGill-Queen's University Press.

Appadurai, A. 1996. *Modernity at Large*. Minneapolis: University of Minnesota Press.

Applebaum, L., and J. Hébert. 1982. *Report of the Federal Cultural Policy Review Committee*. Ottawa: Minister of Supply and Services Canada.

Armstrong, M.E. 1996. TIFF Buyers Focus on Ancillary Markets. *Playback*, 9 September 9:3.

Attallah, P. 1992. Richard Collins and the Debate on Culture and Polity. *Canadian Journal of Communication* 17: 221–36.

– 1996. Canadian Television Exports: Into the Mainstream. In J. Sinclair, E. Jacka, and S. Cunningham, eds, *New Patterns in Global Television: Peripheral Vision*, 161–91. New York: Oxford University Press.

Audley, P. 1994. Cultural Industries Policy: Objectives, Formulation and Evaluation. *Canadian Journal of Communication* 19: 317–52.

Baker, B., and M. Boyd. 1997. *Press Notes: CBC – Ours to Keep – Saskatchewan Committee.* 19 April: http://www.lights.com/~scott/apr19.html. Retrieved 11 February 2003.

Barman, J. 1991. *The West beyond the West: A History of British Columbia.* Toronto: University of Toronto Press.

Barnes, T., D. Edgington, K. Denike, and T. McGee. 1992. Vancouver and the Pacific Rim. In G. Wynn and T. Oke, eds, *Vancouver and Its Regions*, 171–99. Vancouver: UBC Press.

Barnett, C. 1999. Culture, Government and Spatiality: Reassessing the 'Foucault Effect' in Cultural-Policy Studies. *International Journal of Cultural Studies* 2 (3): 369–97.

Baudrillard, J. 1983. *Simulations.* New York: Semiotext(e).

Bawden, J. 1994. Canuck Yucks. *Toronto Star*, 8 October: SW5.

– 1998. Mercer Has Space for Rant. *Toronto Star*, 26 April: E1.

B.C. Film Commission. 1997. *Quick Facts about the B.C. Film Commission.* Vancouver: B.C. Film Commission.

Beginnings. 1996. *Reel West*, March/April: 31.

Bennett, T. 1992. Putting Policy into Cultural Studies. In L. Grossberg, C. Nelson, and P. Treichler, eds, *Cultural Studies*, 23–37. New York: Routledge.

Beynon, H., and R. Hudson. 1993. Place and Space in Contemporary Europe: Some Lessons and Reflections. *Antipode* 25: 177–90.

Bhabha, H. 1994. *The Location of Culture.* New York: Routledge.

Bhabha, H., ed. 1990. *Nation and Narration.* New York: Routledge.

Bird, R., ed. 1988. *Documents of Canadian Broadcasting.* Ottawa: Carleton University Press.

Birnie, P. 1996. Bollywood B.C. *Vancouver Sun*, 3 August: E3, E8.

Black, E. 1996. British Columbia: 'The Spoilt Child of Confederation.' In R.K. Carty, ed., *Politics, Policy, and Government in British Columbia*, 32–44. Vancouver: UBC Press.

Blackwell, R. 2003. Alliance Move Harsh Reality Show. *Globe and Mail*, 17 December: B7.

Bourdieu, P., and L. Wacquant. 1992. *An Invitation to Reflexive Sociology.* Chicago: University of Chicago Press.

Bramham, D. 1997. Hong Kong and Us. *Vancouver Sun*, 3 May: C1-C2.

Brioux, B. 1998. *Da Vinci's* Double. *TV Times*, 27 November: 5.

Business Editors. 2000. Sextant Entertainment Announces Agreement Finalized. *Business Wire*, 8 March.

Butler, J. 1994. *Television: Critical Methods and Applications*. Belmont, Calif.: Wadsworth.

Caddell, I. 1996. States of the Art. *Reel West*, August/September: 7–9.

– 1997. Sunrise Forever. *Reel West*, January/February: 8, 10.

Canada NewsWire. 2003. Dying a Dramatic Death? Canadian Culture Is. http://www.newswire.ca/releases/May2003/13/c0988.html. Retrieved 5 July 2003.

Cantor, M. 1971. *The Hollywood TV Producer: His Work and Audience*. New York: Basic Books.

Caron, A., and P. Belanger. 1993. A Reception Study of American Television Products in Québec. In R. de la Garde, W. Gilsdorf, and I. Wechelsmann, eds, *Small Nations, Big Neighbour: Denmark and Québec/Canada Compare Notes on American Popular Culture*, 133–52. London: John Libbey and Company.

CBC. 1990. News Release. 5 December. Ottawa: Canadian Broadcasting Corporation.

– 1996. *A Vision for the CBC*. 30 January. Ottawa: Canadian Broadcasting Corporation.

CBC Newsworld. 1999. Special on CBC. First aired 17 January.

CBC Research. 1991. *How People Use Television: A Review of TV Viewing Habits*. Ottawa: Canadian Broadcasting Corporation.

Cernetig, M. 1997. Canada Makes China Connection. *Globe and Mail*, 1 July: C6.

CFTPA (Canadian Film and Television Production Association). 2003. Producers Accept Manley and Copps' CTF Offer. 5 June: http://www.cftpa.ca/newsroom/press/06_05_03.html. Retrieved 5 July 2003.

Chow, W. 1997. B.C. Talent Sought for Asian Movies. *Vancouver Sun*, 3 July: D1, D12.

Collins, R. 1990. *Culture, Communication, and National Identity: The Case of Canadian Television*. Toronto: University of Toronto Press.

– 1994. Trading in Culture: The Role of Language. *Canadian Journal of Communication* 19: 377–99.

Come Again, Won't You. 1996. *Playback*, 1 July: 12.

Coombe, R. 1991. Encountering the Postmodern: New Directions in Cultural Anthropology. *Canadian Review of Sociology and Anthropology* 28: 188–205.

Coordinator's Communique. 1997. *4: CBC Unity Train to Roll!* 10 March: http://www.cbucc.org/communique/cc97004.htm. Retrieved 11 February 2003.

The Creative Land: Out on the Edge. 1994. *Maclean's*, 1 July: 38–40.

Creese, G., and L. Peterson. 1996. Making the News: Racializing Chinese Canadians. *Studies in Political Economy* 51: 117–45.

CRTC. 1997a. *Public Notice 1997-25.* 11 March. Ottawa: Canadian Radio-television and Telecommunications Commission.

– 1997b. Decision 97-575. 2 October. Ottawa: Canadian Radio-television and Telecommunications Commission.

– 2002. *Broadcasting Decision CRTC 2002–350.* 6 November. Ottawa: Canadian Radio-television and Telecommunications Commission.

Dalfen, C. 2003. A Goal Worth Fighting For: Canadian Drama on Canadian Television. Speech presented to 24th Banff Television Festival, 9 June.

de Certeau, M. 1984. *The Practice of Everyday Life.* Berkeley: University of California Press.

de la Garde, R. 1993. Dare We Compare? In R. de la Garde, W. Gilsdorf, and I. Wechelsmann, eds, *Small Nations, Big Neighbour: Denmark and Québec/Canada Compare Notes on American Popular Culture*, 25–64. London: John Libbey and Company.

Désaulniers, J.P. 1987. What Does Canada Want? *Media,Culture and Society* 9: 149–57.

Doherty, M. 1998. No Nudity or Violence, Unless It's Essential. *National Post*, 2 December: B4.

Edwards, I. 1996a. Crescent Moves out of Service Production. *Playback*, 29 July: 6.

– 1996b. Studios Boom East and West. *Playback*, 12 August: 22.

– 1996c. U.S. Series Set Sites on Super Natural Vancouver. *Canada on Location*, Spring: 7–10.

– 1997a. B.C. Scene. *Playback*, 13 January: 21–2.

– 1997b. B.C. Scene. *Playback*, 30 June: 12.

– 2002. The Bridge Studios for Sale. *Playback*, 22 July: 1.

Elliott, P. 1972. *The Making of a Television Series: A Case Study in the Sociology of Culture.* London: Constable.

Ellis, D. 1979. *The Evolution of the Canadian Broadcasting System: Objectives and Realities, 1928–1968.* Ottawa: Government of Canada, Department of Communications.

Espinosa, T. 1982. Text-building in a Hollywood Television Series: An Ethnographic Study. PhD diss., Stanford University.

Featherstone, M., ed. 1990. *Global Culture: Nationalism, Globalization and Modernity.* London: Sage.

Feldthusen, B. 1993. Awakening from the National Broadcasting Dream. In D.H. Flaherty and F.E. Manning, eds, *The Beaver Bites Back? American Popu-*

lar Culture in Canada, 42–74. Montreal and Kingston: McGill-Queen's University Press.

Ferguson, W. 1997. *Why I Hate Canadians*. Vancouver: Douglas and McIntyre.

Fiske, J. 1987. *Television Culture*. London: Methuen.

Flaherty, D.H., and F.E. Manning. 1993. Preface. In D.H. Flaherty and F.E. Manning, eds, *The Beaver Bites Back? American Popular Culture in Canada*, xi–xv. Montreal and Kingston: McGill-Queen's University Press.

Foucault, M. 1972. *The Archaeology of Knowledge and the Discourse on Language*. New York: Pantheon Books.

– 1977. *Power/Knowledge: Selected Interviews: 1972–1977*. New York: Pantheon Books.

Fox, F. 1983. *Building for the Future: Towards a Distinctive CBC*. Ottawa: Government of Canada, Department of Communications.

Friedmann, J. 1995. Where We Stand: A Decade of World City Research. In P. Knox and P. Taylor, eds, *World Cities in a World System*, 21–47. Cambridge: Cambridge University Press.

Funding Cuts May Kill Halifax Show. 2003. 15 April: http://novascotia .cbc.ca/ Retrieved 6 June 2003.

Garnham, N. 1979. Contribution to a Political Economy of Mass Communication. *Media, Culture and Society* 1: 124–46.

Gasher, M. 1995. The Audiovisual Locations Industry in Canada: Considering British Columbia as Hollywood North. *Canadian Journal of Communication* 20: 231–54.

The Gatekeepers: Canada's Original Drama Heads. 1997. *Playback*, 14 July: 29–33.

Gathercole, S. 1987. Changing Channels: Canadian Television Needs to Switch. In R. Jackson, D. Jackson, and N. Baxter-Moore, eds, *Contemporary Canadian Politics*, 79–86. Scarborough, Ont.: Prentice-Hall.

Gitlin, T. 1985. *Inside Prime Time*. New York: Pantheon Books.

Glave, J., and Sutherland, J. 1995. WC City: Artists! Writers! Moguls! Eco-Heroes! *Vancouver*, May/June: 49–58.

Goldberg, K. 1990. *The Barefoot Channel: Community Television as a Tool for Social Change*. Vancouver: New Star Books.

Grossberg, L. 1997. *Bringing It All Back Home: Essays on Cultural Studies*. Durham: Duke University Press.

Hall, S. 1990. Cultural Identity and Diaspora. In J. Rutherford, ed., *Identity: Community, Culture, Difference*, 222–37. London: Lawrence and Wishart.

– 1992. The Question of Cultural Identity. In S. Hall, D. Held, and T. McGrew, eds, *Modernity and Its Futures*, 273–321. London: Polity Press.

Harvey, D. 1990. *The Condition of Postmodernity*. Cambridge, Mass.: Blackwell.

Hatten, A. 1987. *The Economic Impact of Expo '86*. Victoria, B.C.: Ministry of Finance and Corporate Relations.

Haysom, I. 1996. Hollywood Lifts Script from Scene-Stealing Northern Movie Industry. *Vancouver Sun*, 20 September: A1, A6.

Hebdige, D. 1988. *Hiding in the Light*. London: Comedia/Routledge.

Heritage Committee. 2003. News Release: Heritage Committee Releases Study on the State of the Canadian Broadcasting System. 11 June. Ottawa: House of Commons.

Hobsbawm, E. 1990. *Nations and Nationalism since 1870*. Cambridge: Cambridge University Press.

Hoskins, Colin, and S. McFadyen. 1992. The Mandate, Structure and Financing of the CBC. *Canadian Public Policy* 18: 275–89.

– 1993. Canadian Participation in Co-productions and Co-ventures. *Canadian Journal of Communication* 18: 219–36.

Hoskins, Colin, S. McFadyen, and A. Finn. 1994. The Environment in Which Cultural Industries Operate and Some Implications. *Canadian Journal of Communication* 19: 353–75.

Hutcheon, L. 1989. *The Politics of Postmodernism*. London: Routledge.

– 1991. *Splitting Images: Contemporary Canadian Ironies*. Oxford: Oxford University Press.

Independent Production. 1997. *Playback*, 21 April: 23.

Jackson, J. 1991. Broadcasting, Centralization, Regionalization, and Canadian Identity. In B. Singer, ed., *Communications in Canadian Society*, 185–99. Scarborough, Ont.: Nelson.

Jensen, J. 1984. An Interpretive Approach to Cultural Production. In W. Roland, ed., *Interpreting Television: Current Research Perspectives*, 98–117. Beverly Hills: Sage.

Jenson, J. 1993. All the World's a Stage: Spaces and Times in Canadian Political Economy. In J. Jenson, R. Mahon, and M. Bienefeld, eds, *Production, Space, Identity: Political Economy Faces the 21st Century*, 143–68. Toronto: Canadian Scholars' Press.

Johnson, B. 1996. 22 Minutes for High Schticking. *Maclean's*, 26 February: 46–51.

Karim, K. 1993. Constructions, Deconstructions, and Reconstructions: Competing Canadian Discourses on Ethnocultural Terminology. *Canadian Journal of Communication* 18: 197–218.

Kellner, D. 1995. *Media Culture: Cultural Studies, Identity and Politics between the Modern and the Postmodern*. London: Routledge.

King, A. 1995. Re-presenting World Cities: Cultural Theory/Social Practice. In P. Knox and P. Taylor, eds, *World Cities in a World System*, 215–31. Cambridge: Cambridge University Press.

Laba, M. 1988. Popular Culture as Local Culture: Regions, Limits and Canadianism. In R. Lorimer and D. Wilson, eds, *Communication Canada: Issues in Broadcasting and New Technologies*, 82–101. Toronto: Kagan and Woo.

Lash, S., and J. Urry. 1987. *The End of Organized Capitalism*. Madison: University of Wisconsin Press.

Laxer, G. 1992. Constitutional Crises and Continentalism: Twin Threats to Canada's Continued Existence. *Canadian Journal of Sociology* 17: 199–222.

Leger, L. 1996. Writers: The Real Story. *Playback*, 17 June: 14, 16.

– 1997. 'Criminals' Emotional Truth Pays Off. *Playback*, 27 January: 28, 39.

Leiren-Young, M. 1995a. Stage Struck. *Hollywood Reporter*, 26 September: S7, S18–S19.

– 1995b. X-Philes. *Hollywood Reporter*, 26 September: S8–S12.

Levin, G. 1998. Pivotal Role Has Lawrence Back in 'Blue.' *USA Today*, 17 February: 9B.

Ley, D. 1994. Social Polarisation and Community Response: Contesting Margins on Vancouver's Downtown Eastside. In F. Frisken, ed., *The Changing Canadian Metropolis: A Public Policy Perspective*, 699–723. Toronto: Canadian Urban Institute.

Ley, D., D. Hiebert, and G. Pratt. 1992. Time to Grow Up? From Urban Village to World City, 1966–91. In G. Wynn and T. Oke, eds, *Vancouver and Its Region*, 234–66. Vancouver: UBC Press.

Lorimer, R. 1994. Of Culture, the Economy, Cultural Production, and Cultural Producers: An Orientation. *Canadian Journal of Communication* 19: 259–89.

MacIntyre, Ken. 1996. *Reel Vancouver*. Vancouver: Whitecap Books.

Magder, T. 1995. Making Canada in the 1990s: Film, Culture, and Industry. In K. McRoberts, ed., *Beyond Quebec: Taking Stock of Canada*, 163–81. Montreal and Kingston: McGill-Queen's University Press.

Mahon, R. 1993. The New Canadian Political Economy Revisited: Production, Space, Identity. In J. Jenson, R. Mahon, and M. Bienefeld, eds, *Production, Space, Identity: Political Economy Faces the 21st Century*, 1–21. Toronto: Canadian Scholars' Press.

Mandate Review Committee, CBC, NFB, Telefilm. 1996. *Making Our Voices Heard: Canadian Broadcasting and Film for the 21st Century*. Ottawa: Department of Canadian Heritage.

Mandel, E., and D. Taras, eds. 1987. *A Passion for Identity*. Toronto: Methuen.

Martin-Barbero, J. 1993. *Communication, Culture and Hegemony: From the Media to Mediations*. London: Sage.

McClarty, L. 1988. *Seeing Things*: Canadian Popular Culture and the Experience of Marginality. In R. Lorimer and D. Wilson, eds, *Communication*

Canada: Issues in Broadcasting and New Technologies, 102–9. Toronto: Kagan and Woo.

Meehan, E. 1994. Conceptualizing Culture as Commodity: The Problem of Television. In H. Newcomb, ed., *Television: The Critical View*, 563–72. New York: Oxford University Press.

Meisel, J. 1991. Stroking the Airwaves: The Regulation of Broadcasting by the CRTC. In B. Singer, ed., *Communications in Canadian Society*, 217–38. Scarborough, Ont.: Nelson.

Mercer, R. 1998. *Streeters: Rants and Raves* from This Hour Has 22 Minutes. Toronto: Doubleday.

MGM/B.C. Government Partnership to Provide 400 New Jobs, Says Premier. 1996. *Reel West*, June/July: 28.

Miller, M.J. 1987. *Turn Up the Contrast: CBC Television Drama since 1952.* Vancouver: University of British Columbia Press.

– 1996. *Rewind and Search: Conversations with the Makers and Decision-makers of CBC Television Drama*. Montreal and Kingston: McGill-Queen's University Press.

Miller, S. 1994. The Grid: Living in Hollywood North. In P. Delaney, ed., *Vancouver: Representing the Postmodern City*, 282–94. Vancouver: Arsenal Pulp Press.

Mitchell, K. 1993. Multiculturalism, or the United Colors of Capitalism? *Antipode* 25: 263–94.

Morley, D., 1992. *Television Audiences and Cultural Studies*. London: Routledge.

– 2000. *Home Territories: Media, Mobility and Identity*. London: Routledge.

Morley, D., and K. Robins. 1995. *Spaces of Identity: Global Media, Electronic Landscapes and Cultural Boundaries*. London: Routledge.

Mulligan, H. 1998. Booked Up: Japanese Turn 'Anne of Green Gables' Fictional Village into a Romantic Destination. *Chicago Tribune*, 8 January: 13:8.

Murdock, G. 1989. Cultural Studies: Missing Links. *Critical Studies in Mass Communication* December: 436–40.

Nederveen Pieterse, J., and B. Parekh, eds. 1995. *The Decolonization of the Imagination: Culture, Knowledge and Power*. London: Zed Books.

Newcomb, H., and R. Alley. 1983. *The Producer's Medium: Conversations with Creators of American Television*. New York: Oxford University Press.

Ontario Scene. 1997. *Playback*, 23 September: 14.

Pevere, G., and G. Dymond 1996. *Mondo Canuck: A Canadian Pop Culture Odyssey*. Scarborough, Ont.: Prentice-Hall.

Posner, M., and J. Adams. 2003. Budget Turns Its Back on TV: Canadian Film and Television Producers Are Fuming after Ottawa Unexpectedly Slashes

Funding. *Globe and Mail*, 20 February: http://globeandmail.com/ Retrieved 4 May 2003.

Public Affairs Department, Vancouver. 1986. *The 1986 World Exposition*. Vancouver: Public Affairs Department.

Raboy, M. 1989. Two Steps Forward, Three Steps Back: Canadian Broadcasting Policy from Caplan-Sauvageau to Bill C-136. *Canadian Journal of Communication* 14: 70–6.

– 1990. *Missed Opportunities: The Story of Canada's Broadcasting Policy*. Montreal and Kingston: McGill-Queen's University Press.

Raboy, M., I. Bernier, F. Sauvageau, and D. Atkinson. 1994. Cultural Development and the Open Economy: A Democratic Issue and a Challenge to Public Policy. *Canadian Journal of Communication* 19: 291–315.

Rasporich, B. 1996. Canadian Humour in the Media: Exporting John Candy and Importing Homer Simpson. In H. Holmes and D. Taras, eds, *Seeing Ourselves: Media Power and Policy in Canada*, 84–98. Toronto: Harcourt Brace.

Rice-Barker, L. 1996. Canadians Cash in at MIPCOM. *Playback*, 21 October: 1, 24–5.

– 1997a. Finance Extends Service Shelter. *Playback*, 13 January: 3.

– 1997b. Growing Up with the Broadcasters. *Playback*, 21 April: 23–4, 39.

Robertson, R. 1990. Mapping the Global Condition: Globalization as the Central Concept. In M. Featherstone, ed., *Global Culture: Nationalism, Globalization, and Modernity*. London: Sage.

Robins, K. 1989. Reimagined Communities? European Image Spaces, beyond Fordism. *Cultural Studies* 3: 145–65.

Rutherford, J. 1990. A Place Called Home: Identity and the Cultural Politics of Difference. In J. Rutherford, ed., *Identity: Community, Culture, Difference*, 9–27. London: Lawrence and Wishart.

Rutherford, P. 1990. *When Television Was Young: Primetime Canada, 1952–1967*. Toronto: University of Toronto Press.

Sassen, S. 1994. *Cities in a World Economy*. London: Pine Forge Press.

Saunders, D. 1997. Exporting Canadian Culture. *Globe and Mail*, 25 January: C1, C3.

Schlesinger, P. 1991. *Media, State and Nation: Political Violence and Collective Identities*. London: Sage.

Seguin, D. 2003. The Battle for *Hollywood North*. *Canadian Business* 76: 54–60.

Sextant Entertainment Group. 2000. *Press Release: Sextant Is Pleased to Announce* The Rumfords. 22 May: http://members.shaw.ca/kevanwong/html /seg/ TheRumfords_PressRelease.html. Retrieved 12 December 2003.

Silj, A. 1988. *East of* Dallas: *The European Challenge to American Television*. London: British Film Institute.

Silverman, D. 1993. *Interpreting Qualitative Data: Methods for Analysing Talk, Text and Interaction*. London: Sage.

Sinclair, J., E. Jacka, and S. Cunningham. 1996. Peripheral Vision. In J. Sinclair, E. Jacka, and S. Cunningham, eds, *New Patterns in Global Television: Peripheral Vision*, 1–32. New York: Oxford University Press.

Skene, W. 1993. *Fade to Black: A Requiem for the CBC*. Vancouver: Douglas and McIntyre.

Smart, A., and J. Smart. 1996. Monster Homes: Hong Kong Immigration to Canada, Urban Conflicts, and Contested Representations of Space. In J. Caulfield and L. Peake, eds, *City Lives and City Forms: Critical Research and Canadian Urbanism*, 36–46. Toronto: University of Toronto Press.

Smith, A. 1990. Towards a Global Culture? In M. Featherstone, ed., *Global Culture: Nationalism, Globalization, and Modernity*, 171–91. London: Sage.

Smith, M. 1995. The Disappearance of World Cities and the Globalization of Local Politics. In P. Knox and P. Taylor, eds, *World Cities in a World System*, 249–66. Cambridge: Cambridge University Press.

Smith, P., and T. Cohn. 1994. International Cities and Municipal Paradiplomacy: A Typology for Assessing the Changing Vancouver Metropolis. In F. Frisken, ed., *The Changing Canadian Metropolis: A Public Policy Perspective*, 613–55. Toronto: Canadian Urban Institute.

Soja, E. 1989. *Postmodern Geographies: The Reassertion of Space in Critical Theory*. London: Verso.

Starowicz, M. 1993. Citizens of Video-America. What Happened to Canadian Television in the Satellite Age. In R. de la Garde, W. Gilsdorf, and I. Wechelsmann, eds, *Small Nations, Big Neighbour: Denmark and Québec/Canada Compare Notes on American Popular Culture*, 83–102. London: John Libbey and Company.

Statistics Canada. 1996. *Government Expenditures on Culture: Data Tables 1994–1995*, 87F001XPE. Ottawa: Education, Culture, and Tourism Division.

Surlin, S., and B. Berlin. 1991. TV, Values, and Culture in U.S.-Canadian Borderland Cities: A Shared Perspective. *Canadian Journal of Communication* 16: 431–9.

Tafler, S. 1985. Why It's Hard to Feel Good about Expo '86. *Globe and Mail Report on Business Magazine*, April: 20–6.

Taylor, P. 1995. Co-productions – Content and Change: International Television in the Americas. *Canadian Journal of Communication* 20:15–20.

Telefilm Canada. 1996. *Annual Report 1995–1996*. Montreal: Telefilm Canada.

– 1997. *Action Plan 1996–1997: Action Plan for the Administration of Telefilm Canada's Funds and Programs*. Montreal: Telefilm Canada.

– 1998. *The Canada Television and Cable Production Fund: Policy Guidelines 1997–1998*. Montreal: Telefilm Canada.

Thacker, R. 1995. English Canada and Other Proximations. *The American Review of Canadian Studies*. Summer and Autumn: 173–7.

Thompson, J. 1995. *The Media and Modernity: A Social Theory of the Media*. Stanford: Stanford University Press.

Thorne, S. 2003. Actors Take Ottawa to Task over Funding. 13 May: http://canadaeast.com/apps/pbcs.dll/article?AID=/20030513/CPN /13536018&cachetime=15. Retrieved 5 July 2003.

Todd G. 1995. 'Going Global' in the Semi-Periphery: World Cities as Political Projects. The Case of Toronto. In P. Knox and P. Taylor, eds, *World Cities in a World System*, 192–212. Cambridge: Cambridge University Press.

Vale, A. 1997. Klymkiw in Action. *Playback*, 14 July: 1, 14, 32.

Vardy, J. 1996. CBC Halifax Could Offer a Few Lessons for Mother Corp. *Financial Post*, 18 May: 21.

Vipond, M. 1992. *The Mass Media in Canada*. Toronto: James Lorimer and Company.

Ward, D., and K. Goldhar. 1997. Optimism Dominates Hong Kong Celebrations in Vancouver. *Vancouver Sun*, 2 July: A11.

Wark, M. 1994. *Virtual Geography: Living with Global Media Events*. Bloomington: Indiana University Press.

Waters, M. 1995. *Globalization*. London: Routledge.

Weaver, R.K. 1992. Political Institutions and Canada's Constitutional Crisis. In R. Kent Weaver, ed., *The Collapse of Canada?*, 7–75. Washington, D.C.: Brookings Institution.

Wernick, A. 1993. American Popular Culture in Canada: Trends and Reflections. In D.H. Flaherty and F.E. Manning, eds, *The Beaver Bites Back? American Popular Culture in Canada*, 293–302. Montreal and Kingston: McGill-Queen's University Press.

Wilson, P. 1996. Clark Joins Lion in Roaring over $5-Million Studio Expansion. *Vancouver Sun*, 30 April: C13.

Winsor, H. 1997. New Content Rules in the Wind, Copps Says. *Globe and Mail*, 15 February: A1, A7.

Wood, C. 1996. British Columbia's Quiet Revolution. *Maclean's*, 12 February: 10–18.

Wyatt, N. 1993. New Brand of CBC Comedy. *Hollywood Reporter*, 10 August: 20.

– 1997. Politics Good for a Laugh: This Hour Thrives on Commons Comedy. *Toronto Star*, 23 July: D18.

Zemans, J. 1995. The Essential Role of National Institutions. In K. McRoberts, ed., *Beyond Quebec: Taking Stock of Canada*, 138–62. Montreal and Kingston: McGill-Queen's University Press.

Index

CULTURAL SPACES

Cultural Spaces explores the rapidly changing temporal, spatial, and theoretical boundaries of contemporary cultural studies. Culture has long been
understood as the force that defines and delimits societies in fixed spaces. The
recent intensification of globalizing processes, however, has meant that it is no
longer possible – if it ever was – to imagine the world as a collection of autonomous, monadic spaces, whether these are imagined as localities, nations,
regions within nations, or cultures demarcated by region or nation. One of the
major challenges of studying contemporary culture is to understand the new
relationships of culture to space that are produced today. The aim of this
series is to publish bold new analyses and theories of the spaces of culture, as
well as investigations of the historical construction of those cultural spaces
that have influenced the shape of the contemporary world.

Series Editors:
Richard Cavell, University of British Columbia
Imre Szeman, McMaster University

Editorial Advisory Board:
Lauren Berlant, University of Chicago
Homi K. Bhabha, Harvard University
Hazel V. Carby, Yale University
Richard Day, Queen's University
Christopher Gittings, University of Western Ontario
Lawrence Grossberg, University of North Carolina
Mark Kingwell, University of Toronto
Heather Murray, University of Toronto
Elspeth Probyn, University of Sydney
Rinaldo Walcott, OISE/University of Toronto

Books in the Series:
Peter Ives, *Gramsci's Politics of Language: Engaging the Bakhtin Circle and the
   Frankfurt School*
Sarah Brophy, *Witnessing AIDS: Writing, Testimony, and the Work of Mourning*
Shane Gunster, *Capitalizing on Culture: Critical Theory for Cultural Studies*
Jasmin Habib, *Israel, Diaspora, and the Routes of National Belonging*
Serra Tinic, *On Location: Canada's Television Industry in a Global Market*